Current
Directions
in
HUMAN
SEXUALITY
AND INTIMATE
RELATIONSHIPS

READINGS FROM THE
ASSOCIATION FOR
PSYCHOLOGICAL SCIENCE

Current Directions

in

HUMAN SEXUALITY AND INTIMATE RELATIONSHIPS

EDITED BY

Terri D. Fisher

Ohio State University

James McNulty

University of Tennessee

Allyn & Bacon

Boston • New York • San Francisco

Mexico City • Montreal • Toronto • London • Madrid • Munich • Paris

Hong Kong • Singapore • Tokyo • Cape Town • Sydney

Acquisitions Editor: Michelle Limoges
Series Editorial Assistant: Lisa Dotson
Marketing Manager: Kate Mitchell
Production Supervisor: Patty Bergin
Editorial Production Service: TexTech International
Manufacturing Buyer: JoAnne Sweeney
Electronic Composition: TexTech International
Cover Designer: Joel Gendron

Library of Congress Cataloging-in-Publication Data

Current directions in human sexuality and intimate relationships / edited by Terri D. Fisher, James McNulty.—1st ed.
   p. cm.
   Includes bibliographical references.

   ISBN-13: 978-0-205-72367-6
   ISBN-10: 0-205-72367-5

1. Sex—Research.   2. Interpersonal relations—Research.   I. Fisher, Terri D.
II. McNulty, James.
   HQ23.C87 2010
   306.7—dc22

                        2009016216

10 9 8 7 6 5 4 3 2 1   13 12 11 10 09

Allyn & Bacon
is an imprint of

                    ISBN-10: 0-205-72367-5
www.pearsonhighered.com ISBN-13: 978-0-205-72367-6

Contents

Introduction

Sex and intimacy both play crucial roles in our lives. Not only are these processes integral to our reproductive lives, they shape who we are in important ways. Our sexual satisfaction and relationship satisfaction are highly correlated, and both are related to health, happiness, and psychological well-being. Interestingly, it is nevertheless relatively uncommon for researchers to simultaneously study sex and relationships.

The scientific study of sex and relationships is rather controversial among the general public. Some people feel that sex and relationships should not be studied scientifically, because to do so would demystify these two areas of life that many people consider "magical." Others object to grant funding for the study of sexual pleasure or love. Nonetheless, more and more researchers have begun to study sexuality and relationships, yielding a great deal of information about these two fundamental areas. This information is valuable in at least two ways. First, research on sex and relationships provides a better understanding of sexual expression and relationship dynamics that serves both public and personal health functions. Second, research in these two areas advances scientific theory and highlights the fact that our sex and relationship satisfaction is multiply determined by the interactive effects of both nature and nurture.

Unfortunately, the study of sex and relationships is sometimes constrained by methodological limitations. An obvious hurdle for sex researchers is the need to rely on self-reports in a variety of domains. Not only are research participants more reluctant to be forthcoming about the most intimate areas of their lives, but their desires to behave in socially appropriate ways may lead men and women to report what they believe is socially appropriate, rather than how they really feel and behave. Further, older adults are less likely to be open about their sexuality than are younger adults, and those with a non-heterosexual orientation might be less inclined to reveal their sexual minority status. In addition, relying on volunteers who are willing to reveal the details of their sexual attitudes and behaviors may impair researchers' abilities to describe the prevalence of those attitudes and behaviors; volunteers may report sexual attitudes that are more sexually permissive than those who choose not to participate, for example. Of course, sex research that is not dependent on self-report helps address these limitations; however a lack of funding and equipment unfortunately makes physiological sex research and other novel approaches less common than questionnaire-based research.

Research on relationships faces impediments as well, some of which are similar to those faced by sex researchers and others that are unique to relationship research. Although many relationship researchers are interested in attitudes and beliefs, constructs that lend themselves nicely to self-report, all factors that ultimately affect the relationship do so through partners' behavioral interactions with one another. And self- and partner-reports of behavior are notoriously unreliable because people frequently lack the insight or desire to accurately report their behavior. Although relationship researchers can rely on observations of many interactions that occur between couples, that research is expensive and time consuming, and thus less common. Another methodological problem facing relationship research is that, whereas relationships are an ongoing process that last over a considerable amount of time, many studies are cross-sectional and thus cannot successfully capture the change that many researchers ultimately want to understand. There is some longitudinal research, and it is becoming more prevalent, but because such studies are very expensive and very labor intensive, the majority of research is cross-sectional.

Despite these and other challenges faced by those who study sexuality and relationships, the articles in this collection of readings are based on sound empirical research using a variety of methods that test hypotheses about the ways sexuality and relationships function and the reasons they function that way. Section 1 addresses some important conceptual, theoretical, and methodological issues, beginning with an examination of the distinction between and possible independence of love and sexual attraction, followed by a couple of articles examining various contextual influences on relationships, and ending with a presentation on an innovative method for studying relationships: speed-dating.

Section 2, on biological foundations, features both applied and theoretical work that leads to an understanding of when, how, and to whom we are attracted. After an initial article discussing the hormonal basis and timing of sexual attraction there are three articles that take an evolutionary perspective on various aspects of sex and attraction, including behaviors that seem to have evolved in humans as the result of sperm competition, concealed ovulation, and what physical appearances were most closely associated with health in ancestral times. The final article explores the neurochemical foundations of the emotional bond between couples.

The third section examines male-female differences in sexuality and relationships. This area holds great interest for researchers and the general public alike, and the articles in this section reflect several different approaches, ranging from theoretical to atheoretical. It is clear from these articles that while many psychologists believe there is consensus as to the significant sex differences in sexuality, other researchers are not so sure, and still others feel the differences are minimal.

Section 4 explores various aspects of sexual orientation, including a discussion of how to define homosexuality as well as a review of various biopsychological factors that may (or may not) contribute to sexual orientation. There are also articles addressing the more interpersonal aspects of sexual orientation, including gay and lesbian couples' family relationships and the concept of sexual prejudice, a negative attitude toward those with a particular sexual orientation.

Section 5 addresses issues that pertain to the formation and maintenance of relationships. Specifically, these articles highlight the complexity of relationships, with each one noting important rewards or costs to relationships. The first addresses relationships among adolescents, noting how the rewards of relationships become more important as adolescents progress toward adulthood. The second article highlights an important conflict people face when trying to maximize their interpersonal rewards—gaining the rewards of closeness without risking the costs of rejection. The third article describes one factor that may determine whether or not people perceive that trying to gain such interpersonal rewards is risky: trust. The fourth article describes one way in which people determine how satisfied they are with their relationship rewards versus costs—they compare the outcomes they have to the outcomes they want.

Finally, Section 6 focuses on some of the costs that ultimately may outweigh the rewards people gain through their relationships, including conflict, infidelity, and violence. The first article in this section describes the nature of conflict, noting what we know and what we do not know about how conflictual interactions shape relationship development. The second article addresses possible explanations for why a large number of people who initially decide to spend their entire lives together are eventually unhappy or leave their relationships. The third article discusses why people may seek relationships with others, while simultaneously attempting to remain in their current relationships. With estimates that as many as half or more relationships may involve some form of violence, the fourth article discusses the personal characteristics of men who perpetrate some of the more severe forms of violence. Finally, the last article discusses the complex relationship between alcohol and the costs of risky sex.

These readings are appropriate for any course dealing with aspects of sexuality and/or relationships, though not every reading may be relevant to a particular course. Nevertheless, given the intrinsic interest in the topics, students may well elect to read even any unassigned articles. We have included questions after each reading to challenge students to think critically about the issues addressed and to encourage them to apply the material to their own lives as well as the lives of others.

Section 1: Theory and Methodology

This opening section addresses several conceptual and methodological issues in sexuality and relationship research. The very first reading addresses a central issue—distinguishing love and sex. Specifically, Lisa Diamond argues that love and sex are distinct processes that do not have to occur together. She suggests that love and sexual desire evolved for different reasons, with sexual desire evolving to facilitate reproduction and love evolving to facilitate child-rearing. In support of this argument, she cites evidence that love and sex are associated with different biochemicals that, in conjunction with culture and socialization, lead to sex differences in the degree to which love and sex are correlated.

Although procreation and child-rearing may be primitive driving forces behind our relationships, our relationships certainly have implications for other aspects of our lives as well. Harry Reis and Andrew Collins provide a broader perspective of the impact relationships have on our lives. For example, they discuss how our social cognitive processes work very differently when we evaluate people who are in relationships with us versus mere acquaintances or strangers. Similarly, they describe how the degree of intimacy we feel with a person affects the onset of our emotional response, its intensity, and whether or not we suppress it. In essence, Reis and Collins argue that understanding our relationships is an essential part of understanding who we are.

Given that relationships play such a fundamental role in our lives, it is important that they function well. Unfortunately, however, all too often, they do not. Benjamin Karney and Thomas Bradbury examine proposals for federal government intervention, specifically in the teaching of values and skills believed to benefit marriages. The authors address why such plans may be insufficient in helping low-income households and argue that to best promote healthy marriages, interventions must acknowledge not only the dyadic processes that occur between partners, but also the broader environment in which those couples spend their lives. Although their analysis focuses mostly on the role of context in shaping marital relationships, the idea that relationships do not occur in a vacuum, but instead are influenced by the surroundings in which they occur, can be generalized to all relationships.

Finally, Eli Finkel and Paul Eastwick describe an innovative and novel research technique that has proved useful: collecting data from speed dating sessions. Utilizing this relatively new way to meet romantic partners, Finkel and Eastwick describe procedures through which researchers can assess the thoughts, feelings, and behaviors of participants as they make naturally occurring decisions regarding real potential relationships. The authors review several studies that have used this method, demonstrating that speed-dating programs can be a useful source of information from both partners, enabling researchers to study relationships as they actually develop (or fail to develop) in a way that may readily generalize to real world situations.

Emerging Perspectives on Distinctions Between Romantic Love and Sexual Desire

Lisa M. Diamond[1]
University of Utah

Abstract

Although sexual desire and romantic love are often experienced in concert, they are fundamentally distinct subjective experiences with distinct neurobiological substrates. The basis for these distinctions is the evolutionary origin of each type of experience. The processes underlying sexual desire evolved in the context of sexual mating, whereas the processes underlying romantic love—or pair bonding—originally evolved in the context of infant-caregiver attachment. Consequently, not only can humans experience these feelings separately, but an individual's sexual predisposition for the same sex, the other sex, or both sexes may not circumscribe his or her capacity to fall in love with partners of either gender. Also, the role of oxytocin in both love and desire may contribute to the widely observed phenomenon that women report experiencing greater interconnections between love and desire than do men. Because most research on the neurobiological substrates of sexual desire and affectional bonding has been conducted with animals, a key priority for future research is systematic investigation of the coordinated biological, behavioral, cognitive, and emotional processes that shape experiences of love and desire in humans.

Keywords

attachment; sexual desire; gender; sexual orientation; evolutionary theory

It is a truism that romantic love and sexual desire are not the same thing, but one might be hard pressed to cite empirical evidence to this effect. In recent years, however, researchers in fields ranging from psychology to animal behavior to neurobiology have devoted increasing attention to the experiences, physiological underpinnings, and potential evolutionary origins that distinguish love and desire. The results of these investigations suggest that romantic love and sexual desire are governed by functionally independent social-behavioral systems that evolved for different reasons and that involve different neurochemical substrates. Furthermore, there are gender differences in the interrelationship between love and desire that may have both biological and cultural origins. This emerging body of theory and research has the potential to profoundly reshape the way we conceptualize human sexuality, gender, sexual orientation, and social bonding.

INDEPENDENCE BETWEEN LOVE AND DESIRE

Sexual desire typically denotes a need or drive to seek out sexual objects or to engage in sexual activities, whereas *romantic love* typically denotes the powerful feelings of emotional infatuation and attachment between intimate partners. Furthermore, most researchers acknowledge a distinction between the earlier "passionate" stage of love, sometimes called "limerence" (Tennov, 1979), and the later-developing "companionate" stage of love, called pair bonding or attachment (Fisher, 1998; Hatfield, 1987). Although it may be easy to imagine sexual desire without romantic love, the notion of "pure," "platonic," or "nonsexual" romantic love is somewhat more controversial. Yet empirical evidence indicates that sexual desire is not a prerequisite for romantic love, even in its earliest, passionate stages. Many men and women report having experienced romantic passion in the absence of sexual desire (Tennov, 1979), and even prepubertal children, who have not undergone the hormonal changes responsible for adult levels of sexual motivation, report intense romantic infatuations (Hatfield, Schmitz, Cornelius, & Rapson, 1988).

Furthermore, extensive cross-cultural and historical research shows that individuals often develop feelings of romantic love for partners of the "wrong" gender (i.e., heterosexuals fall in love with same-gender partners and lesbian and gay individuals fall in love with other-gender partners, as reviewed in Diamond, 2003). Although some modern observers have argued that such relationships must involve hidden or suppressed sexual desires, the straightforward written reports of the participants themselves are not consistent with such a blanket characterization. Rather, it seems that individuals are capable of developing intense, enduring, preoccupying affections for one another regardless of either partner's sexual attractiveness or arousal.

MEASURING THE EXPERIENCE AND SUBSTRATES OF LOVE AND DESIRE

Of course, one's interpretation of such data depends on one's confidence in the methods used to assess and contrast love and desire. Whereas sexual arousal can be reliably and validly assessed by monitoring blood flow to the genitals, no definitive test of "true love" exists. Psychologists have, however, identified a constellation of cognitions and behaviors that reliably characterize (and differentiate between) romantic love and passion across different cultures. As summarized by Tennov (1979), passionate love is a temporary state of heightened interest in and preoccupation with a specific individual, characterized by intense desires for proximity and physical contact, resistance to separation, and feelings of excitement and euphoria when receiving the partner's attention. As passionate love transforms into companionate love, desire for proximity and resistance to separation become less urgent, and feelings of security, care, and comfort predominate.

Some of the most provocative and promising research on love and desire focuses on the neurobiological substrates of these distinctive behaviors and cognitions. Although little direct research in this area has been conducted with humans, converging lines of evidence (reviewed by Fisher, 1998) suggest that the marked experiential differences between love and desire may be partially attributable to their distinct neurochemical signatures. Sexual desire, for example, is directly mediated by gonadal estrogens and androgens (see Diamond, 2003; Fisher, 1998), yet these hormones do not mediate the formation of affectional bonds. Rather, animal research indicates that the distinctive feelings and behaviors associated with attachment formation are mediated by the fundamental "reward" circuitry of the mammalian brain, involving the coordinated action of endogenous opioids, cat-echolamines,[2] and neuropeptides such as oxytocin, which is best known for its role in childbirth and nursing. These neurochemicals regulate a range of emotional, cognitive, behavioral, and biological processes that facilitate social bonding by fostering conditioned associations between specific social partners and intrinsic feelings of reward (reviewed in Carter, 1998).

At the current time, it is not known whether such processes mediate the formation and maintenance of pair bonds between humans, as they have been shown to do in other pair-bonding mammalian species, such as the prairie vole (Carter, 1998). For example, we are only beginning to understand the range of emotional and physical phenomena (other than labor and nursing) that trigger oxytocin release in humans, and whether oxytocin release has consistent effects on subjective experience. Preliminary studies have found fascinating individual differences in the amount of oxytocin released in response to sexual activity, positive emotion, and massage (Carmichael, Warburton, Dixen, & Davidson, 1994; Turner, Altemus, Enos, Cooper, & McGuinness, 1999), and this is a key direction for future research.

Another promising avenue for investigation involves the use of functional magnetic resonance imaging (fMRI) to identify brain regions that are activated during experiences of desire versus infatuation versus attachment. In one preliminary study (Bartels & Zeki, 2000), the brains of individuals who reported being "truly, deeply, and madly in love" were examined under two conditions: while viewing pictures of their beloved and while viewing pictures of other-sex friends. Compared with viewing friends, viewing pictures of loved ones was associated with heightened activation in the middle insula and the anterior cingulate cortex, areas that have been associated in prior research with positive emotion, attention to one's own emotional states, attention to the emotional states of social partners, and even opioid-induced euphoria. Viewing pictures of loved ones was also associated with deactivation in the posterior cingulate gyrus, the amygdala, and the right prefrontal, parietal, and middle temporal cortices, areas that have been associated with sadness, fear, aggression, and depression. Notably, the brain regions that showed distinctive patterns of activity when viewing romantic partners did not overlap with regions typically activated during sexual arousal.

Clearly, much work remains to be done to develop a comprehensive "map" of normative brain activity during both short-term states and longer-term stages of desire, infatuation, and attachment; to examine changes in brain activity as individuals move between these states and stages within specific relationships; and to explore whether inter-individual differences in personality and relationship quality moderate such patterns. Perhaps most important, however, we require a greater understanding of the functional implications of different coordinated patterns of activation and deactivation.

THE EVOLUTIONARY ORIGINS OF LOVE AND DESIRE

Given the accumulating evidence that love and desire are, in fact, functionally independent phenomena with distinct neurobiological substrates, a natural question is, *why*? After all, most individuals end up falling in love with partners to whom they are sexually drawn, and this seems to make good evolutionary sense given that pair bonding with one's sexual partner is a good way to ensure that the resulting offspring have two dedicated parents instead of just one. This view assumes, however, that the basic biobehavioral mechanisms underlying affectional bonding evolved for the purpose of reproductive mating, and this may not be the case. Although these processes would clearly have conferred reproductive benefits on early humans, some researchers have argued that they originally evolved for an altogether different purpose: infant-caregiver attachment.

Bowlby (1982) conceptualized attachment as an evolved behavioral system designed to keep infants in close proximity to caregivers (thereby maximizing infants' chances for survival). Attachment establishes an intense affectional bond between infant and caregiver, such that separation elicits feelings of distress and proximity elicits feelings of comfort and security. Other evolutionary theorists have argued that this system was eventually co-opted for the purpose of keeping reproductive partners together to rear offspring (Hazan & Zeifman, 1999). In other words, adult pair bonding may be an *exaptation*—a system that originally evolved for one reason, but comes to serve another. The fundamental correspondence between infant-caregiver attachment and adult pair bonding is supported by extensive research documenting that these phenomena share the same core emotional and behavioral dynamics: heightened desire for proximity, resistance to separation, and utilization of the partner as a preferred target for comfort and security (Hazan & Zeifman, 1999). Even more powerful evidence is provided by the voluminous animal research documenting that these two types of affectional bonding are mediated by the same opioid- and oxytocin-based neural circuitry (Carter, 1998).

This view helps to explain the independence between love and desire, because sexual desire is obviously irrelevant to the process of infant-caregiver bonding. Yet even if one grants that affectional bonding and sexual mating are fundamentally distinct processes that evolved for distinct purposes, the question still remains: Why do the majority of human adults fall in love only with partners to whom they are sexually attracted? One reason is obviously cultural: Most human societies have strong and well-established norms regarding what types of feelings and behaviors are appropriate for different types of adult relationships, and they actively channel adults into the "right" types of relationships through a variety of social practices. Additionally, however, both human and animal data suggest that attachments are most likely to form between individuals that have extensive proximity to and contact with one another over a prolonged period of time (Hazan & Zeifman, 1999). Sexual desire provides a powerful motive for such extended contact, increasing the likelihood that the average adult becomes attached to sexual partners rather than platonic friends.

IMPLICATIONS REGARDING GENDER AND SEXUAL ORIENTATION

Psychologists have long noted that one of the most robust gender differences regarding human sexuality is that women tend to place greater emphasis on relationships as a context for sexual feelings and behaviors than do men (Peplau, 2003). For example, many lesbian and bisexual women report that they were never aware of same-sex desires until after they fell in love with a particular woman (Diamond, 2003). One potential reason for this gender difference is that women appear more likely than men to have their first experiences of sexual arousal in the context of a heterosexual dating relationship, rather than the solitary context of masturbation. Another potential contributor to this gender difference is that historically women have been socialized to restrict their sexual feelings and behaviors to intimate emotional relationships—ideally, marital ties—whereas males have enjoyed more social license regarding casual sexual relations.

Yet our emerging understanding of the neurochemical substrates of love and desire raises the intriguing possibility that biological factors might also contribute to this gender difference. Specifically, several of the neurochemicals that mediate mammalian bonding processes—most notably, oxytocin, vasopressin, and dopamine—also mediate sexual behavior, and these neurochemicals often show hormone-dependent, gender-specific patterns of functioning. For example, female rats have far more extensive oxytocin brain circuits than do male rats, perhaps to facilitate oxytocin-dependent caregiving behaviors, and oxytocin interacts with estrogen to regulate female rats' sexual receptivity (Panksepp, 1998). Among humans, women show greater oxytocin release during sexual activity than do men, and some women show correlations between oxytocin release and orgasm intensity (Carmichael et al., 1994). Such findings raise the provocative possibility that women's greater emphasis on the relational context of sexuality—that is, their greater experience of links between love and desire—may be influenced by oxytocin's joint, gender-specific role in these processes (in addition to culture and socialization).

Furthermore, the fact that women sometimes develop same-sex desires as a result of falling in love with female friends (a phenomenon rarely documented among men) might be interpreted to indicate that oxytocin-mediated links between love and desire make it possible for a woman's affectionally triggered desires to "override" her general sexual orientation. In other words, whereas the fundamental independence between love and desire means that individuals' sexual orientations do not necessarily circumscribe their capacity for affectional bonding, the biobehavioral links between love and desire may make it possible for either experience to trigger the other (Diamond, 2003). Although this might be true for both sexes, it is perhaps more likely for women because of both gender-specific oxytocin-mediated processes and the greater cultural permission for women to develop strong affectional bonds with members of their own sex (for a similar argument regarding same-sex female bonds and gender-differentiated patterns of stress response, see Taylor et al., 2000).

These notions run counter to the conventional notion that lesbians and gay men fall in love only with same-sex partners and heterosexuals fall in love only with other-sex partners. Yet this conventional notion is also contradicted by cross-cultural, historical, and even animal research. For example, given sufficient cohabitation, both male and female prairie voles have been induced to form nonsexual bonds with same-sex partners (DeVries, Johnson, & Carter, 1997), although these bonds form more quickly and are more robust among females. One fascinating area for future research concerns the conditions under which humans form and maintain sexual and affectional relationships that run counter to their established patterns of desire and affection, the implications of such phenomena for later experience and development, and the specific role played by cognitive, behavioral, emotional, and biological mechanisms in regulating such processes.

Historically, it has been assumed that sexual arousal is a more basic, biologically mediated phenomenon than is romantic love, and therefore is more amenable to scientific study. Yet this assumption is outmoded. Research has demonstrated that the distinct behaviors and intense feelings associated with affectional bonds are governed not only by culture and socialization, but also by evolved, neurochemically mediated processes that are a fundamental legacy of our mammalian heritage. Future research on the nature and functioning of these processes in humans will not only provide researchers with novel tools to investigate age-old debates (can you fall in love with two people at once?), but will also make critical contributions to understanding the basic experience of human intimacy and how it is shaped by gender and sexual orientation over the life course.

Recommended Reading

Carter, C.S. (1998). (See References)
Diamond, L.M. (2003). (See References)
Fisher, H.E. (1998). (See References)
Hazan, C., & Zeifman, D. (1999). (See References)

Notes

1. Address correspondence to Lisa M. Diamond, Department of Psychology, University of Utah, 380 South 1530 East, Room 502, Salt Lake City, UT 84112-0251; e-mail: diamond@psych.utah.edu.

2. The release of catecholamines (most notably, dopamine, epinephrine, and norepinephrine) is associated with a variety of physiological responses that prepare the body to "fight or flee" a stressor (e.g., increased heart rate, blood pressure, and blood glucose levels). In contrast, endogenous opioids are known for their role in diminishing endocrine, cardiovascular, and behavioral stress responses, and are particularly well known for blunting the experience of pain. For this reason, they are often called "the body's own pain killers." These neuropeptides also play a role in the subjective experience of pleasure and reward, and facilitate learning and conditioning.

References

Bartels, A., & Zeki, S. (2000). The neural basis of romantic love. *NeuroReport, 11*, 3829–3834.
Bowlby, J. (1982). *Attachment and loss: Vol. 1: Attachment* (2nd ed.). New York: Basic Books.
Carmichael, M.S., Warburton, V.L., Dixen, J., & Davidson, J.M. (1994). Relationships among cardiovascular, muscular, and oxytocin responses during human sexual activity. *Archives of Sexual Behavior, 23*, 59–79.
Carter, C.S. (1998). Neuroendocrine perspectives on social attachment and love. *Psychoneuroendocrinology, 23*, 779–818.
DeVries, A.C., Johnson, C.L., & Carter, C.S. (1997). Familiarity and gender influence social preferences in prairie voles *(Microtus ochrogaster). Canadian Journal of Zoology, 75*, 295–301.
Diamond, L.M. (2003). What does sexual orientation orient? A biobehavioral model distinguishing romantic love and sexual desire. *Psychological Review, 110*, 173–192.
Fisher, H.E. (1998). Lust, attraction, and attachment in mammalian reproduction. *Human Nature, 9*, 23–52.

Hatfield, E. (1987). Passionate and companionate love. In R.J. Sternberg & M.L. Barnes (Eds.), *The psychology of love* (pp. 191–217). New Haven, CT: Yale University Press.

Hatfield, E., Schmitz, E., Cornelius, J., & Rapson, R.L. (1988). Passionate love: How early does it begin? *Journal of Psychology and Human Sexuality, 1,* 35–52.

Hazan, C., & Zeifman, D. (1999). Pair-bonds as attachments: Evaluating the evidence. In J. Cassidy & P.R. Shaver (Eds.), *Handbook of attachment theory and research* (pp. 336–354). New York: Guilford.

Panksepp, J. (1998). *Affective neuroscience: The foundations of human and animal emotions.* New York: Cambridge University Press.

Peplau, L.A. (2003). Human sexuality: How do men and women differ? *Current Directions in Psychological Science, 12,* 37–40.

Taylor, S.E., Klein, L.C., Lewis, B.P., Gruenewald, T.L., Gurung, R.A.R., & Updegraff, J.A. (2000). Biobehavioral responses to stress in females: Tend-and-befriend, not fight-or-flight. *Psychological Review, 107,* 411–429.

Tennov, D. (1979). *Love and limerence: The experience of being in love.* New York: Stein and Day.

Turner, R.A., Altemus, M., Enos, T., Cooper, B., & McGuinness, T. (1999). Preliminary research on plasma oxytocin in normal cycling women: Investigating emotion and interpersonal distress. *Psychiatry, 62,* 97–113.

Critical Thinking Questions

1. What are the implications of Diamond's ideas for our understanding of sexual orientation?

2. What are the implications of Diamond's ideas for our cultural norm of having one partner to meet all needs?

This article has been reprinted as it originally appeared in *Current Directions in Psychological Science*. Citation information for this article as originally published appears above.

Relationships, Human Behavior, and Psychological Science

Harry T. Reis[1]
University of Rochester

W. Andrew Collins
University of Minnesota

Abstract

Extensive evidence attests to the importance of relationships for human well-being, and evolutionary theorizing has increasingly recognized the adaptive significance of relationships. Psychological science, however, has barely begun to consider how relationships influence a broad array of basic social, cognitive, emotional, and behavioral processes. This article discusses contemporary theory and research about the impact of relationship contexts, citing examples from research on social cognition, emotion, and human development. We propose that the validity and usefulness of psychological science will be enhanced by better integration of relationship contexts into theories and research.

Keywords

relationship; social cognition; emotion; development

A recent cartoon in the *New Yorker* depicts a middle-aged, probably long-married couple reading quietly in their living room. The man turns to his wife and says, "I can't remember which one of us is me." This cartoon embodies an idea whose time has come in the psychological sciences: that human behavior varies significantly depending on relationship contexts and the cognitive, emotional, and social mechanisms that have evolved for recognizing, evaluating, and responding to those contexts—who else is present and who else is affected by, or has had an effect on, present circumstances. This idea follows from the uncontroversial but often overlooked fact that most human activity involves coordinating one's actions with the actions of others, and that the relative success or failure of such coordination is a principal determinant of productivity and well-being, whether in families, friendships, organizations, neighborhoods, or societies.

Psychological science rarely integrates relationship contexts into its theories and research. One reason for this gap has been the historical focus of psychology on the behavior of individuals.

Another has been a shortage of valid concepts, empirical knowledge, and rigorous methods for introducing relationship processes into mainstream psychological research. Recent advances in relationship science—empirical research on relationship processes and their effects—suggest that this void may soon be filled. A virtual explosion of research has provided analytical and methodological tools that allow most psychological or behavioral processes to be investigated from a relationship perspective. The premise of this article is that such investigations will advance the completeness and accuracy of psychological science.

WHY RELATIONSHIPS MATTER

Abundant evidence attests that associations, often powerful ones, exist between the quality and quantity of relationships and diverse outcomes, including mortality rates, recovery from coronary artery bypass surgery, functioning of the immune system, reactions to stress, psychiatric disturbance, and life satisfaction. These effects do not appear to be artifacts of personality, temperament, behavior, or lifestyles, but instead reflect the direct influence of relationship events on biological processes (e.g., Kiecolt-Glaser & Newton, 2001).

How did the processes by which relationship events affect human biology evolve? Many accounts posit that living and working in small, cooperative groups has been the primary survival strategy for the human species, because social organization buffered early humans from the dangers of the natural environment. Thus, it was adaptive for the human mind to develop a series of mechanisms—Bugental (2000) called them the "algorithms of social life"—for regulating social relations. Social organization is composed of interlocking relationships among individuals within a social network.

Although no definitive list of innate systems for regulating social relations and responding to social circumstances exists, many processes of long-standing interest among behavioral researchers are likely candidates: cooperation and competition, adherence to social norms, coalition formation, attachment, face perception, social inclusion and exclusion, communication of emotion, romantic jealousy, empathy, and commitment, for example. These processes are not applied equally to all of an individual's contacts, but rather are applied selectively, depending on the existing relationship and the particular problem to be solved. People become psychologically attached primarily to caregivers and intimates, and cooperation predominates within in-groups. Social interaction involves determining what sort of relationship exists and therefore which processes are most relevant. Growing evidence that these processes are manifested in nonhuman species and that they are governed to some extent by nonconsciously regulated neurobiological systems suggests that responsiveness to relationship contexts is deeply wired into human architecture.

Relationships may be characterized in terms of the properties that describe the involved parties' interdependence with each other—the manner in which individuals alter their behavior in order to coordinate with others' actions and preferences. Thus, persons in relationships respond (or not) to each other's wishes, concerns, abilities, and emotional expressions; they modify their behavior to be together (or not); they allocate tasks between themselves; they react to each other's behaviors and circumstances, misfortune, and happiness; and they take the fact of their interdependence into account in organizing everyday life and longer-term plans. Central to most conceptualizations of relationship is the idea that these patterns of mutual influence are more informative about relationships than are nominal categories (e.g., spouses, co-workers, friends) or simple static descriptors (e.g., length of acquaintance, nature or degree of affect).

Evidence for differential effects of relationship contexts is available in many areas of research. We next describe three such areas to illustrate the importance of such evidence for psychological science.

SOCIAL COGNITION

Much research has investigated the cognitive processes by which individuals perceive, interpret, and respond to their social environments. In most such studies, no relationship exists between the subjects and the objects of thought, who are often, for example, strangers, hypothetical people described by the experimenter, famous persons, or social groups. Even when a relationship does exist, its possible influence on the results obtained is rarely considered. This approach tacitly implies that the principles governing cognition about people who are familiar or close do not differ materially from the principles governing cognition about acquaintances and strangers (or, for that matter, inanimate objects). Increasingly, theory and research challenge this assumption.

Take, for example, one of the most robust social-cognitive phenomena: the *self-serving attributional bias*, which refers to the fact that people give themselves more credit for success and less responsibility for failure than they give strangers. This bias, reported in virtually every textbook in the field, is not observed when the self is compared with close relationship partners, who are accorded the same attributional generosity as is the self (Sedikides, Campbell, Reeder, & Elliot, 1998). Other phenomena that reflect self-serving biases also vary depending on the closeness of the relationship.

Another example concerns the well-documented *self-referential effect*: the enhancement of memory when information is encoded with reference to the self, rather than, for example, another person. This effect is significantly smaller when the other person is an intimate rather than a stranger or acquaintance (Symons & Johnson, 1997). Partners in close or committed relationships typically adopt an interdependent frame of reference ("we," rather than "you and I"), perhaps because, following the logic of a connectionist model, close relationships entail a greater number of direct connections and overlapping links than distant relationships do (Smith, Coats, & Walling, 1999). Even more suggestive is a recent neural imaging study (Lichty et al., 2004) showing substantial overlap—most strongly, in the right superior frontal gyrus and prefrontal cortex—in the brain regions activated by hearing one's own name and hearing the name of a close friend, but no overlap in the areas of activation associated with hearing one's own name and hearing the name of a familiar (but not close) other person. The degree of overlap in the own-name and close-friend conditions was more pronounced to the extent that the relationship with the other was experienced as a close relationship.

Relationship context may also influence social cognition when the close partner is not present. A long-standing and sophisticated program of experimentation has shown that representations of significant others from one's past may affect one's inferences, recollections, evaluations, and feelings about a new acquaintance when the new acquaintance resembles the significant other (and thereby activates mental schemas associated with the preexisting relationship; Andersen & Chen, 2002).

It has long been recognized that social cognition is designed to facilitate the individual's transit through social life. These and similar studies represent an advance in psychological science, demonstrating that which particular social-cognitive process is activated, and the output of its operation, depends critically on the nature of the ongoing relationship between the cognizer and relevant others. Moreover, Bugental (2000) has argued that evolved brain mechanisms tend to be specialized, perhaps as distinct modules, to fit the varying role requirements of different relationship contexts. If so, humans' extraordinary capacity to quickly recognize (within milliseconds) close friends or even distant acquaintances expedites activation of different cognitive processes with different partners.

EMOTION

Ever since Darwin emphasized the social communicative function of emotion in the survival of species, researchers have recognized that emotions have both evolutionary significance and relevance to social life. It is thus somewhat ironic that "interpersonal functions [of emotion] have generally been given short shrift in comparison to intrapersonal functions . . . [although most researchers] believe that emotions are brought into play most often by the actions of others, and, once aroused, emotions influence the course of interpersonal transactions" (Ekman & Davidson, 1994, p. 139). Although not all interpersonal transactions involve partners in ongoing relationships, many do. Consequently, many researchers now acknowledge that affect should be examined in its relationship context.

Several emotions are intrinsically relationship-specific; they are unlikely to arise outside of relationships (e.g., jealousy, maternal and romantic love, grief over loss). For most other emotions, the likelihood, intensity, and nature of expression typically are influenced by the individual's relationship with the target of the emotion. For example, a rude bus driver likely elicits a weaker and different response than a rude spouse, junior colleague, or teenaged daughter. This observation accords with the definition of emotion as a response to environmental events that have significance for personal well-being. Different relationships necessarily imply different consequences for personal well-being.

Diverse studies demonstrate links between the emotion-eliciting power of situations and their relationship context. For example, the intensity of elicited emotions, particularly the so-called hot emotions, varies with the closeness of a relationship. This pattern can be explained by Berscheid and Ammazzalorso's (2001) emotion-in-relationships model, according to which expectancy violations are the cause of emotion. The more interdependent two persons are, the stronger, more numerous, and more consequential their expectations of each other, and thus, the more intense the emotions they elicit. Moreover, people's willingness to communicate about emotional experience depends on their relationship with the person with whom they are communicating. Studies conducted by the first author and his colleagues indicate that people are more willing to express both positive and negative emotions to the extent that a relationship is intimate, trusting, and communal (i.e., a relationship in which partners are responsive to each other's needs), regardless of whether the emotion was triggered by the partner or someone else. Similarly, emotional displays may be suppressed when the emotion is perceived to have relationship-impairing potential. For example, East Asians are more likely than European Americans to suppress certain emotion displays, perhaps reflecting their greater potential to harm relationships in collectivist than in individualist cultures. Although the tendency to experience emotion is widely believed to be hard-wired, behavioral responses to emotion-eliciting events may be shaped to a significant extent by interactions within close relationships.

A further example of the links between emotion and relationship context is that in communal relationships, relative to less caring ones, individuals are more likely to show empathic compassion for a partner's misfortune, better understand each other's emotions (the occasional instance of motivated misunderstanding notwithstanding), and are more likely to share in each other's emotional experience through such processes as emotional contagion, physiological synchrony, vicarious arousal, and rapport (Clark, Fitness, & Brissette, 2001).

Thus, attention to relationship contexts advances understanding of emotional experience and expression.

RELATIONSHIPS AND DEVELOPMENT

Rudimentary social interaction skills are evident at birth, or soon thereafter. Newborns attend to the faces of members of their species. Other innate mechanisms for relating to others (e.g., attachment, or a proximity-seeking bond between child and caregiver) begin to emerge shortly after birth. Infants contribute to these early relationships by orienting clearly and consistently to their caregivers, and caregivers contribute by attending closely to their infants' behavior and emotions. Patterns of exchange and interdependence are apparent from the early weeks of life. A key sign of the importance of early relationships is that infants reliably turn to caregivers for reassurance and confidence in the face of threatening or stressful circumstances, a phenomenon known as the *secure base*. A critical mass of research now shows that these and other such abilities provide an essential infrastructure for many vital activities (relating to other people, exploring the environment, striving for achievement, solving problems creatively, caring for children and other people in need, engaging in health-promoting behavior) throughout life. Moreover, it is increasingly evident that the development of these abilities (and their underlying psychological traits) depends on the child's early relationships.

Caregiver-child pairs vary in the degree to which their relationships readily and unambiguously provide the secure base and the resulting emergent sense of security. Existing evidence indicates a substantial degree of continuity between early experiences and diverse relationships during childhood, adolescence, and adulthood. Discontinuities between earlier and later relationships typically are related to pronounced disruptions or stressors in the intervening years. Several explanations have been suggested for these temporal links. One possibility is that unsatisfying or restricted early relationships disrupt normal development, in turn affecting later behavior and relationships. Research with nonhuman species and with human children reared in orphanages with inadequate care arrangements has shown that even minor deprivation of contact with responsive individuals results in abnormal development of the brain and hormonal systems that regulate coping with stress (Gunnar, 2000). One researcher (Siegel, 1999) has even proposed that the "mind" develops at the intersection of neurophysiological processes and interpersonal relations. A more limited possibility is that early relationships are key sources of expectations about social relations. These "residues" of early relationships have been found repeatedly to be related to the characteristics of later relationships in childhood, adolescence, and adulthood (Roisman, Madsen, Hennighausen, Sroufe, & Collins, 2001). Little evidence supports one popular alternative hypothesis—that the long-term implications of attachment security are better attributed to individual differences in temperament (Thompson, 1998).

The evidence is compelling that relationships are significant in nearly every domain of activity. From infancy to old age, having friends and relating successfully to other people is associated with desirable outcomes in virtually all human domains: school, work, coping with negative events, adaptation during life transitions, parenthood, self-worth, and emotional well-being (Hartup & Stevens, 1997). This fact underscores the adaptive significance of relationships in human evolution and highlights the need to study development as a process that unfolds in relational contexts.

CONCLUDING COMMENT

Diverse emerging evidence indicates that relationship contexts have the potential to influence a diverse array of cognitive, emotional, and behavioral processes. Important challenges remain if these trends are to be cultivated into a systematic body of knowledge. Chief among these challenges is the necessity for identifying and evaluating the boundaries for relationship-context effects, and articulating their operation in a theoretically integrated way: To what extent do which different interpersonal circumstances affect the operation of which processes? Similarly, which individual differences moderate the degree to which interpersonal circumstances influence relationship outcomes and their behavioral effects? Other key questions for further advances in this area of research concern mechanisms. Although the evidence we have cited is suggestive, it remains to be determined how the external reality of relating is translated into the internal reality of basic cognitive, emotional, and biological processes. Finally, the rudimentary theoretical and methodological tools currently available must be supplemented by additional, even more sophisticated models and techniques. Such work promises to allow psychological science to more fully capitalize on a cherished axiom: that behavior is a product of the interaction between the properties of the person and the properties of the environment. To individuals, few features of the environment have greater salience or impact than whom they are with (or thinking about), and the nature of their relationship with that person. Fuller integration of the role of relationship contexts at all levels of psychological theorizing, research, and application is likely to augment the validity and utility of psychological science.

Recommended Reading

Berscheid, E. (1999). The greening of relationship science. *American Psychologist, 54,* 260–266.

Collins, W.A., & Laursen, B. (Eds.). (1999). *Minnesota Symposium on Child Psychology: Vol. 30. Relationships as developmental contexts.* Mahwah, NJ: Erlbaum.

Hinde, R.A. (1997). *Relationships: A dialectical perspective.* East Sussex, England: Psychology Press.

Kelley, H.H., Berscheid, E., Christensen, A., Harvey, J., Huston, T., Levinger, G., McClintock, E., Peplau, L.A., & Peterson, D. (1983). *Close relationships*. New York: Freeman.

Reis, H.T., Collins, W.A., & Berscheid, E. (2000). The relationship context of human behavior and development. *Psychological Bulletin, 126*, 844–872.

Acknowledgments—We gratefully acknowledge the enormous contributions of Ellen Berscheid to the conceptual framework from which this article emerged.

Note

1. Address correspondence to Harry Reis, Department of Clinical and Social Sciences in Psychology, University of Rochester, Rochester, NY 14627; e-mail: reis@psych.rochester.edu.

References

Andersen, S.M., & Chen, S. (2002). The relational self: An interpersonal social-cognitive theory. *Psychological Review, 109*, 619–645.

Berscheid, E., & Ammazzalorso, H. (2001). Emotional experience in close relationships. In M. Hewstone & M. Brewer (Eds.), *Black-well handbook of social psychology* (Vol. 2, pp. 308–330). Oxford, England: Blackwell.

Bugental, D. (2000). Acquisition of the algorithms of social life: A domain-based approach. *Psychological Bulletin, 126*, 187–219.

Clark, M., Fitness, J., & Brissette, I. (2001). Understanding people's perceptions of relationships is crucial to understanding their emotional lives. In M. Hewstone & M. Brewer (Eds.), *Blackwell handbook of social psychology* (Vol. 2, pp. 253–278). Oxford, England: Blackwell.

Ekman, P., & Davidson, R. (Eds.). (1994). *The nature of emotion: Fundamental questions*. New York: Oxford.

Gunnar, M.R. (2000). Early adversity and the development of stress reactivity and regulation. In C. Nelson (Ed.), *Minnesota Symposium on Child Psychology: Vol. 31. The effects of adversity on neurobehavioral development* (pp. 163–200). Mahwah, NJ: Erlbaum.

Hartup, W.W., & Stevens, N. (1997). Friendships and adaptation in the life course. *Psychological Bulletin, 121*, 355–370.

Kiecolt-Glaser, J., & Newton, T. (2001). Marriage and health: His and hers. *Psychological Bulletin, 127*, 472–503.

Lichty, W., Chyou, J., Aron, A., Anderson, A., Ghahremani, D., & Gabrieli, J. (2004, October). *Neural correlates of subjective closeness: An fMRI study*. Poster presented at the annual meeting of the Society for Neuroscience, San Diego, CA.

Roisman, G.I., Madsen, S., Hennighausen, K., Sroufe, L.A., & Collins, W.A. (2001). The coherence of dyadic behavior across parent-child and romantic relationships as mediated by the internalized representation of experience. *Attachment & Human Development, 3*, 156–172.

Sedikides, C., Campbell, W., Reeder, G., & Elliot, A. (1998). The self-serving bias in relational context. *Journal of Personality and Social Psychology, 74*, 378–386.

Siegel, D.J. (1999). *The developing mind: Toward a neurobiology of interpersonal experience*. New York: Guilford.

Smith, E.R., Coats, S., & Walling, D. (1999). Overlapping mental representations of self, in-group, and partner: Further response time evidence and a connectionist model. *Personality and Social Psychology Bulletin, 25*, 873–882.

Symons, C., & Johnson, B. (1997). The self-reference effect in memory: A meta-analysis. *Psychological Bulletin, 121*, 371–394.

Thompson, R.A. (1998). Early sociopersonality development. In W. Damon (Series Ed.) & N. Eisenberg (Vol. Ed.), *The handbook of child psychology* (Vol. 3, pp. 25–104). New York: Wiley.

Critical Thinking Questions

1. Think of the important relationships you currently have or have had in the past. How do they, and did they, shape who you are?

2. When might relationships have the strongest (or weakest) influence on us?

3. The authors suggest that relationships may hold adaptive significance in human evolution. Discuss this possibility in terms of the caregiver-child relationship.

This article has been reprinted as it originally appeared in *Current Directions in Psychological Science*. Citation information for this article as originally published appears above.

Contextual Influences on Marriage: Implications for Policy and Intervention

Benjamin R. Karney[1]
RAND Corporation
Thomas N. Bradbury
University of California, Los Angeles

Abstract

Current proposals to promote and strengthen marriage among low-income populations focus on values and behavioral skills as primary targets of intervention. Marital
research that examines contextual influences on marriage calls these emphases into
question. Ethnographic and survey research reveal no evidence that populations experiencing higher rates of divorce value healthy marriages any less than other populations do. Longitudinal and observational research reveals two mechanisms through
which the environment of a marriage may enhance or constrain effective relationship
maintenance. First, some environments contain fewer sources of support and pose
more severe challenges than others, presenting marriages in those environments with
greater burdens than marriages in more supportive environments are faced with. Second, when demands external to the marriage are relatively high, even couples with
adequate coping skills may have difficulty exercising those skills effectively. Together,
such findings suggest that successful policies and interventions to strengthen marriages need to acknowledge the environments within which marriages take place.

Keywords

marriage; family policy; stress; relationship maintenance

To improve the well-being of low-income populations, federal policymakers
have begun to emphasize the role of healthy marriages in shaping adult and child
outcomes. The justification for this emphasis on marriage has been correlational research demonstrating that stable, fulfilling marriages are associated
with improved physical and mental health and higher educational and economic
achievement for parents and children and that the absence of such relationships
is associated with poorer health and economic outcomes (e.g., Amato, 2001;
Kiecolt-Glaser & Newton, 2001). Assuming that the parents' relationship plays
a causal role in these associations, policymakers have proposed allocating over
1.5 billion dollars over the next 5 years to fund activities that support couples in
forming and maintaining healthy marriages. Legislation currently being debated
in the House and Senate specifies eight allowable activities for this funding, all
of which involve some form of relationship education—e.g., teaching the value
of stable marriages or teaching relationship and communication skills. Federal
policy seems to be guided by two perspectives: one emphasizing values and
another focusing on skills as primary determinants of marital outcome.

One challenge to applying educational interventions to low-income families
stems from the fact that, although the target populations for these initiatives

have been selected exclusively on the basis of their environment (i.e., low socio-economic status), the models guiding educational interventions generally do not address the role of the environment in determining marital outcomes. Behaviorally oriented relationship education, for example, places the responsibility for marital success or failure squarely on the couple, without regard for how their relationship may be affected by the context within which their marriage takes place. Recent marital research that has directly examined the effects of context on couples' relationships calls this emphasis into question. Cross-sectional surveys and longitudinal studies of newlywed couples have begun to identify paths through which communication, problem solving, and other relationship processes may be constrained or enhanced by supports or demands present in a marriage's context. The emerging picture suggests that even skilled and relatively satisfied couples may have difficulty interacting effectively under conditions of stress or diminished resources. Thus, current research on contextual influences on marriage suggests broadening the focus of interventions and policies designed to support healthy families among low-income populations.

FAMILY VALUES: WHO HAS THEM? WHO NEEDS THEM?

Marriages are unquestionably less frequent and less stable in low-income populations. Survey data reveal that, compared to those in high-income populations, women in low-income populations are half as likely to be married, twice as likely to divorce if married, and several times more likely to bear children outside of marriage (Bramlett & Mosher, 2002; Singh, Matthews, Clarke, Yannicos, & Smith, 1995). The case for offering values education to these individuals rests on the assumption that people in low-income populations do not appreciate the benefits of stable, healthy marriages as much as do people in high-income populations, in which marriage is more common and divorce less common.

In fact, there has been little research on attitudes toward family issues in low-income populations, but what research does exist indicates that members of these populations may value marriage more, not less, than members of middle- or high-income groups do. For example, Edin (2000) conducted lengthy interviews with unmarried mothers receiving welfare, asking them to describe their attitudes and intentions toward marriage. Far from minimizing the importance of marriage, these mothers reported strongly positive feelings about the institution and expressed their own intentions to marry. They described their decisions to postpone marriage as having little to do with their values and more to do with their belief that their current economic circumstances and available partners would be unlikely to lead to an enduring marriage over time. Thus, members of low-income populations may postpone marriage not because they value it too little but rather because they value it so much that they are unwilling to enter into a marriage that has a high risk of ending in divorce.

It is important to note that Edin's data exclude low-income men, who are notoriously underrepresented in family research. However, quantitative survey data from low-income men and women paint a similar picture. A recent survey commissioned by the state of Florida examined family structures and attitudes in

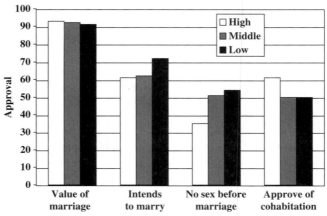

Fig. 1. Attitudes toward family issues by household income (high, middle, low). The low-income groups that report the highest rates of divorce, premarital sex, and cohabitation also express the lowest approval of them.

a representative sample (Karney, Garvan, & Thomas, 2003). Over 6,000 residents of Florida, Texas, California, and New York were asked in telephone interviews about their own experiences of marriage and families and about their opinions regarding marriage and family issues. Confirming the pattern in the broader census data, low-income respondents were far more likely than high-income respondents to be unmarried, to be divorced, and to be raising children outside of marriage. At the same time, however, compared to middle- or high-income respondents, members of low-income populations on average expressed the same or more positive attitudes toward traditional family structures (see Fig. 1). For example, when asked to rate their agreement with the statement "A happy, healthy marriage is one of the most important things in life," low-income respondents indicated that they agreed or strongly agreed at the same rate as did middle- and high-income respondents. When unmarried respondents were asked if they would like to be married someday, members of low-income households were substantially more likely than members of middle- or high-income households to say yes.

Existing research offers little justification for allocating limited resources toward values education for low-income populations. At least among women in this population, promarriage values appear to be in place already, and in any case such values may not be sufficient to bring about stable, fulfilling relationships.

CONTEXTUAL INFLUENCES ON MARRIAGE

Whereas there is little evidence that values are associated with decisions to enter into or postpone marriage, there is growing evidence to suggest that the quality of a couple's communication and problem solving is associated with marital outcomes over time (Heyman, 2001; Johnson et al., 2005). Furthermore, several studies provide evidence that premarital education programs focusing on communication can affect problem solving and that such programs may have long-term benefits for marriages (e.g., Halford, Sanders, & Behrens, 2001).

Despite this evidence, the existing research has been limited in two main ways. First, research on marital interaction and premarital education programs has addressed primarily white, college-educated, middle-class samples. In terms of their risk of experiencing marital dysfunction, the support available to them, and the demands they face outside of the marriage, such samples differ greatly from the low-income populations of interest to policymakers. It remains an open question whether programs developed within middle-class populations can be effective for improving the marriages of low-income couples. Second, when assessing relationship processes like problem solving and support, researchers have assumed that such processes are generally stable in the absence of intervention. Research on marital interactions in particular has treated the quality of a couple's communication as a stable, trait-like condition of the relationship that accounts for later marital outcomes. Far less frequent has been research on how marital interactions and relationship processes themselves may vary and develop over time. As a result, the conditions that encourage or discourage effective interactions in marriage remain poorly understood.

Current research on the effects of context and environmental stress on marital processes is beginning to illuminate both of these issues. Drawing from cross-sectional survey research, researchers have begun to examine relationship processes across a wide range of contexts and cultures, to understand how the predictors of marital success may differ depending on the context within which particular marriages form and develop. Using intensive longitudinal designs, researchers have begun to identify the correlates of variability in relationship processes within couples over time, in order to understand the forces that support or constrain couples in their efforts to maintain their relationships. Although it has long been known that marriages under stress report lower marital quality and are at increased risk of dissolution (e.g., Hill, 1949), research adopting these approaches has now elaborated on the mechanisms through which context affects marriage.

Context Shapes the Content of Marital Interactions

An emphasis on relationship skills reflects the assumption that the way couples communicate is more important than the specific issues they discuss. One reason that this assumption has gone unchallenged may be that studies have examined couples in a relatively narrow and privileged segment of the population whose problems are, on average, relatively mild. Surveying a broader range of the population, however, confirms that the couples in different contexts may face different sorts of marital problems. For example, when respondents rated the severity of potential relationship problems in the survey cited earlier (Karney et al., 2003), communication was rated as a relatively severe problem regardless of household income, although it was rated most severe in high-income households (see Fig. 2). Drugs and infidelity, in contrast, were rated as more severe problems by low-income households. Research on middle-class newlyweds indicates that spouses tend to report more severe relationship problems during periods of relatively high stress than they do during periods of relatively low stress (Neff & Karney, 2004). Not surprisingly, the more severe the problems discussed by a couple, the more negatively their communication is rated by objective observers

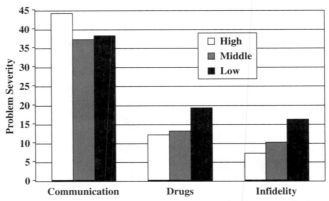

Fig. 2. Severity of specific relationship problems by household income (high, middle, low). Although couples at all income levels report problems with communication, low-income couples are more likely to report problems with drugs or infidelity.

(Vogel & Karney, 2002). Thus, independent of spouses' relationship skills, marriages taking place in more stressful contexts may be more challenging simply due to the increased severity of the obstacles that couples must face inside and outside of their marriages. Interventions that acknowledge those obstacles may prove more effective than interventions addressing communication skills alone.

Context Affects Spouses' Ability to Interact Effectively

When the context of a marriage contains many demands and few sources of support, spouses not only have more severe problems to cope with but may also have diminished ability to exercise the coping skills they possess. A 4-year study of 172 middle-class newlywed couples (Karney, Story, & Bradbury, 2005) revealed that couples experiencing relatively high levels of chronic stress (e.g., financial difficulties, lack of social support, inadequate employment) not only reported lower marital satisfaction overall but also seemed to have more difficulty maintaining their satisfaction over time. Relative to couples reporting better conditions, those reporting high levels of chronic stress experienced a steeper decline in marital satisfaction over the early years of marriage, a finding that held even after these couples' initially lower levels of satisfaction was controlled for. Moreover, for wives experiencing chronic stress, marital satisfaction was especially reactive to increases in acute stress, such that the same negative life events were associated with steeper declines in satisfaction for stressed wives than they were for less stressed wives.

Why would marital satisfaction be more difficult to maintain when conditions outside of the marriage are more adverse? The activities that maintain relationships take time and energy, so those activities should be harder to undertake under adverse conditions. Supporting this view is an independent study of 82 middle-class newlyweds that examined how spouses' willingness to forgive their partners' negative behaviors was associated with changes in their levels of stress over time (Neff & Karney, 2004). Within-couple analyses revealed that individuals who could excuse their partners' negative behaviors during intervals of relatively low stress were more likely to blame their partners for those same behaviors during periods of relatively high stress. In other words, spouses who are capable of making adaptive responses appear to be less likely to do so when facing challenges outside of their marriages.

It is worth noting that both of these studies sampled from a population experiencing a relatively narrow range of stress. In samples that included severely disadvantaged families, Conger and colleagues (e.g., Conger, Rueter, & Elder, 1999) also showed that economic strain inhibits effective relationship maintenance. Together, such studies begin to suggest how stressful environments come to be associated with negative marital outcomes. Stressful environments not only present couples with more challenges, but they diminish those couples' ability to deal with their challenges effectively.

IMPLICATIONS FOR MARITAL INTERVENTIONS AND POLICIES

Given what is currently known about the effects of context on marriage and marital processes, there are two reasons to expect that, by themselves, interventions developed for middle-class couples may not be adequate to support marriages among the low-income couples of interest to policymakers. First, the skills relevant to solving the problems faced by middle- and upper-income couples may not be relevant to the types of problems (e.g., substance abuse, domestic violence, infidelity) that low-income couples are more likely than other populations to face. Second, even if a set of valuable relationship skills could be identified and taught, those skills may be difficult or impossible to practice in the context of low-income marriage. Effective problem solving will matter little, for example, to couples who have few opportunities to interact together due to demands outside the marriage. Providing such couples with relationship skills training without also addressing the external forces that impede couples' ability to practice those skills may be akin to offering piano lessons to people with no access to a piano.

Providing a solid empirical foundation for interventions to promote and support low-income marriage requires basic research on marriage in this population, not only to identify the processes that make for successful relationships among low-income couples, but also to describe the circumstances that make those processes more or less likely. The unfortunate irony is that, just as this research is needed to inform policy, funding for research on marital outcomes has been explicitly removed from consideration at the National Institute of Mental Health, formerly the major source of support for marital research.

The drive to provide services that improve the lives of low-income families thus presents marital research with a challenge and an opportunity. The challenge is to find ways to specify the minimum conditions that must be met before behavioral skills training can have a positive impact on low-income marriages. The opportunity is the chance to reexamine what is known about the significant predictors of marital outcome in this new context, and thereby to establish which of those predictors are not only significant, but substantial.

Recommended Reading

Bradbury, T.N. & Karney, B.R. (2004). Understanding and altering the longitudinal course of marriage. *Journal of Marriage and Family, 66,* 862–879.

Edin, K., & Kefalas, M. (2005). *Promises I can keep: Why poor women put motherhood before marriage.* Berkeley: University of California Press.

Cherlin, A.J. (2004). The deinstitutionalization of American marriage. *Journal of Marriage and Family, 66,* 848–861.

Acknowledgments—Preparation of this article was supported by Grant R01MH59712 from the National Institute of Mental Health awarded to the first author, and Grant R01MH48764 from the National Institute of Mental Health awarded to the second author.

Note

1. Address correspondence to Benjamin R. Karney, RAND Corporation, 1776 Main Street, P.O. Box 2138, Santa Monica, CA 90407-2138; e-mail: bkarney@rand.org.

References

Amato, P.R. (2001). Children of divorce in the 1990s: An update of the Amato and Keith (1991) meta-analysis. *Journal of Family Psychology, 15,* 355–370.

Bramlett, M.D., & Mosher, W.D. (2002). *Cohabitation, marriage, divorce, and remarriage in the United States* (Vital and Health Statistics Series 23, No. 22). Hyattsville, Maryland: National Center for Health Statistics.

Conger, R.D., Rueter, M.A., & Elder, G.H. (1999). Couple resilience to economic pressure. *Journal of Personality and Social Psychology, 76,* 54–71.

Edin, K. (2000). What do low-income single mothers say about marriage? *Social Problems, 47,* 112–133.

Halford, W.K., Sanders, M.R., & Behrens, B.C. (2001). Can skills training prevent relationship problems in at-risk couples? Four-year effects of a behavioral relationship education program. *Journal of Family Psychology, 15,* 750–768.

Heyman, R.E. (2001). Observation of couple conflicts: Clinical assessment applications, stubborn truths, and shaky foundations. *Psychological Assessment, 13,* 5–35.

Hill, R. (1949). *Families under stress.* New York: Harper & Row.

Johnson, M.D., Cohan, C.L., Davila, J., Lawrence, E., Rogge, R.D., Karney, B.R., Sullivan, K.T., & Bradbury, T.N. (2005). Problem-solving skills and affective expressions as predictors of change in marital satisfaction. *Journal of Consulting and Clinical Psychology, 73,* 15–27.

Karney, B.R., Garvan, C.W., & Thomas, M.S. (2003). *Family formation in Florida: 2003 baseline survey of attitudes, beliefs, and demographics relating to marriage and family formation.* Gainesville, FL: University of Florida.

Karney, B.R., Story, L.B., & Bradbury, T.N. (2005). Marriages in context: Interactions between chronic and acute stress among newlyweds. In T.A. Revenson, K. Kayser, & G. Bodenmann (Eds.), *Emerging perspectives on couples' coping with stress* (pp. 13–32). Washington, DC: American Psychological Association.

Kiecolt-Glaser, J.K., & Newton, T.L. (2001). Marriage and health: His and hers. *Psychological Bulletin, 127,* 472–503.

Neff, L.A., & Karney, B.R. (2004). How does context affect intimate relationships? Linking external stress and cognitive processes within marriage. *Personality and Social Psychology Bulletin, 30,* 134–148.

Singh, G.K., Matthews, T.J., Clarke, S.C., Yannicos, T., & Smith, B.L. (1995). *Annual summary of births, marriages, divorces, and deaths: United States, 1994* (Monthly Vital Statistics Report, Vol. 43, No. 13). Atlanta, GA: National Center for Health Statistics.

Vogel, D.L., & Karney, B.R. (2002). Demands and withdrawal in newlyweds: Elaborating on the social structure hypothesis. *Journal of Social and Personal Relationships, 19,* 685–702.

Critical Thinking Questions

1. How might policymakers more effectively intervene to promote the marriages of low-income couples?

2. In addition to the socioeconomic issues on which the current article focused, what are some contextual variables that may influence how relationships function?

3. Do you think there might be thoughts or behaviors that can benefit certain relationships but hurt others?

4. What environmental stressors affect your relationships?

This article has been reprinted as it originally appeared in *Current Directions in Psychological Science*. Citation information for this article as originally published appears above.

Speed-Dating

Eli J. Finkel[1] and Paul W. Eastwick
Northwestern University

Abstract

Scholars have recently begun to harness the immense power of speed-dating procedures to achieve important and novel insights into the dynamics of romantic attraction. Speed-dating procedures allow researchers to study romantic dynamics dyadically, with regard to potentially meaningful relationships, and with strong external validity. This article highlights the strengths and promise of speed-dating procedures, reviews some of their most exciting contributions to our understanding of the social psyche, and illustrates how scholars can employ speed-dating and its straightforward variants to study topics relevant to diverse subfields of psychological science.

Keywords

speed-dating; romantic attraction; relationships; thin slices; social relations model

In the late 1990s, Rabbi Yaacov Deyo invented speed-dating to help Jewish singles in Los Angeles meet each other. In Deyo's clever paradigm, individuals interested in meeting potential romantic partners go on approximately 10 to 25 very brief (e.g., 4-minute) "dates" with a series of desired-sex partners. After the event, participants report whether they would ("yes") or would not ("no") be interested in corresponding with each speed-dating partner again in the future. If two participants reply "yes" to each other, they are a *match,* and the host of the speed-dating event provides them with the opportunity to contact each other, perhaps to arrange a more traditional date.

Readers with no first-hand exposure to Deyo's speed-dating paradigm might become exhausted by the mere *notion* of going on 10 to 25 blind dates in one night. Fortunately, speed-dating bears little resemblance to traditional blind dates. A better analogy for a speed-dating event is a party or other social gathering where individuals hope to meet other singles. Compared to such social gatherings, however, speed-dating offers several advantages to participants, including the assurance that the people they meet are also interested in meeting romantic partners, the ability to give to each partner unambiguous acceptance or rejection feedback without having to do so face-to-face, and the comfort of knowing that the suffering inflicted by a bad date will be mercifully brief.

What led to Deyo's invention of speed-dating? As the details of his life are somewhat hazy, we use guesswork to fill in the gaps: Deyo must have long been a social psychology fanatic who delighted in those all-too-rare articles describing well-controlled studies from the 1960s and '70s in which scholars randomly assigned participants to go on blind dates with each other (e.g., Byrne, Ervin, & Lamberth, 1970; Walster, Aronson, Abrahams, & Rottmann, 1966). Later, during the 1990s, he must have voraciously consumed the scholarly literature on interpersonal perception, becoming enthralled by Nalini Ambady's research on perceptions based on "thin slices" of social behavior (e.g., Ambady, Bernieri, & Richeson, 2000;

Ambady & Rosenthal, 1992) and by David Kenny's research on perceptions at "zero acquaintance" (e.g., Kenny, 1994). This evidence that individuals can make accurate and differentiated social judgments based on strikingly brief social observations or interactions surely caused Deyo to conclude that singles could probably evaluate each other's romantic potential within a few short moments. He augmented the blind date with speed to help people meet romantic partners as efficiently as possible.

Of course, this "social psychology fanatic" theory of speed-dating's birth is fictional. It does, however, accurately situate speed-dating procedures squarely in the mainstream of social psychological theory and methodology.

THE SCIENTIFIC POWER OF SPEED-DATING PROCEDURES

Speed-dating incorporates a variety of extant methodological and statistical innovations (see Eastwick & Finkel, in press; for a nuts-and-bolts manual for conducting speed-dating studies, see Finkel, Eastwick, & Matthews, 2007). For example, importing the *speed* aspect of the "thin slices" and "zero acquaintance" literatures allows scholars to examine the opening moments of romantic attraction with supercharged efficiency (e.g., dozens of times during a 2-hour speed-dating event rather than just once during a traditional, 2-hour blind date) and to explore why a given individual desires certain romantic partners but not others. In this article, we discuss how scholars can use speed-dating to (a) study dyadic processes, (b) examine real relationships in real time, and (c) enjoy strong external validity.

Dyadic Processes

One advantage of speed-dating is that its procedures allow scholars to study both members of a given dyad. Because romantic attraction involves two individuals simultaneously perceiving and being perceived, scholars may fail to investigate (or even recognize) important attraction phenomena if their methods do not allow them to consider the dyad as the unit of analysis.

Many widespread empirical procedures examine romantic attraction from only one person's perspective. For example, scholars may (a) present participants with information about a target person (e.g., a photograph and attitude information) and then assess participants' attraction to him or her (e.g., Byrne, 1971), or even (b) bolster psychological realism by having participants report their attraction for a research confederate (e.g., Dutton & Aron, 1974). Although such methods are powerful and valuable—especially insofar as they can readily accommodate diverse experimental manipulations—they fail to capture essential dyadic features of romantic-attraction dynamics, such as the uncertainty and evaluation apprehension that both individuals frequently experience during the interaction.

Speed-dating procedures overcome this limitation, as each speed-date involves two participants who simultaneously explore their romantic potential with the other person. For example, a heterosexual speed-dating event attended by 20 men and 20 women would include 400 separate dyadic interactions. Among other advantages, this efficient accumulation of dyadic interactions allows scholars to harness the power of the statistical procedures underlying Kenny's (1994) social relations model. For example, scholars can distinguish among three independent reasons why Laura experienced sexual desire for Tim following their speed-date: (a) Laura tended to have a crush on all the men at the event (her standards are low), (b) all the women at the event tended to have a crush on Tim (he is consensually desirable), or (c) Laura experienced some unique "chemistry" with Tim that stimulated her desire for him beyond her desire for the typical man and beyond the desire of the typical woman for Tim.

Speed-dating data also provide scholars with an optimal means of exploring inherently dyadic processes such as reciprocity of liking. Such reciprocity can emerge in two distinct ways: *dyadic reciprocity*, which refers to the desire that two individuals share uniquely with each other, and *generalized reciprocity*, which refers to the tendency for individuals who generally desire others to be desired in return (Kenny, 1994). One recent speed-dating study (Eastwick, Finkel, Mochon, & Ariely, 2007) revealed a positive dyadic-reciprocity effect (if Laura romantically desired Tim more than she desired the other men, he desired her more than he desired the other women) and a negative generalized-reciprocity effect (if Laura romantically desired the men at the event more than the other women did, those men desired her *less* than they desired the other women at the event; see left half of Fig. 1). Neither effect differed by participant sex, and both were robust beyond any physical attractiveness effects.

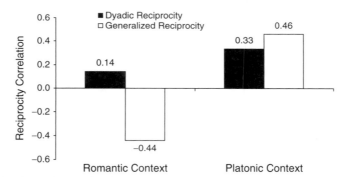

Fig. 1. Dyadic and generalized reciprocity correlations in platonic and romantic (speed-dating) contexts. The romantic-context correlations come from a speed-dating study (Eastwick, Finkel, Mochon, & Ariely, 2007), whereas the platonic-context correlations come from the three previous studies employing one-to-one sequential interactions between strangers (see Kenny, 1994). The reported values are Fisher z-transformed correlations (the Pearson correlations for the four bars, from left to right, are .14, −.41, .32, and .43; see Eastwick, Finkel, Mochon, & Ariely, 2007; Kenny, 1994).

Correlations are measures of agreement that can vary from −1.00 to +1.00; a value of 1.00 indicates complete agreement, a value of −1.00 indicates complete disagreement, and a value of .00 indicates that two scores are unrelated to each other. For example, the −.44 generalized reciprocity correlation in the romantic context indicates that the more individuals tended to experience nonselective romantic desire for others, the *less* they were romantically desired in return. In contrast, the .46 generalized reciprocity correlation in the platonic context indicates that the more individuals tended to experience nonselective platonic liking for others, the *more* they were liked in return.

These results suggest that unselective romantic desire smacks of desperation and turns people off, although this adverse consequence may be unique to romantic contexts. Three other studies employing dyadic interactions with strangers in nonromantic contexts (see Kenny, 1994) yielded both positive dyadic and positive generalized reciprocity effects: Individuals who platonically liked others were liked in return, regardless of whether their liking was selective or unselective (see right half of Fig. 1).

Real Relationships

A second advantage of speed-dating is that it allows social scientists to study initial attraction dynamics between two individuals who could plausibly pursue a meaningful romantic relationship together in the near future. Scholars can study such dynamics in real time (rather than with retrospective reports or with hypothetical scenarios) and with regard to consequential dating behaviors. Participants' behavior on their speed-dates (which can be videotaped and coded), and their "yessing" and e-mailing decisions, can powerfully influence their romantic lives over the ensuing days, weeks, and beyond.

A recent speed-dating study (Eastwick & Finkel, 2008) explored the possibility that reports about hypothetical relationships may not map onto actual relationship dynamics. This study reexamined the well-replicated and well-publicized findings that men prefer physical attractiveness in a mate more than women do and that women prefer good earning prospects in a mate more than men do (e.g., Buss, 1989). When reporting before their speed-dating event on their preferences for an ideal partner and for a speed-dating partner—abstract, hypothetical partners, as in previous research—men stated that they preferred physically attractive partners more than women stated that they did, and women stated that they preferred partners with strong earning prospects more than men stated that they did (Eastwick & Finkel, 2008; see left half of Fig. 2).

But the story does not end there: Speed-dating procedures allow scholars to ask whether these sex differences in *stated preferences* correspond to preferences for actual, flesh-and-blood partners. Meta-analyzing across 17 different measures of romantic attraction from the speed-dating event and the ensuing month (e.g., "yessing," date initiation, romantic passion), no reliable sex differences emerged in the degree to which speed-daters' judgments of targets' physical attractiveness or earning prospects inspired their romantic interest in those targets (Eastwick & Finkel, 2008; see right half of Fig. 2). These null effects for sex were not moderated by participants' pursuit of short-term versus long-term mating goals, and they could not be explained by participants settling for nonideal partners due to fear of rejection.

That those sex differences emerging so reliably when participants report on hypothetical partners disappear when they report on flesh-and-blood partners raises a fascinating question: Do individuals have accurate introspective access to their preferences in a live romantic context? Each Northwestern Speed-Dating Study participant met approximately 12 opposite-sex speed-daters. Therefore, we could assign a unique score (an *in-vivo preference*) representing how well a given participant's judgments of each partner's physical attractiveness or earning

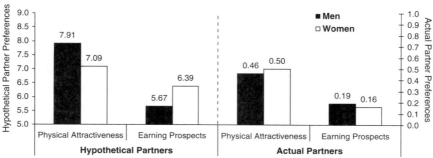

Fig. 2. Men's and women's preferences for physical attractiveness and earning prospects regarding hypothetical partners and actual partners. Participants reported their hypothetical partner preferences for a given characteristic (physical attractiveness or earning prospects) on scales ranging from 1 to 9, with higher values reflecting stronger preferences for that characteristic. For clarity of presentation, these hypothetical ratings average across participants' preferences in an ideal partner and in a speed-dating partner. Participants' actual partner preferences reflect the correlation of their evaluation of a specific speed-dating partner's characteristics and their romantic attraction to him or her (across 17 measures of romantic attraction). The sex differences for hypothetical partners are statistically significant both for physical attractiveness and for earning prospects, but they fail to approach significance in either case for actual partners. The values reported in the right half of the figure are Fisher z-transformed correlations (the Pearson correlations for the four bars, from left to right, are .43, .46, .19, and .16; see Eastwick & Finkel, 2008).

prospects predicted her or his romantic attraction toward that partner. Remarkably, stated preferences were not correlated with in-vivo preferences, suggesting that those preferences individuals report regarding hypothetical partners may not predict whom they desire after a face-to-face meeting (Eastwick & Finkel, 2008). At a broader level, individuals seem to lack accurate introspective access to the preferences they will exhibit when encountering potential dating partners (see also Iyengar, Simonson, Fisman, & Mogilner, 2005; Todd, Penke, Fasolo, & Lenton, 2007); this lack of insight echoes classic research suggesting that individuals are frequently unable to report accurately *why* they exhibit a particular response (e.g., "liking") to a stimulus (Nisbett & Wilson, 1977).

External Validity

A third advantage of speed-dating procedures is that they exhibit stronger external validity than do many other highly controlled procedures for studying romantic attraction. For example, speed-dating is an activity that millions of people pursue outside of the laboratory. One benefit of speed-dating's widespread appeal is that scholars can access impressive participant samples. One study employing a diverse sample of 10,526 real-world speed-daters (mean age, 33) revealed that attraction to speed-dating partners is driven (a) more by generally agreed-upon mate values than by idiosyncratic or similarity-based mating tendencies and (b) more by observable characteristics such as attractiveness, height, and age than by less observable characteristics such as education, religion, or the desire to have children

(Kurzban & Weeden, 2005). The size and diversity of this study's sample make its conclusions especially compelling.

Given speed dating's appeal across sociodemographic categories, scholars can readily employ it to investigate how race and ethnicity moderate romantic attraction. For example, one study demonstrated that individuals who grew up in geographical locations characterized by relatively strong (versus weak) opposition to interracial marriage are more likely to prefer same-race over different-race speed-dating partners (Fisman, Iyengar, Kamenica, & Simonson, 2008). Although this finding emerged in a sample of Columbia University graduate students, scholars could collaborate with speed-dating companies to examine whether it replicates when comparing events hosted in locations characterized by strong versus weak opposition to interracial marriage. Speed-dating scholars could employ similar procedures (and have already begun to do so) to replicate other race-related findings, including the finding that female speed-daters tend to prefer same-race over different-race partners more than male speed-daters do (Fisman et al., 2008; Kurzban & Weeden, 2005) and the finding that White participants who endorse political conservatism are more likely than their liberal counterparts to report reduced romantic desire for racial minority romantic partners compared to White romantic partners (Eastwick, Richeson, & Finkel, 2008).

POTENTIAL LIMITATIONS OF SPEED DATING

Although many researchers have become avid supporters of speed-dating's scientific potential, such procedures, as with all methodological innovations, should be evaluated with caution (Eastwick & Finkel, in press; Finkel et al., 2007). For example, although speed-dating possesses strong external validity in certain ways, it might lack it in others. After all, speed-dating events do differ in several notable ways from traditional ways that romantic partners meet, and these differences might appeal only to a small subset of singles. Such external-validity concerns, however, are hardly unique to speed-dating. Scholars have yet to establish (a) how romantic relationships beginning at church socials differ from those beginning at work, at the beach, or on the subway (e.g., perhaps relationships beginning at church benefit from spiritual rather than sexual compatibility, whereas relationships beginning at the beach show the opposite pattern); or (b) how the personalities of individuals who meet partners in one setting differ from the personalities of individuals who meet partners in others (e.g., perhaps speed-daters have exceptionally strong—or exceptionally weak—social skills). Future research could fruitfully explore whether certain means of meeting partners are better suited to some people than to others.

A second potential concern is that speed-dating might fail to foster romantic attraction. The scholarly value of speed-dating procedures would diminish substantially if speed-daters only rarely become attracted to each other or only rarely initiate postevent contact (relative to parallel frequencies in other contexts). Fortunately, preliminary evidence suggests that speed-dating may be an especially effective means of introducing people who subsequently pursue follow-up dates with each other (Eastwick & Finkel, in press; Finkel et al., 2007).

CONCLUDING COMMENTS

In the decade since Rabbi Deyo invented speed-dating, it has become a major phenomenon extending well beyond Western culture. Its core structure is readily amenable to adaptation, even for populations that might not generally encourage dating. For example, devout Muslims have adapted speed-dating procedures to include parental chaperones (MacFarquhar, 2006). Entrepreneurs have also adapted speed-dating procedures for nonromantic activities such as speed-networking, speed-interviewing, and speed-friending. Given that speed-dating procedures and its nonromantic variants involve dyadic processes, real social dynamics in real time, and strong external validity, they promise to help scholars gain new insights into the social dynamics relevant to research domains such as decision making, prejudice, emotion, memory, social development, and personality (to name but a few). For example, cognitive or social psychologists could employ speed-friending procedures to study the association of interpersonal liking with subsequent memory for the interaction, and industrial/organizational psychologists could employ speed-networking procedures to study whether individuals' likelihood of exchanging business cards depends upon each dyad's personality similarity. The possibilities are endless.

Recommended Reading

Eastwick, P.W., & Finkel, E.J. (2008). (See References). An in-depth speed-dating exploration of sex differences in romantic partner preferences and the disconnect between stated and in-vivo preferences.

Eastwick, P.W., & Finkel, E.J. (in press). (See References). An overview of why speed-dating has so much promise as a tool for studying initial romantic attraction and early relationship development.

Finkel, E.J., Eastwick, P.W., & Matthews, J. (2007). (See References). A conceptual and methodological primer—a "how-to guide"—for scholars interested in conducting their own speed-dating studies.

Fisman, R., Iyengar, S.S., Kamenica, E., & Simonson, I. (2008). (See References). An excellent study investigating the roles of race and gender in "yessing" decisions.

Kurzban, R., & Weeden, J. (2005). (See References). This early speed-dating article does a superb job illustrating the power of speed-dating procedures.

Acknowledgments—The authors, who contributed equally to this article, thank Candida Abrahamson and Jennifer Richeson for their insightful feedback.

Note

1. Address correspondence to Eli Finkel or Paul Eastwick, Northwestern University, Department of Psychology, 2029 Sheridan Road, Swift Hall #102, Evanston, IL, 60208-2710; e-mail: finkel@northwestern.edu or p-eastwick@northwestern.edu.

References

Ambady, N., Bernieri, F.J., & Richeson, J.A. (2000). Toward a histology of social behavior: Judgmental accuracy from thin slices of the behavioral stream. In M.P. Zanna (Ed.), *Advances in experimental social psychology* (Vol. 32, pp. 201–271). San Diego, CA: Academic Press.

Ambady, N., & Rosenthal, R. (1992). Thin slices of expressive behavior as predictors of interpersonal consequences: A meta-analysis. *Psychological Bulletin, 111,* 256–274.

Buss, D.M. (1989). Sex differences in human mate preferences: Evolutionary hypotheses tested in 37 cultures. *Behavioral and Brain Sciences, 12,* 1–49.

Byrne, D. (1971). *The attraction paradigm.* New York: Academic Press.

Byrne, D., Ervin, C.R., & Lamberth, J. (1970). Continuity between the experimental study of attraction and real-life computer dating. *Journal of Personality and Social Psychology, 16,* 157–165.

Dutton, D.G., & Aron, A.P. (1974). Some evidence for heightened sexual attraction under conditions of high anxiety. *Journal of Personality and Social Psychology, 30,* 510–517.

Eastwick, P.W., & Finkel, E.J. (2008). Sex differences in mate preferences revisited: Do people know what they initially desire in a romantic partner? *Journal of Personality and Social Psychology, 94,* 245–264.

Eastwick, P.W., & Finkel, E.J. (in press). Speed-dating: A powerful and flexible paradigm for studying romantic relationship initiation. In S. Sprecher, A. Wenzel, & J. Harvey (Eds.), *Handbook of relationship initiation.* New York: Guilford.

Eastwick, P.W., Finkel, E.J., Mochon, D., & Ariely, D. (2007). Selective versus unselective romantic desire: Not all reciprocity is created equal. *Psychological Science, 18,* 317–319.

Eastwick, P.W., Richeson, J.A., & Finkel, E.J. (2008). *Is love colorblind? Political orientation and interracial romantic desire.* Unpublished manuscript, Northwestern University.

Finkel, E.J., Eastwick, P.W., & Matthews, J. (2007). Speed-dating as an invaluable tool for studying romantic attraction: A methodological primer. *Personal Relationships, 14,* 149–166.

Fisman, R., Iyengar, S.S., Kamenica, E., & Simonson, I. (2008). Racial preferences in dating. *Review of Economic Studies, 75,* 117–132.

Iyengar, S.S., Simonson, I., Fisman, R., & Mogilner, C. (2005, January). *I know what I want but can I find it? Examining the dynamic relationship between stated and revealed preferences.* Paper presented at the Annual Meeting of the Society for Personality and Social Psychology (SPSP), New Orleans, LA.

Kenny, D.A. (1994). *Interpersonal perception: A social relations analysis.* New York: Guilford.

Kurzban, R., & Weeden, J. (2005). Hurrydate: Mate preferences in action. *Evolution and Human Behavior, 26,* 227–244.

MacFarquhar, N. (2006, September 19). It's Muslim boy meets girl, but don't call it dating. *New York Times,* p. A1.

Nisbett, R.E., & Wilson, T.D. (1977). Telling more than we can know: Verbal reports on mental processes. *Psychological Review, 84,* 231–259.

Todd, P.M., Penke, L., Fasolo, B., & Lenton, A.P. (2007). Different cognitive processes underlie human mate choices and mate preferences. *Proceedings of the National Academy of Sciences, USA, 104,* 15011–15016.

Walster, E., Aronson, V., Abrahams, D., & Rottmann, L. (1966). Importance of physical attractiveness in dating behavior. *Journal of Personality and Social Psychology, 4,* 508–516.

Critical Thinking Questions

1. In addition to those outlined in this article, what other questions could be addressed through speed-dating studies?

2. What questions could not be addressed through speed-dating studies?

3. What are some of the advantages and disadvantages of this procedure?

This article has been reprinted as it originally appeared in *Current Directions in Psychological Science.* Citation information for this article as originally published appears above.

Section 2: Biological Foundations of Sex and Relationships

Although people often speak of "chemistry" when referring to the spark that attracts them to another person, it is likely that they rarely consider all of the biological underpinnings of sexuality and relationships. Many of the emotions we have in our relationships are strongly shaped by a host of biological agents, such as our hormones, our neurotransmitters, and our various brain structures. Thus, a complete understanding of sexuality and relationships is not possible without an understanding of their biological foundations.

In the first article of this section, Martha McClintock and Gilbert Herdt argue that the emergence of sexuality is a developmental *process* rather than an event. Contrary to common belief, sexual attraction appears to exist in children well before gonadarche, the maturation of the ovaries or testes. McClintock and Herdt report that sexual attraction in males and females develops around the age of ten due to the maturing of the adrenal glands (*adrenarche*) which secrete significant levels of androgens. Through their presentation of data and logic, McClintock and Herdt argue against many alternative cultural, social, and learning-based explanations for why sexual attraction appears to emerge prior to puberty.

For the majority of people, unlike most other animals, sex and relationships are intimately intertwined. Is the tendency of humans to form intimate bonds with their sexual partners shaped purely by culture, or are there biological underpinnings to the formation of such bonds? J. Thomas Curtis and Zuoxin Wang (2003) review evidence from studies of various species of voles (a type of rodent) suggesting that biology may play a role in the tendency to bond with partners. Specifically, Curtis and Wang describe evidence for the involvement of four neurochemicals—vasopressin, oxytocin, dopamine, and corticosterone—in forging lasting connections between partners.

Consider that a man who mates with a woman who has other sexual partners cannot be assured that he will be the father of her offspring. Todd Shackelford and Aaron Goetz argue that the male mating system has developed a means of dealing with the sperm of other men—potential competitors in the race to spread genes. Drawing on some examples from the animal kingdom, they argue that there are several areas in which there are human adaptations to sperm competition, including the size of testes, the shape of the penis, the amount of sperm contained within ejaculate, and sexual arousal in situations that suggest the presence of the sperm of other men. Most controversially, they argue that men with partners who have had the opportunity to be unfaithful are more inclined to engage in coercive sexual interactions with that partner.

The article by Steven Gangestad, Randy Thornhill, and Christine Garver-Apgar is a nice illustration of science. Specific hypotheses are deduced from theory—in this case, evolutionary psychology. Then, data are collected to support or refute those predictions—in this case, using behaviors that would be expected in the present day. According to the *adaptationist* hypothesis, women can maximize their reproductive fitness by extrarelational mating during ovulation, a practice that works against the reproductive interests of their male partners. Indeed, the research they describe provides substantial evidence that women are attracted to different qualities in a man when they are ovulating than during the rest of their menstrual cycle. Further, not surprising from an evolutionary perspective, men appear to have developed various mate-guarding strategies to make it less likely that their primary partners will mate with other men during ovulation, such as greater vigilance during ovulation.

Although some degree of beauty may be in the eye of the beholder, ratings of physical attractiveness are remarkably consistent, even across cultures. What is it about a face that makes it attractive? In the final article of this section, Bernhard Fink and Ian Penton-Voak review evidence suggesting that humans may have evolved a preference for three facial qualities because those qualities were likely to have reflected the health and thus fertility of a potential mate to ancestral humans: symmetry, averageness, and hormone markers. Of course, these features alone do not account for everything that makes a face attractive to a particular person. Indeed, Fink and Penton-Voak go on to review evidence that explains how various individual differences may develop according to previous experience and current context.

Rethinking Puberty: The Development of Sexual Attraction

Martha K. McClintock[1] and Gilbert Herdt

Department of Psychology, The University of Chicago, Chicago, Illinois

A youth remembers a time when he was sitting in the family room with his parents watching the original "Star Trek" television series. He reports that he was 10 years old and had not yet developed any of the obvious signs of puberty. When "Captain Kirk" suddenly peeled off his shirt, the boy was titillated. At 10 years of age, this was his first experience of sexual attraction, and he knew intuitively that, according to the norms of his parents and society, he should not be feeling this same-gender attraction. The youth relating this memory is a self-identified gay 18-year-old in Chicago. He also reports that at age 5 he had an absence of sexual attractions of any kind, and that even by age 8 he had not experienced overt awareness of sexual attraction. By age 10, however, a profound transformation had begun, and it was already completed by the time he entered puberty; sexual attraction to the same gender was so familiar to him (Herdt & Boxer, 1993) that it defined his selfhood.

Recent findings from three distinct and significant studies have pointed to the age of 10 as the mean age of first sexual attraction—well before puberty, which is typically defined as the age when the capacity to procreate is attained (Timiras, 1972). These findings are at odds with previous developmental and social science models of behavioral sexual development in Western countries, which suggested that *gonadarche* (final maturation of the testes or ovaries) is the biological basis for the child's budding interest in sexual matters. Earlier studies postulated that the profound maturational changes during puberty instigate the transition from preadolescent to adult forms of sexuality that involve sexual attraction, fantasy, and behavior (Money & Ehrhardt, 1972). Thus, adult forms of sexuality were thought to develop only after gonadarche, typically around ages 12 for girls and 14 for boys, with early and late bloomers being regarded as "off time" in development (Boxer, Levinson, & Petersen, 1989). But the new findings, which locate the development of sexual attraction before these ages, are forcing researchers to rethink the role of gonadarche in the development of sexual attraction as well as the conceptualization of puberty as simply the product of complete gonadal maturation.

Many researchers have conflated puberty and gonadarche, thinking that the two are synonymous in development. The new research on sexual orientation has provided data that invalidate the old model of gonadarche as the sole biological cause of adult forms of sexuality. To the extent that sexual attraction is affected by hormones, the new data indicate that there should be another significant hormonal event around age 10. Indeed, there is: the maturation of the adrenal glands during middle childhood, termed *adrenarche*. (The adrenal glands[2] are the biggest nongonadal source of sex steroids.) This biological process, distinctively different from gonadarche, may underlie the development not only of sexual attraction, but of cognition, emotions, motivations, and social behavior as well.

This observation, in turn, leads to a redefinition of prepubertal and pubertal development.

GONADARCHE IS NOT A SUFFICIENT EXPLANATION

Previous biopsychological models of sexual development have attributed changes in adolescent behavior to changes in hormone levels accompanied by gonadarche (Boxer et al., 1989), presumably because of a focus on the most dramatic features of gonadal development in each gender: menarche in girls and spermarche in boys. If gonadarche were responsible for first sexual attractions, then the mean age of the development of sexual attractions should be around the age of gonadarche. Moreover, one would expect a sex difference in the age of first attraction, corresponding to the sex difference in age of gonadarche: 12 for girls and 14 for boys. Neither of these predictions however, has been borne out by recent data.

In three studies attempting to illuminate the sources of sexual orientation, adolescents have been asked to recall their earliest sexual thoughts; their answers are surprising. One study (Herdt & Boxer, 1993) investigated the development of sexual identity and social relations in a group of self-identified gay and lesbian teenagers (ages 14–20, with a mean age of 18) from Chicago. The mean age for first same-sex attraction was around age 10 for both males and females. Moreover, sexual attraction marked the first event in a developmental sequence: same-sex attraction, same-sex fantasy, and finally same-sex behavior (see Table 1).

This evidence provides a key for understanding sexuality as a process of development, rather than thinking of it as a discrete event, which emerges suddenly at a single moment in time. Virtually all models of adolescent sexual development, from Anna Freud and Erik Erikson up to the present, have been based on the gonadarche model (Boxer et al., 1989). It conceptualizes the development of sexuality as a precipitous, singular, psychological event, fueled by intrinsic changes in hormone levels. Gonadarche is seen as a "switch," turning on desire and attraction, and hence triggering the developmental sequelae of adult sexuality.

Instead, the new data suggest a longer series of intertwined erotic and gender formations that differentiate beginning in middle childhood. Indeed, the psychological sequence of attraction, fantasy, and behavior may parallel the well-known Tanner stages, which are routinely used by clinicians to quantify the process of physical development during puberty (Timiras, 1972). For example, in girls, onset of sexual attraction may co-occur with Tanner Stage II (development

Table 1. *Ages (years) at which males and females recall having their first same-sex attraction, fantasy, and activity (from Herdt & Boxer, 1993)*

	Males			Females		
Developmental event	M	SD	n	M	SD	n
First same-sex attraction	9.6	3.6	146	10.1	3.7	55
First same-sex fantasy	11.2	3.5	144	11.9	2.9	54
First same-sex activity	13.1	4.3	136	15.2	3.1	49

of breast buds); sexual fantasy may co-occur with Tanner Stage III (enlargement of mammary glands); and sexual behavior may co-occur with Tanner Stage IV (full breast development), with each psychosexual stage reflecting a different stage of hormonal development. If so, then we may begin to look for a biological mechanism for psychosexual development in the physiological basis for these early Tanner stages that occur prior to the final gonadal maturation that enables procreation.

The generality of these psychological findings is substantiated by two other recent studies that also reported the age of first sexual attraction to be around 10 (see Fig. 1). Pattatucci and Hamer (1995) and Hamer, Hu, Magnuson, Hu, and Pattatucci (1993) asked similar retrospective questions of two distinctive samples of gay- and lesbian-identified adults in the United States. Unlike the Chicago study (Herdt & Boxer, 1993), these studies gathered information from subjects throughout the United States and interviewed adults who were mostly in their mid-30s (range from 18 to 55). They also used different surveys and

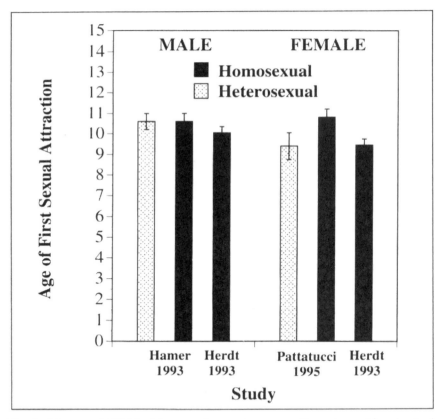

Fig. 1. Mean age (±SEM) of first sexual attraction reported by males and females, both homosexual and heterosexual. The data are reported in three studies: Herdt and Boxer (1993), Pattatucci and Hamer (1995), and Hamer, Hu, Magnuson, Hu, and Pattatucci (1993).

interview methodologies. Nevertheless, all three studies pinpointed 10 to 10.5 as the mean age of first sexual attraction. Admittedly, none of the studies was ideal for assessing early development of sexuality; the age of first recalled sexual attraction may not be the actual age. Nonetheless, this work is an essential part of the systematic investigation of same-gender attractions in children.

The question then arises whether there is a similar developmental pattern among heterosexuals. We know of no reason to assume that heterosexuals and homosexuals would have different mechanisms for the activation of sexual attraction and desire. Fortunately, we could test this hypothesis because both Pattatucci's and Hamer's samples had comparison groups of heterosexuals. Indeed, the reported age of first attraction was the same for heterosexually as for homosexually identified adults (only the attraction was toward the opposite sex). Thus, regardless of sexual orientation or gender, the age of initial sexual attraction hovered just over age 10. In sum, the switch mechanism responsible for "turning on" sexual attraction seems to be operating at the same time both for boys and for girls, and regardless of whether their sexual orientation is toward the same or opposite gender.

Thus, we surmise that the maturation of the gonads cannot explain the data found independently by these three studies in different samples and geographic areas. There is no known mechanism that would enable the gonads to supply sufficient levels of hormones at that age to cause sexual attraction, because they are not fully developed. The mean age of sexual attraction is the same in both genders and in both structural forms of sexual orientation; therefore, the biological counterpart in both genders and in both structural forms of sexual orientation of sexual attraction is probably the same. These constraints effectively eliminate gonadarche as a candidate to explain the observed findings.

ADRENARCHE IN MIDDLE CHILDHOOD

In the pediatric literature, it is well recognized that children between the ages of 6 and 11 are experiencing a rise in sex steroids. These hormones come from the maturing adrenal glands. Adrenarche is clinically recognized primarily by the onset of pubic hair, but it also includes a growth spurt, increased oil on the skin, changes in the external genitalia, and the development of body odor (New, Levine, & Pang, 1981; Parker, 1991). Nonetheless, both the psychological literature and the institutions of our culture regard this period of middle childhood as hormonally quiescent. Freud's (1905/1965) classic notion of a "latency" period between ages 4 to 6 and puberty perhaps best distills the cultural prejudices. In contrast, we have hypothesized that the rise in adrenal steroid production is critical for understanding interpersonal and intrapsychic development in middle childhood.

Both male and female infants have adult levels of sex steroids during the first days of life, and their adrenal androgens also approach the adult range (see Fig. 2). After a few months, the sex hormone levels begin to fall to a very low level and then remain low until the maturation of the adrenal glands and gonads. When children are between 6 and 8 years of age, their adrenal glands begin to mature. Specifically, the adrenal cortex begins to secrete low levels of androgens, primarily dehydroe-piandrosterone (DHEA; see Fig. 2) (Parker, 1991). The metabolism

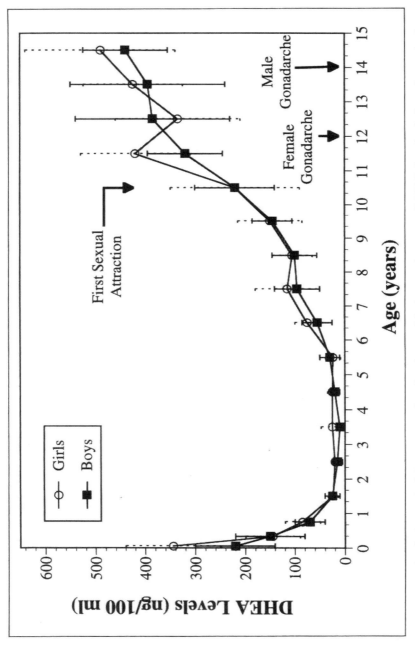

Fig. 2. Mean levels (±*SEM*) of the primary adrenal androgen dehydroepiandrosterone (DHEA) from birth through gonadarche in boys (solid error bars) and girls (dashed error bars). (Data redrawn from De Peretti & Forest, 1976.)

45

of DHEA leads to both testosterone and estradiol, the primary sex steroids in men and women.

It is noteworthy that both girls and boys experience a rise in androgens, although androgens are typically misidentified as male hormones. Moreover, there is no sex difference in the age at which these androgens begin to rise or the rate at which they do so. After adrenarche, an individual's level of androgens plateaus until around 12 years of age in girls and 14 years of age in boys, whereupon gonadarche triggers a second hormonal rise into the adult range (Parker, 1991).

In adults, the androgens that are produced by the adrenal cortex and their metabolites are known to have psychological effects in a variety of developmental areas relating to aggression, cognition, perception, attention, emotions, and sexuality. Although adult levels of DHEA are not reached until after gonadarche, levels of this hormone do increase significantly around age 10 (see Fig. 2; De Peretti & Forest, 1976), when they become 10 times the levels experienced by children between 1 and 4 years of age. It is plausible that this marked increase in androgen levels alters the brain, and thus behavior, either by modifying neural function or by permanently altering cellular structure.

WHAT IS SPECIAL ABOUT THE FOURTH GRADE?

We considered the hypothesis that the age of first sexual attraction is similar for boys and girls, both homosexual and heterosexual, because there is some marked change in environmental stimuli, socialization, or cognitive abilities around the age of 10. If so, then the 10-fold rise in DHEA would be only correlated with the emergence of sexuality and should not be considered its direct cause.

A major weakness of the idea that environmental stimuli lead to the emergence of sexual attraction at age 10 is the fact that, in the United States, there is no marked cultural prompt for sexuality in a 10-year-old. Children this age are typically in fourth grade. To our knowledge, there is no overt change in social expectations between Grades 3 and 4, or between Grades 4 and 5, that might account for the developmental emergence of sexual attraction at age 10. In U.S. culture, the typical ages for the so-called rites of passage are 12 to 13, when the adolescent becomes a "teenager," or around 15 to 16, when the driver's license is issued. Perhaps between Grades 5 and 6 (or, depending on the school system, between Grades 6 and 7), we might identify a critical change during the transition from elementary to middle school. Yet all of these culturally more prominent transitions occur later than age 10. Other subtle changes, such as girls wearing ornate earrings or boys forming preteenage groups, may occur around age 10, but these social factors seem too weak to adequately explain the sudden emergence of sexual attraction before anatomical changes are noteworthy in the child.

We also considered the possibility that although the social environment does not change at age 10, sexual attraction arises at this age because of an increase in the child's cognitive capability to perceive and understand the sexual and social environment. When the child becomes cognitively capable of understanding sexual interactions among adults, the child is capable also of imitating and putting into action the behaviors he or she has observed. This may be a plausible explanation for development of an awareness of sexual attraction in heterosexuals, and no doubt plays a role in the development of sexuality (after all, people typically do not develop sexuality in a vacuum). But does the explanation hold for children who are sexually attracted to the same gender?

The simple social-learning hypothesis predicts that as soon as children become aware of a strong cultural taboo on the expression of homosexual feelings, they should inhibit or even extinguish these desires in subsequent sexual development. We would therefore expect to find that homosexuals would reveal same-sex attraction significantly later than the age when heterosexuals reveal opposite-sex attraction. But this is not the case.

If 10-year-old children are simply mimicking the sexual behavior most commonly seen in adults (and the biological ability to actually carry out the behavior will arise only with gonadarche), then, given the predominant culture, all 10-year-old boys should demonstrate sexual attraction toward females, and all 10-year-old girls should show sexual attraction toward males. However, this also is not the case.

Other criticisms of simple learning-theory hypotheses regarding sexual development are well known and need not be repeated here (Abramson & Pinkerton, 1995). However, the Sambia of Papua New Guinea (Herdt, 1981) provide particularly compelling counterevidence to a simple learning theory model. The Sambia provide powerful reinforcement for same-gender relations by institutionalizing the practice of men inseminating boys over a period of many years, beginning at age 7 to 10. The goal of the men is to masculinize and "grow" the youths into competent reproductive adult men. This intensive training and reinforcement of sexual relationships between males does not result in exclusive homosexuality in adulthood. Instead, adult Sambia men reveal marked bifurcation of their sexual interest; they generally stop all same-gender relations after marriage and enjoy sexual relations with women.

THE RELATIONSHIP BETWEEN ADRENARCHE AND SEXUALITY: CAUSE OR CORRELATION?

Does the inability of the hypotheses of gonadarche and social learning to explain the data imply that adrenarche is the key to the emergence of sexual attraction at age 10? That question cannot yet be answered conclusively. It is entirely possible that the sequential changes in attraction, fantasy, and behavior result from major structural changes in the brain that have their etiology in sources other than sex steroids. However, there has been no documented evidence for such neural structures as of yet. Moreover, if structural changes in the brain do prove to be the cause of the emergence of sexual attraction, modification of all current sexual developmental models and theories will still be needed because they assume that adult desires and behaviors develop from gonadarche.

A change in the nervous system that results from hormones released at adrenarche does look like the most likely developmental mechanism for several reasons. First, girls and boys experience their first sexual attraction, but not gonadarche, at the same age. Second, DHEA, the primary androgen released by the adrenal, is intimately linked with testosterone and estradiol, the major adult sex hormones. Their dynamic relationship is based on the fact that they share many of the fundamental features of steroid function: metabolic pathways that produce the steroids, binding proteins in the blood that carry them to their target tissue, and receptors that enable the cells in the target tissue, including the brain, to change their function in response to the hormonal information. Third, these androgens are known to affect the sexual fantasies and behavior of adolescents and adults, and it is plausible that the same hormones would have similar effects at an earlier age.

RETHINKING PUBERTY: IMPLICATIONS FOR MANY DOMAINS

Given the strong possibility that the currently popular model of puberty is limited, if not incorrect, researchers need to rethink puberty and test the new models in a wide range of psychological disciplines. Adrenarche clearly raises androgens to significant levels, and if these hormones are responsible for the effects seen in sexual attraction, then they are likely to affect a wide range of other behaviors: aggression, cognition, perception, attention, arousal, emotions, and, of course, sexual identity, fantasy, and behavior.

Even if it turns out that hormones released from the adrenal glands are not responsible for the onset of sexual attraction, the behavioral data themselves demonstrate that the concept of puberty must be greatly elaborated and its various stages unpacked. Indeed, Freud's idea of a latency period is seriously flawed. The current behavioral work reinforces the well-established clinical understanding that puberty is composed of at least two separate maturational processes: adrenarche and gonadarche. Any psychosocial research that uses puberty as a stage in development needs to break down the relevant developmental and social behaviors into these two different stages. Researchers need to take into account the hormonal fact that the start of puberty in normal individuals is around ages 6 to 8 and the end of puberty is not until around ages 15 to 17.

The idea of sexuality developing in stages is nothing new to social scientists. But the idea that sexuality is a continuous process that begins from the inside, well before gonadarche, and extends into adulthood is a conceptual advance. These new data from sexual orientation research force a reevaluation of the social and health models of sexual development. No longer can the brain at puberty be treated as a black box, which is suddenly able to process sexual stimuli *de novo* at the time of gonadal change.

Although adrenarche may not be the answer to all the riddles of sexual development, the new data from the developmental and social study of sexual identity have triggered a major conceptual advance in the understanding of both puberty and sexual development as psychobiological phenomena.

Recommended Reading

Becker, J.B., Breedlove, S.M., & Crews, D. (Eds.). (1992). *Behavioral endocrinology.* London: MIT Press.

Boxer, A., & Cohler, B. (1989). The life-course of gay and lesbian youth: An immodest proposal for the study of lives. In G. Herdt (Ed.), *Gay and lesbian youth* (pp. 315–335). New York: Harrington Park Press.

Korth-Schütz, S.S. (1989). Precocious adrenarche. In F.G. Maguelone (Ed.), *Pediatric and adolescent endocrinology* (pp. 226–235). New York: Karger.

Rosenfield, R.L. (1994). Normal and almost normal precocious variations in pubertal development: Premature pubarche and premature thelarche revisited. *Hormone Research, 41*(Suppl. 2), 7–13.

Acknowledgments—We extend our profound thanks to Colin Davis, who coordinated the data and helped substantially with manuscript preparation; to Ruvance Pietrz, who edited text and figures; and to Amanda Woodward for her insightful and constructive comments. This work was supported by National Institute of Mental Health MERIT Award R37 MH41788 to Martha K. McClintock.

Notes

1. Address correspondence to Martha K. McClintock, 5730 Woodlawn Ave., Chicago, IL 60637; e-mail: mkml@midway.uchicago.edu.

2. The adrenal glands are small, pyramidal glands located above the kidneys. They produce hormones that affect metabolism, salt regulation, response to stress, and reproductive function, in part by binding in the brain and altering neural function.

References

Abramson, P., & Pinkerton, S. (Eds.). (1995). *Sexual nature, sexual culture*. Chicago: University of Chicago Press.

Boxer, A., Levinson, R.A., & Petersen, A.C. (1989). Adolescent sexuality. In J. Worell & F. Danner (Eds.), *The adolescent as decision-maker* (pp. 209–244). San Diego: Academic Press.

De Peretti, E., & Forest, M.G. (1976). Unconjugated dehydroepiandrosterone plasma levels in normal subjects from birth to adolescence in humans: The use of a sensitive radioimmunoassay. *Journal of Clinical Endocrinology and Metabolism, 43*, 982–991.

Freud, S. (1965). *Three essays on the theory of sexuality*. New York: Basic Books. (Original work published 1905)

Hamer, D.H., Hu, S., Magnuson, V.L., Hu, N., & Pattatucci, A.M.L. (1993). A linkage between DNA markers on the X chromosome and male sexual orientation. *Science, 261*, 321–327.

Herdt, G. (1981). *Guardians of the flutes*. New York: McGraw-Hill.

Herdt, G., & Boxer, A. (1993). *Children of horizons*. New York: Beacon Press.

Money, J., & Ehrhardt, A. (1972). *Man, woman, boy, girl*. Baltimore: Johns Hopkins University Press.

New, M.I., Levine, L.S., & Pang, S. (1981). Adrenal androgens and growth. In M. Ritzen (Ed.), *The biology of normal human growth: Transactions of the First Karolinska Institute Nobel Conference* (pp. 285–295). New York: Raven Press.

Parker, L.N. (1991). Adrenarche. *Endocrinology and Metabolism Clinics of North America, 20*(1), 71–83.

Pattatucci, A.M.L., & Hamer, D.H. (1995). Development and familiality of sexual orientation in females. *Behavior Genetics, 25*, 407–420.

Timiras, P.S. (1972). *Developmental physiology and aging*. New York: Macmillan.

Critical Thinking Questions

1. According to McClintock and Herdt, sexual attraction typically begins between the ages of eight and ten years of age. What are the implications of this for schools?

2. What are the implications of the findings reported in the article for our under- standing of the etiology of sexual orientation?

3. If childhood is not a time of sexual latency, why do you think Freud believed that it was?

This article has been reprinted as it originally appeared in *Current Directions in Psychological Science*. Citation information for this article as originally published appears above.

Adaptation to Sperm Competition in Humans

Todd K. Shackelford[1] and Aaron T. Goetz
Florida Atlantic University

Abstract

With the recognition, afforded by recent evolutionary science, that female infidelity was a recurrent feature of modern humans' evolutionary history has come the development of a unique area in the study of human mating: sperm competition. A form of male–male postcopulatory competition, sperm competition occurs when the sperm of two or more males concurrently occupy the reproductive tract of a female and compete to fertilize her ova. Males must compete for mates, but if two or more males have copulated with a female within a sufficiently short period of time, sperm will compete for fertilizations. Psychological, behavioral, physiological, and anatomical evidence indicates that men have evolved solutions to combat the adaptive problem of sperm competition, but research has only just begun to uncover these adaptations.

Keywords

sperm competition; anti-cuckoldry; sexual conflict; female infidelity; evolutionary psychology

Male flour beetles sometimes fertilize females with a rival male's sperm. This "fertilization by proxy" occurs when the mating male's aedeagus (reproductive organ) translocates the sperm of another male into the female's reproductive tract (Haubruge, Arnaud, Mignon, & Gage, 1999). The sperm of a male that a female has copulated with can adhere to a subsequent male's aedeagus because these insects' genitalia have chitinous spines designed to facilitate removal of rival male sperm prior to deposition of self-sperm into a female's reproductive tract. This phenomenon was predicted and observed by researchers who study sperm competition. Although not yet documented empirically, humans also may experience fertilization by proxy (Gallup & Burch, 2004). More generally, a rapidly growing literature indicates that sperm competition has been an important selection pressure during human evolution.

Sperm competition is intrasexual (male–male) competition that occurs after the initiation of copulation. Whereas Darwin and others identified *pre*copulatory adaptations associated with intrasexual competition (e.g., horns on beetles, status seeking in men), researchers studying sperm competition aim to identify *post*copulatory adaptations. Thus, an alternative way of thinking about sexual selection is that there is not only competition between males for mates, but competition between males for fertilizations.

Sperm competition is the inevitable consequence of males competing for fertilizations. If females mate in a way that concurrently places sperm from two or more males in their reproductive tracts, this generates selection pressures on males. If these selection pressures are recurrent throughout a species' evolutionary history, males will evolve tactics to aid their sperm in outcompeting rivals' sperm for fertilizations. These tactics may take the form of anatomical, physiological,

and psychological adaptations. Although revolutionary for its time, the first definition of sperm competition, "the competition within a single female between
the sperm of two or more males for the fertilization of the ova" (Parker, 1970,
p. 527), does not capture the full spectrum of male anatomy, physiology, psychology, and behavior associated with sperm competition.

SPERM COMPETITION AS AN ADAPTIVE PROBLEM IN HUMANS

For species that practice social monogamy—the mating system in which males
and females form long-term pair bonds but also pursue extra-pair copulations
(i.e., "affairs")—it is the extra-pair copulations by females that creates the primary context for sperm competition. A male whose female partner engages in an
extra-pair copulation is at risk of cuckoldry—the unwitting investment of resources
into genetically unrelated offspring—and its associated costs, which include loss
of the time, effort, and resources the male spent attracting his partner and the
misdirection of his current and future resources to a rival's offspring. Consequently, in species with paternal investment in offspring, selection often favors
the evolution of adaptations that decrease the likelihood of being cuckolded.
Anti-cuckoldry tactics fall into three categories: *preventative tactics,* designed to
prevent female infidelity; *sperm competition tactics,* designed to minimize conception risk in the event of female infidelity; and *differential paternal investment,*
designed to allocate paternal investment prudently in the event that female infidelity may have resulted in conception.

The extent to which sperm competition occurred in ancestral human populations would have depended largely on rates of female sexual infidelity and
cuckoldry. Current estimates of worldwide cuckoldry rates range from 1.7% to
29.8% (Anderson, 2006). Although current estimates of cuckoldry rates provide
only a proxy of the occurrence of cuckoldry throughout human evolutionary history, even the most conservative estimates of these rates would have generated
sufficient selection pressures on males to avoid the costs of cuckoldry. Moreover,
the ubiquity and power of male sexual jealousy provides evidence of an evolutionary history of female infidelity and thus perhaps also of sperm competition.
Male sexual jealousy can evolve only if female sexual infidelity was a recurrent
feature of human evolutionary history, and female infidelity increases the likelihood that sperm from two or more men occupied concurrently the reproductive
tract of a particular woman. This suggests that sexual selection, in the form of
sperm competition, has been an important selection pressure during recent
human evolution. If this is the case, then specific adaptations to sperm competition may have evolved.

ADAPTATIONS TO SPERM COMPETITION IN HUMANS

In this section, we discuss adaptations men may have evolved in response to an
evolutionary history of sperm competition. We limit our discussion of these adaptations to testis size, ejaculate adjustment, semen displacement, sexual arousal,

and forced in-pair copulation, as these adaptations have been investigated more rigorously than others.

Testis Size

Across a range of animal species, males have relatively larger testes in species with more intense sperm competition. Because larger testes produce more sperm, a male with larger testes can better compete by inseminating a female with more sperm. Among the great apes, testes size varies predictably with the risk of sperm competition. In gorillas, female promiscuity and sperm competition are rare, and the gorilla's testes are relatively small, making up just 0.03% of their body weight. Chimpanzees, in contrast, are highly promiscuous and, accordingly, males have relatively large testes, making up 0.30% of their body weight. The size of human testes falls between these two extremes at 0.08% of body weight, suggesting intermediate levels of female promiscuity and sperm competition in our evolutionary past (Shackelford & Goetz, 2006).

Ejaculate Adjustment

The number of sperm recruited into a given ejaculate is not constant. Although the physiology is not well understood, there is evidence that sperm number can be adjusted even moments before ejaculation (reviewed in Shackelford, Pound, & Goetz, 2005). A key hypothesis derived from sperm competition theory is that males will adjust the number of sperm they inseminate into a female as a function of the risk that their sperm will encounter competition from the sperm of other males. Baker and Bellis (1993) documented a negative relationship between the proportion of time a couple has spent together since their last copulation and the number of sperm ejaculated at the couple's next copulation. As the proportion of time a couple spends together since their last copulation decreases, there is a predictable increase in the probability that the man's partner has been inseminated by another male. Additional analyses documented that the proportion of time a couple spent together since their last copulation negatively predicts sperm number ejaculated at the couple's next copulation, but not at the man's next masturbation (Baker & Bellis, 1993). Inseminating into a female more sperm following a separation may function to outnumber or "flush out" sperm from rival men that may be present in the reproductive tract of the woman.

Inspired by Baker and Bellis's (1993) demonstration of male physiological adaptations to sperm competition, Shackelford et al. (2002) documented that human male psychology may include psychological adaptations to decrease the likelihood that a rival man's sperm will fertilize a partner's ovum. For example, men who spent a greater proportion of time apart from their partners since the couples' last copulation—and, therefore, face a higher risk of sperm competition—report that their partners are more sexually attractive, have more interest in copulating with their partners, and believe that their partners are more interested in copulating with them, relative to men spent a lesser proportion of time apart from their partners. These effects were independent of relationship satisfaction, total time since last copulation, and total time spent apart, which rules out several alternative explanations (although other plausible alternative mechanisms remain to be evaluated). These perceptual changes may motivate men to copulate as soon as possible with their partners, thereby entering their sperm into competition with any rival sperm that may be present in their partners' reproductive tracts.

Semen Displacement

Features of the penis may have evolved in response to the selective pressures of sperm competition. The penis of the damselfly is equipped with spines that can remove up to 99% of the sperm stored in a female, and the penis of the tree cricket is designed structurally to remove rival sperm prior to insemination of the male's own ejaculate. Spines, ridges, and knobs on the penis of some waterfowl are positioned in a way to displace rival sperm, and these protuberances are larger in species for which the intensity of sperm competition is greater.

The human penis does not have barbs and spines for removing rival sperm, but recent evidence suggests that the human penis may have evolved to function, in part, as a semen-displacement device. Using artificial genitals and simulated semen, Gallup et al. (2003) tested the hypothesis that the human penis is designed to displace semen deposited by other men in the reproductive tract of a woman. The results indicated that artificial phalluses with a glans and coronal ridge that approximated a human penis displaced more simulated semen than did a phallus that did not have such features. When the penis is inserted into the vagina, the frenulum of the coronal ridge makes semen displacement possible by allowing semen to flow back under the penis alongside the frenulum and collect on the anterior of the shaft behind the coronal ridge. Displacement of simulated semen occurred when a phallus was inserted at least 75% of its length into the artificial vagina.

That the penis must reach an adequate depth before semen is displaced suggests that displacing rival semen may require specific copulatory behaviors. Following allegations of female infidelity or separation from their partners (contexts in which the likelihood of rival semen being present is relatively greater), both men and women report that men thrusted the penis more deeply and more quickly into the vagina at the couple's next copulation (Gallup et al., 2003), behaviors likely to increase semen displacement. In an independent study, Goetz et al. (2005) investigated men's copulatory behaviors when under a high risk of sperm competition. Men mated to women who placed them at high risk of sperm competition were more likely to use specific copulatory behaviors arguably designed to displace rival semen (e.g., more frequent thrusts, deeper thrusts) than were men mated to women who did not place them at high risk of sperm competition.

Sexual Arousal

Men's sexual fantasies often involve sex with multiple, anonymous partners—behavior that would have had fitness payoffs in ancestral environments. It has been suggested, however, that although men might desire and seek sexual variety and the absence of competition with other men, cues of sperm competition risk also might be sexually arousing. Because sexual arousal increases the rate of sperm transport in the vas deferens, Pound (2002) argued that ancestral males might have benefited from being aroused to cues of sperm competition. When faced with cues of sperm competition, sexual arousal would have resulted in an increase in sperm transport upon ejaculation, thus enabling men to compete more effectively in such contexts.

Pound hypothesized that men, therefore, will be more aroused by sexually explicit images incorporating cues of sperm competition than by comparable material in which such cues are absent. Content analyses of sexually explicit images on Internet sites and of commercial "adult" video releases revealed that depictions of sexual activity involving a woman and multiple men are more prevalent than those involving a man and multiple women, indicating that the former category may be preferred by men. Additionally, an online survey of self-reported preferences and an online preference study that unobtrusively assessed image selection yielded corroborative results. Pound argued that the most parsimonious explanation for these results is that male sexual arousal in response to visual cues of sperm competition reflects the functioning of psychological mechanisms that would have motivated adaptive patterns of copulatory behavior in ancestral males exposed to evidence of female promiscuity.

Pound's hypothesis recently has been supported by experimental evidence that men viewing images depicting cues to sperm competition produce more competitive ejaculates than men viewing comparable images in which cues to sperm competition are absent (Kilgallon & Simmons, 2005). Kilgallon and Simmons documented that men produce a higher percentage of motile sperm in their ejaculates after viewing sexually explicit images of two men and one woman (sperm competition images) than after viewing sexually explicit images of three women. More generally, these results support the hypothesis that men adjust their ejaculates in accordance with sperm competition theory.

Forced In-Pair Copulation

Noting that instances of forced in-pair copulation (i.e., partner rape) followed extra-pair copulations in waterfowl and anecdotal reports that forced in-pair copulation in humans often followed accusations of female infidelity, Thornhill and Thornhill (1992) hypothesized that sexual coercion in response to cues of a partner's sexual infidelity might function in humans to introduce a man's sperm into his partner's reproductive tract at a time when there is a high risk of extra-pair paternity. Goetz and Shackelford (2006a) found empirical support for this hypothesis. In two studies, Goetz and Shackelford found that men's sexual coercion in the context of an intimate relationship was related positively to his partner's infidelities. According to men's self-reports and women's partner-reports, men who use more sexual coercion in their relationships are mated to women who have been or are likely to be unfaithful. The hypothesis that sexual coercion and forced in-pair copulation may be a sperm competition tactic has been supported directly and indirectly in at least half a dozen studies (reviewed in Goetz & Shackelford, 2006b).

CONCLUSION AND FUTURE DIRECTIONS

Sperm competition was first identified as a form of postcopulatory competition between males by Geoff Parker in the 1970s. Since then, evolutionary biologists and behavioral ecologists have described many anatomical, physiological, and behavioral adaptations to sperm competition in many nonhuman species. The question as to whether sperm competition has been an important selection pressure during human evolution remains somewhat controversial, and further research is needed to establish the extent to which this might be the case. As outlined in this article, however, there is mounting evidence that aspects of men's sexual psychology and behavior, such as their attraction to and sexual interest in their partners, their copulatory behaviors, and sources of sexual arousal, may reflect adaptations to sperm competition.

Although we focused on men's adaptations to sperm competition, women are not passive sperm receptacles. An important avenue for future research is to identify adaptations not only in men but also in women. Sexual conflict between males and females produces a coevolutionary arms race between the sexes, in which an advantage gained by one sex selects for counteradaptations in the other sex. Thus, men's adaptations to sperm competition are likely to be met by counteradaptations in women (e.g., mechanisms that increase retention of sperm inseminated by men with "good genes"; see Shackelford et al., 2005), and the study of such mechanisms is an important direction for future research.

Recommended Reading

Platek, S.M., & Shackelford, T.K. (Eds.). (2006). *Female infidelity and paternal uncertainty*. New York: Cambridge University Press.
Shackelford, T.K., & Goetz, A.T. (2006). (See References)
Shackelford, T.K., & Pound, N. (Eds.). (2006). *Sperm competition in humans*. New York: Springer.
Shackelford, T.K., Pound, N., & Goetz, A.T. (2005). (See References)

Acknowledgments—The authors contributed equally to this article.

Note

1. Address correspondence to Todd K. Shackelford, Florida Atlantic University, Department of Psychology, 2912 College Avenue, Davie, FL 33314; e-mail: tshackel@fau.edu.

References

Anderson, K.G. (2006). How well does paternity confidence match actual paternity? Evidence from worldwide nonpaternity rates. *Current Anthropology, 47*, 513–520.
Baker, R.R., & Bellis, M.A. (1993). Human sperm competition: Ejaculate adjustment by males and the function of masturbation. *Animal Behaviour, 46*, 861–885.
Gallup, G.G., & Burch, R.L. (2004). Semen displacement as a sperm competition strategy in humans. *Evolutionary Psychology, 4*, 12–23.
Gallup, G.G., Burch, R.L., Zappieri, M.L., Parvez, R.A., Stockwell, M.L., & Davis, J.A. (2003). The human penis as a semen displacement device. *Evolution and Human Behavior, 24*, 277–289.
Goetz, A.T., & Shackelford, T.K. (2006a). Sexual coercion and forced in-pair copulation as sperm competition tactics in humans. *Human Nature, 17*, 265–282.
Goetz, A.T., & Shackelford, T.K. (2006b). *Sexual coercion in intimate relationships: A comparative analysis of the effects of women's infidelity and men's dominance and control.* Manuscript submitted for publication.
Goetz, A.T., Shackelford, T.K., Weekes-Shackelford, V.A., Euler, H.A., Hoier, S., Schmitt, D.P., & LaMunyon, C.W. (2005). Mate retention, semen displacement, and human sperm competition:

A preliminary investigation of tactics to prevent and correct female infidelity. *Personality and Individual Differences, 38,* 749–763.

Haubruge, E., Arnaud, L., Mignon, J., & Gage, M.J.G. (1999). Fertilization by proxy: Rival sperm removal and translocation in a beetle. *Proceedings of the Royal Society of London B, 266,* 1183–1187.

Kilgallon, S.J., & Simmons, L.W. (2005). Image content influences men's semen quality. *Biology Letters, 1,* 253–255.

Parker, G.A. (1970). Sperm competition and its evolutionary consequences in the insects. *Biological Reviews, 45,* 525–567.

Pound, N. (2002). Male interest in visual cues of sperm competition risk. *Evolution and Human Behavior, 23,* 443–466.

Shackelford, T.K., & Goetz, A.T. (2006). Comparative evolutionary psychology of sperm competition. *Journal of Comparative Psychology, 120,* 139–146.

Shackelford, T.K., LeBlanc, G.J., Weekes-Shackelford, V.A., Bleske-Rechek, A.L., Euler, H.A., & Hoier, S. (2002). Psychological adaptation to human sperm competition. *Evolution and Human Behavior, 23,* 123–138.

Shackelford, T.K., Pound, N., & Goetz, A.T. (2005). Psychological and physiological adaptations to sperm competition in humans. *Review of General Psychology, 9,* 228–248.

Thornhill, R., & Thornhill, N.W. (1992). The evolutionary psychology of men's coercive sexuality. *Behavioral and Brain Sciences, 15,* 363–421.

Critical Thinking Questions

1. Shackelford and Goetz present some convincing explanations for aspects of male sexual structures and functions. Can you think of alternative reasons why these structures and functions evolved?

2. During ovulation, women strongly prefer men with more masculine facial features and deeper voices, who are more confident and dominant in their behavior. They also become more sexually attracted to men other than their primary partners than they are during the rest of their cycle. What are the implications of this for relationships, reproduction, and paternity?

This article has been reprinted as it originally appeared in *Current Directions in Psychological Science*. Citation information for this article as originally published appears above.

Adaptations to Ovulation: Implications for Sexual and Social Behavior

Steven W. Gangestad[1]and Christine E. Garver-Apgar
Department of Psychology

Randy Thornhill
Department of Biology, University of New Mexico

Abstract

In socially monogamous species in which males heavily invest in offspring, there arises an inevitable genetic conflict between partners over whether investing males become biological fathers of their partners' offspring. Humans are such a species. The ovulatory-shift hypothesis proposes that changes in women's mate preferences and sexual interests across the cycle are footprints of this conflict. When fertile (mid-cycle), women find masculine bodily and behavioral features particularly sexy and report increased attraction to men other than current partners. Men are more vigilant of partners when the latter are fertile, which may reflect evolved counteradaptations. This adaptationist hypothesis has already generated several fruitful research programs, but many questions remain.

Keywords

mating; evolutionary psychology; attraction

Human sex can result in conception only about 20% of the time: from 5 days before ovulation to the day of ovulation. Yet unlike in humans' close primate relatives, human females lack conspicuous sexual swellings that vary across the cycle, and people have sex throughout the cycle. Continuous receptivity, however, need not imply that women's sexual interests or preferences remain constant. Indeed, it would be surprising if selection had not forged psychological adaptations in one or both sexes to be sensitive to conception risk—and recent research confirms this expectation. The ways people are sensitive to it provide keys to understanding how selection shaped human sexual relations. In short, romantic relationships take shape out of people's adaptive design for cooperating with partners—often lovingly—in pursuit of shared interests, in conjunction with each sex's adaptive design for pursuing its own interests (or those of same-sex ancestors) that conflict with those of partners.

EVOLUTIONARY BACKGROUND: MATE CHOICE FOR GENES

Over evolutionary time, natural selection sifts through available genetic variants, saving those that promote success within a species' niche and discarding others. Our genes are typically "good genes" that have passed a test of time. But some aren't. Genes mutate. Though each gene is copied correctly 99.99+% of the time, sperm or eggs commonly contain one or more new copying errors. Because mutations typically have minor effects (much as slight impurities in a tank of gas subtly compromise car performance), most survive multiple generations before being eliminated. On average, an individual probably has several tens if not hundreds of mutations. Additionally, although the world to which humans must adapt is constant in many ways (e.g., its gravitational fields), in other subtle-but-profound ways it is not. Pathogens constantly evolve to better thrive in the human body, and humans must change merely to keep pace. Despite selection on thousands of ancestral generations to resist pathogens, humans do not possess sure-fire defenses against them.

The ubiquity of maladapted genes may explain why sex evolved. A gene mutated in an asexual, cloning organism persists in all descendants. Sexual organisms pass on just half of their genes to offspring, and what may make sex worthwhile is that offspring need not get all maladapted genes; some offspring get fewer than either parent.

Through good fortune and bad, not everyone has the same number of maladapted genes. The best way to minimize maladapted genes in offspring is to mate with someone lacking them. While mate choosers cannot directly compare DNA copying errors in suitors, they can do so indirectly—for precisely the reason that choosing mates with good genes is important: Genes affect their bearers' performance. Selection ensures that mate choosers evolve to be attuned and attracted to elements of performance that are sensitive to poorly adapted genes within the species—whether it be growth, the ability to physically dominate or outwit others, or possessing "good looks."

TRADE-OFFS BETWEEN MATERIAL AND GENETIC BENEFITS

In relatively few species do both females and males intensively nurture offspring. Humans may be one. While questions remain about how and to what extent men nurture their own offspring in foraging societies, in most societies men and women typically form socially monogamous pairs and men attempt to direct resources (meat, protection, direct care, money) to mates and offspring. Chimpanzees, bonobos, and gorillas don't share this pattern and are probably poor models of human sexual relations. As many bird species form social pairs, however, theories about their mating may offer insight into how selection shaped human sexual psychologies.

Many socially monogamous birds are not sexually monogamous. On average across species, 10 to 15% of offspring are fathered by males other than social partners—so-called "extra-pair" males. Multiple reasons that females seek extra-pair mates are being investigated, but one is that male assistance in raising offspring doesn't eliminate selection pressure on females to obtain good genes. Not all females can pair up with males with high genetic fitness. Those who don't could potentially benefit from getting social partners' cooperation in raising offspring but getting other males' genes. This pattern has been elegantly demonstrated in the collared flycatcher. A large male forehead patch advertises good genes. Females don't prefer large-patched males as social partners, as they work less hard at the nest. Small-patched males, however, are more likely to be cuckolded and large-patched males the biological fathers. Indeed, females time extra-pair copulations to occur during peak fertility, favoring paternity by extra-pair partners.

More generally, in socially monogamous species in which pairs have males as close neighbors, an inevitable conflict between the sexes arises. All else being equal, females mated to males not possessing the best genes could benefit by getting genes from someone else. At the same time, selection operates on investing males to prevent cuckoldry (e.g., by mate guarding or being able to recognize offspring not their own). Selection hence operates on each sex against the interests of the other sex; thus "sexually antagonistic adaptations" evolve. Depending on which sex evolves more effective adaptations (which may depend on ecological factors affecting the ease with which males guard their mates, the relative value of good genes, the amount of assistance males give females, etc.), the actual extra-pair sex rate may be high (20% or more) or low (5% or less). Even when it is low, however, the genetic conflict exists and sexually antagonistic adaptations may evolve.

THE OVULATORY-SHIFT HYPOTHESIS

We (Gangestad & Thornhill, 1998) proposed to look for human adaptations that are footprints of these selection forces, based on the fact we began with: Women are fertile during a brief window of their cycles. If ancestral females benefited from multiple mating to obtain genetic benefits but at some potential cost of losing social mates, selection may have shaped preferences for indicators of those benefits to depend on fertility status: maximal at peak fertility and less pronounced outside the fertile period. Cycle shifts should furthermore be specific to when women evaluate men as short-term sex partners (i.e., their "sexiness") rather than as long-term, investing mates (Penton-Voak et al., 1999). The logic is that costs do not pay when benefits cannot be reaped.

Over a dozen recent studies show that female preferences clearly do shift. At mid-cycle, normally ovulating, non-pill-using women particularly prefer physical symmetry, masculine facial and vocal qualities, intrasexual competitiveness, and various forms of talent.

The Scent of Symmetrical Men   Asymmetry on bilateral traits that are symmetrical at the population level (e.g., finger lengths, ear dimensions, wrist width) reflects developmental instability, perturbations due to mutations, pathogens, toxins, and other stresses. Developmental instability, in turn, could affect numerous other features of men, including their scent. In four studies, men wore tee-shirts for two nights and women rated the attractiveness of the shirts' scents. All studies found that, when they were fertile, women particularly preferred the scent of symmetrical men (see Fig. 1). When women were not fertile, they had no preference for symmetrical men's scents. Although the chemical mediating this effect has not been identified, data and theory suggest the existence of androgen-derived substances, the scent of which women evaluate more positively when fertile.

Masculine Faces   Male and female faces differ in various ways. Most notably, men have broader chins and narrower eyes (due to development of the brow ridge). Men vary, however, in the extent to which they possess masculine facial features. Women's preference for more masculine faces is more pronounced when they are fertile than when they are infertile, particularly when they rate

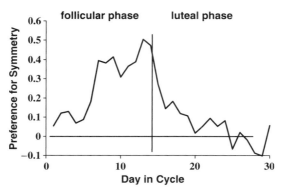

Fig. 1. Women's preference for the scent of symmetrical men as a function of their day in the cycle ($N = 141$). The vertical line corresponds to women's average day of ovulation. The follicular and luteal phases precede and follow ovulation, respectively. Each woman's ratings of scent attractiveness (a sum of ratings of pleasantness and sexiness) were measured against men's physical symmetry. Data are compiled from three separate studies: Gangestad & Thornhill (1998), Thornhill & Gangestad (1999), and Thornhill et al. (2003).

men's sexiness, not their attractiveness as long-term mates (e.g, Penton-Voak et al., 1999; Johnston, Hagel, Franklin, Fink, & Grammer, 2001).

Behavioral Displays of Social Presence and Intrasexual Competitiveness   We (Gangestad, Simpson, Cousins, Garver-Apgar, & Christensen, 2004) had women view videotapes of men being interviewed for a potential lunch date. Men independently rated as confident and who acted toward their male competitors in condescending ways were found more sexy by women when the women were fertile than they were when the women were not fertile (see Fig. 2).

Vocal Masculinity   When rating men's short-term attractiveness, women find masculine (deep) voices more attractive at mid-cycle than they do at other times (Puts, 2005).

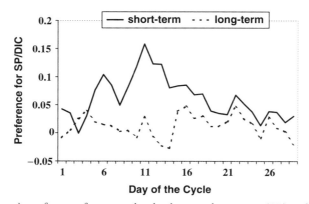

Fig. 2. Women's preference for men who display social presence (SP) and direct intrasexual competitiveness (DIC) as short-term partners (solid line) and as long-term partners (dotted line), as a function of day of their cycle ($N = 238$). From Gangestad et al. (2004).

Talent Versus Wealth   Haselton and Miller (in press) found that, when faced with trade-offs between talent (e.g., creativity) and wealth, women choose talent more often when fertile than they do when nonfertile, but only when evaluating men's short-term mating attractiveness.

All of these characteristics may well have been indicators of good genes ancestrally. Not all positive traits are sexier mid-cycle, however. Traits particularly valued in long-term mates (e.g., promising material benefits) do not appear to be especially attractive to fertile women. For instance, follow-up analyses showed that while the women in the Gangestad et al. (2004) study found arrogant, confrontative, and physically attractive men particularly sexy mid-cycle, their attraction to men perceived to be kind, intelligent, good fathers, and likely to be financially successful—traits particularly valued in long-term mates— didn't change across the cycle. And men judged to be faithful were rated as less sexy mid-cycle than at other times (see also Thornhill et al., 2003).

SHIFTS IN WOMEN'S SEXUAL INTERESTS

Patterns of women's sexual interests also shift across the cycle. In one study, normally ovulating women reported thoughts and feelings over the previous 2 days twice: once when fertile (as confirmed by a luteinizing hormone surge, 1–2 days before ovulation) and once when infertile. When fertile, women reported greater sexual attraction to and fantasy about men other than their primary partners than they did at other times—but their level of attraction to primary partners at this time was no greater than it was when they were infertile (Gangestad, Thornhill, & Garver, 2002; cf. Pillsworth, Haselton, & Buss, 2004).

In fact, however, the ovulatory-shift hypothesis expects a more finely textured pattern. On average, ancestral women could have garnered genetic benefits through extra-pair mating, but those whose primary partners had good genes could not. Selection thus should have shaped interest in extra-pair men mid-cycle to itself depend on partner features; only women with men who, relatively speaking, lack purported indicators of genetic benefits should be particularly attracted to extra-pair men when fertile. We (Gangestad, Thornhill, & Garver-Apgar, 2005) tested this prediction in a replication and extension of Gangestad et al. (2002). Romantically involved couples participated. Again, individuals privately filled out questionnaires twice, once when the female was fertile and once during her luteal phase. Men's symmetry was measured. Once again, women reported greater attraction to extra-pair men and not their primary partners when fertile. Effects, however, were moderated by the symmetry of women's partners. At high fertility, women with relatively asymmetrical partners were more attracted to extra-pair men—and less attracted to their own partners—than when they were infertile. No such effects were found during the luteal phase. Controlling for relationship satisfaction, another important predictor of women's attraction to extra-pair men, did not diminish the effect of partner symmetry. (See also Haselton & Gangestad, in press.)

MALE COUNTERSTRATEGIES ACROSS THE CYCLE

If women have been under selection to seek good genes mid-cycle, men should have been under selection to take additional steps to prevent them from seeking extra-pair sex at this time. Multiple studies indicate that they do so by being more vigilant, proprietary, or monopolizing of mates' time during those times (e.g., Gangestad et al., 2002; Haselton & Gangestad, in press).

There are several candidate cues of fertility status men might use. Three studies found that men find the scent of ovulating women particularly attractive (e.g., Thornhill et al., 2003) and one found that men judge women's faces more attractive mid-cycle. If women's interests change across the cycle, their behavior might too. Whatever the cues, women are unlikely to have been designed through selection to send them. As noted at the outset, women do not have obvious sexual swellings mid-cycle, and they have sex throughout the cycle. These features may well be due to selection on women to suppress signs of fertility status. Men, nonetheless, should be selected to detect byproducts of fertility status not fully suppressed. Consistent with this idea, we (Gangestad et al., 2002) found that enhanced male vigilance of partners mid-cycle (as reported by women) was predicted by enhanced female interest in extra-pair men and not their partners. Men may be particularly vigilant of their partners mid-cycle, when their partners least want them to be.

ADDITIONAL OVULATORY ADAPTATIONS AND BYPRODUCTS

Women's preferences and biases may shift not only toward certain men, but away from clearly undesirable mating options (e.g., incest, rape; e.g., Chavanne & Gallup, 1998). Fessler and Navarrete (2003) assessed women's disgust in several domains: maladaptive sex such as incest and bestiality, food aversiveness, and filth. Only disgust to maladaptive sex rose with fertility.

Women can identify male faces as male more quickly when fertile (e.g., Macrae, Alnwick, Milne, & Schloerscheidt, 2002). This effect is perhaps a byproduct of greater salience of masculine features in male faces associated with their preference when women are fertile. Adaptive ovulatory shifts in preferences, sexual interests, and biases may produce a variety of other byproducts.

CONCLUSION

In any socially monogamous species in which males heavily invest in offspring, there is an inevitable genetic conflict between partners over where the female obtains genes for her offspring. Changes across the ovulatory cycle in women's and men's behavior may contain telltale signs of this conflict.

Many questions remain unanswered. Which female mate preferences strengthen mid-cycle; which don't? Is the pattern consistent with the good-genes hypothesis? Some preferences may be for compatible genes, ones that complement those of the mate chooser (e.g., dissimilar major histocompatibility complex [MHC] genes). Are preferences for compatibility maximal mid-cycle (see Thornhill et al., 2003)? How do male-partner features (e.g., symmetry, MHC dissimilarity) or relationship characteristics (e.g., satisfaction) affect female sexual interest mid-cycle? Do cycle shifts endure across women's reproductive lifespan? Are they robust across human populations? How, precisely, do men behave differently toward fertile partners and what cues mediate changes? Do women resist partners' proprietary actions more mid-cycle? What proximate mechanisms (e.g., hormones) mediate cycle shifts? (Changes in female preferences for the scent of symmetrical men are best predicted by corresponding changes in women's testosterone [positively] and progesterone [negatively], but other candidates [e.g., estrogen, luteinizing hormone] are possible.) Do men's hormones (e.g., testosterone) fluctuate in response to female partners' ovulatory status?

An evolutionary approach uniquely views ovulation as a highly important event around which psychological adaptations might evolve. Alternative nonevolutionary approaches could not have predicted a priori or accounted for these findings. More generally, then, the ovulatory-shift hypothesis illustrates the heuristic value of an adaptationist perspective, guiding researchers to explore domains otherwise unexplored and generating fruitful predictions not offered by other approaches.

Recommended Reading

Gangestad, S.W., Thornhill, R., & Garver-Apgar, C.E. (in press). Adaptations to ovulation. In D.M. Buss (Ed.), *Evolutionary Psychology Handbook*. Boston: Allyn-Bacon.

Jennions, M.D., & Petrie, M. (2000). Why do females mate multiply?: A review of the genetic benefits. *Biological Reviews, 75,* 21–64.

Kappeler, P.M., & van Schaik, C.P. (Eds.) (2004). *Sexual selection in primates: New and comparative perspectives.* Cambridge, U.K.: Cambridge University Press.

Rice, W.R., & Holland, B. (1997). The enemies within: Intragenomic conflict, interlocus contest evolution (ICE), and the intraspecific Red Queen. *Behavioral Ecology and Sociobiology, 41,* 1–10.

Note

1. Address correspondence to Steve Gangestad, Department of Psychology, University of New Mexico, Albuquerque, NM 87111; email: sgangest@unm.edu.

References

Chavanne, T.J., & Gallup, G.G. (1998). Variation in risk taking behavior among female college students as a function of the menstrual cycle. *Evolution and Human Behavior, 19,* 27–32.

Fessler, D.M.T., & Navarrete, C.D. (2003). Domain-specific variation in disgust sensitivity across the menstrual cycle. *Evolution and Human Behavior, 324,* 406–417.

Gangestad, S.W., Simpson, J.A., Cousins, A.J., Garver-Apgar, C.E., & Christensen, P.N. (2004). Women's preferences for male behavioral displays change across the menstrual cycle. *Psychological Science, 15,* 203–207.

Gangestad, S.W., & Thornhill, R. (1998). Menstrual cycle variation in women's preference for the scent of symmetrical men. *Proceedings of the Royal Society of London, B, 262,* 727–733.

Gangestad, S.W., Thornhill, R., & Garver, C.E. (2002). Changes in women's sexual interests and their partners' mate retention tactics across the menstrual cycle: Evidence for shifting conflicts of interest. *Proceedings of the Royal Society of London, B, 269,* 975–982.

Gangestad, S.W., Thornhill, R., & Garver-Apgar, C.E. (2005). Female sexual interests across the ovulatory cycle depend on primary partner developmental instability. *Proceedings of the Royal Society of London, B, 272,* 2023–2027.

Haselton, M.G., & Gangestad, S.W. (in press). Conditional expression of female desires and male mate retention efforts across the human ovulatory cycle. *Hormones and Behavior.*

Haselton, M.G., & Miller, G.F. (in press). Evidence for ovulatory shifts in attraction to artistic and entrepreneurial excellence. *Human Nature.*

Johnston, V.S., Hagel, R., Franklin, M., Fink, B., & Grammer, K. (2001). Male facial attractiveness: Evidence for hormone mediated adaptive design. *Evolution and Human Behavior, 23,* 251–267.

Macrae, C.N., Alnwick, K.A., Milne, A.B., & Schloerscheidt, A.M. (2002). Person perception across the menstrual cycle: Hormonal influences on social-cognitive functioning. *Psychological Science, 13,* 532–536.

Penton-Voak, I.S., Perrett, D.I., Castles, D., Burt, M., Kobayashi, T., & Murray, L.K. (1999). Female preference for male faces changes cyclincally. *Nature, 399,* 741–742.

Pillsworth, E.G., Haselton, M.G., & Buss, D.M. (2004). Ovulatory shifts in female sexual desire. *Journal of Sex Research, 41,* 55–65.

Puts, D.A. (2005). Mating context and menstrual phase affect women's preference for male voice pitch. *Evolution and Human Behavior, 26,* 388–397.

Thornhill, R., & Gangestad, S.W. (1999). The scent of symmetry: A human pheromone that signals fitness? *Evolution and Human Behavior, 20,* 175–201.

Thornhill, R., Gangestad, S.W., Miller, R., Scheyd, G., McCollough, J., & Franklin, M. (2003). MHC, symmetry and body scent attractiveness in men and women (*Homo sapiens*). *Behavioral Ecology, 14,* 668–678.

Critical Thinking Questions

1. Humans, unlike many species, have concealed ovulation. Nonetheless, even though men cannot consciously recognize when women are ovulating, they do seem to prefer certain aspects of ovulating women. Do you think that human mating patterns would be substantially different if there were more obvious signs of ovulation in women?

2. Why do you think humans have developed concealed ovulation? What are the advantages and disadvantages?

This article has been reprinted as it originally appeared in *Current Directions in Psychological Science*. Citation information for this article as originally published appears above.

Evolutionary Psychology of Facial Attractiveness

Bernhard Fink[1] and Ian Penton-Voak

Ludwig-Boltzmann-Institute for Urban Ethology, Vienna, Austria (B.F.), and Department of Psychology, University of Stirling, Stirling, Scotland, United Kingdom (I.P.-V.)

Abstract

The human face communicates an impressive number of visual signals. Although adults' ratings of facial attractiveness are consistent across studies, even cross-culturally, there has been considerable controversy surrounding attempts to identify the facial features that cause faces to be judged attractive or unattractive. Studies of physical attractiveness have attempted to identify the features that contribute to attractiveness by studying the relationships between attractiveness and (a) symmetry, (b) averageness, and (c) nonaverage sexually dimorphic features (hormone markers). Evolutionary psychology proposes that these characteristics all pertain to health, suggesting that humans have evolved to view certain features as attractive because they were displayed by healthy individuals. However, the question remains how single features that are considered attractive relate to each other, and if they form a single ornament that signals mate quality. Moreover, some researchers have recently explained attractiveness preferences in terms of individual differences that are predictable. This article briefly describes what is currently known from attractiveness research, reviews some recent advances, and suggests areas for future researchers' attention.

Keywords

face; attractiveness; mate choice; evolutionary psychology

An obsession with beauty is not unique to modern Western culture but can be found around the world in almost all societies that have been studied. Several studies have shown that members of different ethnic groups share common attractiveness standards, suggesting that the constituents of beauty are neither arbitrary nor culture bound. Beauty and sexual attractiveness seem to be almost interchangeable concepts, and people of different social classes, ages, and sexes tend to rate human faces similarly. Evolutionary psychologists have suggested that such a ubiquitous phenomenon as beauty may reflect human psychological adaptations and mate preferences. Certainly, the high consensus of people's judgments of facial attractiveness is consistent with the theory of biologically based standards of beauty. Evolutionary psychology has focused on the perception of three major cues that may underpin biologically significant assessments of mate value: (a) symmetry, (b) averageness, and (c) nonaverage sexually dimorphic features.

SYMMETRY

Bilateral symmetry of physical traits is hypothesized to reflect an overall high quality of development, especially the ability to resist environmental perturbations during development. Hence, a symmetrical face may signal the ability of an individual to cope with the challenges of his or her environment. Symmetry of bilateral traits is positively correlated with genetic heterozygosity (i.e., the presence of different variants of a gene on homologous chromosomes) in many animals, including humans, and may signal an outbred mate or provide information on an individual's genetic diversity in defense against parasites. Numerous studies have demonstrated that assessments of attractiveness are sensitive to facial symmetry. Preferences for symmetric faces may thus have some adaptive value.

Despite several studies demonstrating the direct effects of symmetry on rated attractiveness, other research suggests that symmetry can be associated with attractiveness for reasons other than direct effects of symmetry per se. Scheib, Gangestad, and Thornhill (1999) found a relationship between women's attractiveness ratings of faces and symmetry even when symmetry cues were removed by presenting only the left or right half of each face. These results suggest that attractive features other than symmetry can be used to assess physical condition. Symmetry may simply covary with these other features rather than acting as a primary cue to attractiveness. Other researchers have offered an alternative account of the symmetry-attractiveness link, arguing that symmetry is more readily perceived by the visual system than other perceptual cues are. Consequently, it may be the case that the human preference for facial symmetry is not the result of evolved psychological adaptations, but rather is a by-product of the perceptual system's design.

AVERAGENESS

Preference for average traits in some facial features could have evolved because in many heritable traits, the average denotes heterozygosity. Studies indicate that computer-generated average faces are rated as more attractive than almost all of the individual faces they are constructed from. It has been known for some time, however, that average faces can be made more attractive by manipulating specific features to make them nonaverage. In a recent study, however, Halberstadt and Rhodes (2000) found a strong relationship between averageness and attractiveness also for nonface objects like drawings of dogs, birds, and watches. It may be that humans have a general attraction to prototypical exemplars, and that their attraction to average faces is a reflection of this more general propensity. Exactly what features contribute to the preference for averageness, and whether these effects represent an adaptation or byproducts of other adaptations, remains unclear.

HORMONE MARKERS

In many species, including humans, testosterone production and metabolism mobilizes resources to encourage males to attract and compete for mates. Testosterone affects a number of facial features. In pubertal males, a high testosterone-to-estrogen ratio facilitates the lateral growth of the cheekbones, mandibles, and chin; the forward growth of the bones of the eyebrow ridges; and the lengthening of the lower facial bone. Because testosterone suppresses the immune system, such

67

"masculine" traits may represent an honest signal of quality, as the individual with high testosterone has successfully coped with its somewhat debilitating effects.

Hormone markers are also present in females. The signaling value of many female body features is linked to age and reproductive condition, both of which correspond to a woman's ratio of estrogen to testosterone. Attractive features (e.g., prominent cheekbones) correspond to high ratios and signal fertility, but estrogen in women could be a handicapping sex hormone as testosterone is in men. Thus, markers of high estrogen may reliably signal that a female's immune system is of such high quality that it can deal with the toxic effects of high estrogen.

In this context, skin condition is presumed to reliably signal aspects of female mate value. Human males, universally, are expected to be most sexually attracted by female skin that is free of lesions, eruptions, warts, moles, cysts, tumors, acne, and hirsutism. The absence or presence of body hair is a sexually dimorphic characteristic, and relative hairlessness and smooth skin in women may signal fertility because of its association with low androgen and high estrogen. Skin infection may denote a disturbance of the production of androgen and estrogen and reduced reproductive ability. Empirical evidence shows that women's facial skin texture affects males' judgments of their facial attractiveness, and homogeneous (smooth) skin is most attractive (Fink, Grammer, & Thornhill, 2001). Males evaluate females' skin texture in addition to the characteristics of age and facial shape in judging facial beauty.

The link between hormone markers and attractiveness in male faces is, however, complex. Although some studies support the hypothesis that women prefer masculinized male faces, other studies indicate that women do not have clear preferences for such traits in males. Perrett et al. (1998) showed that females' preferences regarding male faces are apparently driven by stereotypical personality attributions: Highly masculinized male faces were perceived as less warm, less honest, and more dominant than feminized male faces. Such attributions may have a kernel of truth, as high testosterone has been linked with antisocial behavior in men.

However, the variability in women's preferences for hormone markers seems to represent some of the best evidence for evolved adaptations in the facial attractiveness literature. The studies demonstrating this variability fall into two categories, those investigating the influence of menstrual-cycle phase on women's preferences in male faces and those investigating individual differences in perceptions of the attractiveness of men's faces. Varying female preferences may reflect alternative tactics in a conditional mating strategy that trades off cues to supposedly good genes against other factors, such as sociability.

ATTRACTIVENESS AND THE MENSTRUAL CYCLE

The menstrual phase has been shown to influence females' perception of male attractiveness. Specifically, females exhibit a shift in preference toward a more masculine male face during the phase of their menstrual cycle when likelihood of conception is high (Johnston, Hagel, Franklin, Fink, & Grammer, 2001; Penton-Voak et al., 1999). Trends in the data indicate that this shift may be influenced by a woman's relationship status (i.e., women show larger shifts toward masculinity when judging attractiveness in the context of a potential short-term relationship than in the context of a potential long-term relationship). Furthermore, women in relationships tend to show larger cyclic shifts than women who are not in relationships.

These shifts in preferences have been interpreted as representing adaptive trade-offs in mate choice. Females choose a relatively feminine face (possibly indicating prosociality, or acting in ways that tend to benefit other people without the prospect of an external personal benefit, and willingness to invest in offspring) when they are unlikely to conceive, yet may prefer more masculine faces when sex is likely to result in pregnancy (so that they may gain heritable benefits). Taken together, these studies provide strong evidence for a hormone-mediated adaptive design. A female's attraction to testosterone markers on a male's face may be influenced by her estrogen/progesterone ratio. This suggests that the neural mechanism responsible for generating positive feelings toward male faces is sensitive to levels of hormones circulating in the blood.

INDIVIDUAL DIFFERENCES IN PERCEPTIONS OF ATTRACTIVENESS

Clearly, individual differences in attractiveness judgments exist, as not all people find exactly the same faces attractive. Recently, however, studies have indicated that certain psychological factors influence preferences in a predictable way. Johnston et al. (2001) compared women who scored low on a psychological "masculinity" test with those who received higher scores and found that the low scorers showed a larger preference shift across the menstrual cycle, had lower self-esteem, and had a greater preference for male facial dominance cues in potential short-term mates. Johnston et al. supposed that father-daughter bonding could enhance a female's self-esteem and reduce her sensitivity to male dominance cues, whereas a lack of attachment could have the reverse effect. Additional evidence for experiential influences on attractiveness judgments comes from a recent study (Perrett et al., 2002) demonstrating that, in adulthood, the offspring of older parents were less impressed by youth in a potential partner than were the children of younger parents.

Moreover, in a study comparing females who did and did not consider themselves to be physically attractive, those who considered themselves physically attractive showed a greater preference for two proposed markers of quality in male faces: masculinity and symmetry (Little, Burt, Penton-Voak, & Perrett, 2001). This finding can be interpreted in terms of a conditional strategy, as this increased preference for masculine faces was seen only when judgments were made in the context of a long-term relationship. Potentially, women with high mate value may be able to elicit different behaviors from masculine-looking men than women with lower mate value. Recently, a similar varying preference for masculinity has been found using women's facial attractiveness and waist-to-hip ratio, rather than self-rated attractiveness, as the putative measures of female viability.

BEAUTY: A SINGLE ORNAMENT OF MATE QUALITY?

Symmetry, averageness, and hormone markers probably have interacting effects on the perception of attractiveness. The question of how these features relate to one another, then, is important. Research has focused mainly on the analysis of single features and their contribution to attractiveness, but this approach may be inherently limited, as attractiveness may not be reducible to the analysis of a single feature. The ecological literature suggests two alternative explanations of how features relate to one another: the *multiple-message hypothesis* and the *redundant-signal hypothesis* (Møller & Pomianowski, 1993). According to the former, each ornament signals a specific, unique property of the condition of an individual. This hypothesis corresponds to the *multiple-fitness model* of Cunningham, Roberts, Wu, Barbee, and Druen (1995), which states that perceived attractiveness varies across multiple dimensions, rather than a single dimension, with each feature signaling a different aspect of mate value.

The redundant-signal hypothesis also suggests that there are multiple features, each signaling a different aspect of mate quality, but adds that these features are considered against one another in arriving at an evaluation. That is, according to this hypothesis, mate choosers pay attention to several sexual ornaments in combination to obtain a better estimate of general condition than if they paid attention to any single ornament. In a recent study, Grammer, Fink, Juette, Ronzal, and Thornhill (2001) showed that this hypothesis is better than the multiple-message hypothesis for explaining how signals actually contribute to female attractiveness, although its validity for the assessment of male attractiveness remains to be investigated. Support for the redundant-signal hypothesis also comes from Thornhill and Grammer (1999). They asked participants to judge the attractiveness of the same women in each of three poses (face, front nude with face covered, and back nude) and found a significant positive correlation between the ratings for the three poses in both Austrian and U.S. participants. Because the attractiveness features of the face, back, and front are all related to estrogen, the correlation of the ratings of the different pictures implies that women's faces and bodies form what amounts to a single ornament of honest mate value.

BEAUTY HAS A REWARD VALUE

Another influential component of attractiveness is eye gaze, as eye contact is an important part of social interaction. Gaze provides different levels of meaning (e.g., social attention or even "mind reading" through eye gaze) depending on the status, disposition, and emotional state of the sender and receiver of the contact. In an experiment in which participants viewed faces varying in attractiveness and direction of eye gaze, Kampe, Frith, Dolan, and Frith (2001) showed that brain activity in the ventral striatum (a brain area associated with prediction of reward) reflected an interaction of the two variables. Specifically, when eye gaze was directed toward the viewers, activity in the ventral striatum increased as attractiveness increased, and when eye gaze was directed away from the viewers, activity in this area decreased as attractiveness increased. Thus, depending on the direction of gaze, perceived attractiveness can activate brain regions that are strongly linked to reward, and eye contact with attractive individuals appears to be more "rewarding" than eye contact with less attractive individuals.

This finding has been confirmed by Aharon et al. (2001), who showed that discrete categories of beautiful faces have differing reward values and differentially activate reward circuitry in human subjects. Functional magnetic resonance imaging shows that passive viewing of beautiful female faces activates the brain's reward circuitry, but studies in which the attractiveness of male faces was rated indicate that aesthetic evaluation may be separate from reward assessment.

CONCLUSION

If we accept that evolutionary processes have shaped our psychological adaptations, it seems likely that human beings evolved mechanisms for detecting and assessing cues of mate value. Furthermore, these mechanisms are presumed to be highly resistant to cultural modification, although many cultural markers of attractiveness (e.g., body decoration) clearly contribute to interpersonal attraction. Recently, research has indicated that cues to attractiveness are integrated to form a single ornament of mate value. The slightest introspection, however, informs us that individuals differ in their judgments of attractiveness. Such individual differences may reflect the operation of adaptive conditional mating strategies that trade off cues to genetic and direct benefits, as well as individual differences in experience across the life span.

Despite the general consensus among evolutionary psychologists that facial attractiveness reflects adaptations that discriminate the mate value of individuals, there are still open questions that remain to be solved. Future research should direct further attention to how variations in life history affect attractiveness judgments. Also, we take it for granted that features like facial symmetry, facial averageness, and hormone markers reflect immune-system competence, but research is still needed to provide empirical evidence for this assumption. However, to date, the adaptationists' perspective seems to provide a fruitful framework that should help us to gain further insight into the question whether beauty is only "skin deep" or rather lies in the adaptation of the beholder.

Recommended Reading

Rhodes, G., & Zebrowitz, L. (Eds.). (2001). *Advances in visual cognition: Vol. 1. Facial attractiveness—Evolutionary, cognitive, cultural and motivational perspectives.* Westport, CT: Ablex.

Thornhill, R., & Gangestad, S.W. (1999). Facial attractiveness. *Trends in Cognitive Sciences, 3,* 452–460.

Note

1. Address correspondence to Bernhard Fink, Ludwig-Boltzmann-Institute for Urban Ethology, Althanstrasse 14, A-1090 Vienna, Austria; e-mail: bernhard.fink@ieee.org.

References

Aharon, I., Etcoff, N., Ariely, D., Chabris, C.F., O'Connor, E., & Breiter, H.C. (2001). Beautiful faces have variable reward value: fMRI and behavioral evidence. *Neuron, 32,* 537–551.

Cunningham, M.R., Roberts, A.R., Wu, C.-H., Barbee, A.P., & Druen, P.B. (1995). Their ideas of beauty are, on the whole, the same as ours: Consistency and variability in the cross-cultural perception of female attractiveness. *Journal of Personality and Social Psychology, 68,* 261–279.

Fink, B., Grammer, K., & Thornhill, R. (2001). Human (*Homo sapiens*) facial attractiveness in relation to skin texture and color. *Journal of Comparative Psychology, 115*(1), 92–99.

Grammer, K., Fink, B., Juette, A., Ronzal, G., & Thornhill, R. (2001). Female faces and bodies: N-dimensional feature space and attractiveness. In G. Rhodes & L. Zebrowitz (Eds.), *Advances in visual cognition: Vol. 1. Facial attractiveness—Evolutionary, cognitive, cultural and motivational perspectives* (pp. 97–125). Westport, CT: Ablex.

Halberstadt, J., & Rhodes, G. (2000). The attractiveness of non-face averages: Implications for an evolutionary explanation of the attractiveness of average faces. *Psychological Science, 11,* 285–289.

Johnston, V.S., Hagel, R., Franklin, M., Fink, B., & Grammer, K. (2001). Male facial attractiveness: Evidence for hormone mediated adaptive design. *Evolution and Human Behavior, 22,* 251–267.

Kampe, K.K., Frith, C.D., Dolan, R.J., & Frith, U. (2001). Reward value of attractiveness and gaze. *Nature, 413,* 589.

Little, A.C., Burt, D.M., Penton-Voak, I.S., & Perrett, D.I. (2001). Self-perceived attractiveness influences human preferences for sexual dimorphism and symmetry in male faces. *Proceedings of the Royal Society of London B, 268,* 39–44.

Møller, A.P., & Pomianowski, A. (1993). Why have birds got multiple sexual ornaments? *Behavioral Ecology and Sociobiology, 32,* 167–176.

Penton-Voak, I.S., Perrett, D.I., Castles, D.L., Kobayashi, T., Burt, D.M., Murray, L.K., & Minamisawa, R. (1999). Female preference for male faces changes cyclically. *Nature, 399,* 741–742.

Perrett, D.I., Lee, K.J., Penton-Voak, I., Rowland, D., Yoshikawa, S., Burt, D.M., Henzi, S.P., Castles, D.L., & Akamatsu, S. (1998). Effects of sexual dimorphism on facial attractiveness. *Nature, 394,* 884–887.

Perrett, D.I., Penton-Voak, I.S., Little, A.C., Tiddeman, B.P., Burt, D.M., Schmidt, N., Oxley, R., Kinloch, N., & Barrett, L. (2002). Facial attractiveness judgements reflect learning of parental age characteristics. *Proceedings of the Royal Society of London B, 269,* 873–880.

Scheib, J.E., Gangestad, S.W., & Thornhill, R. (1999). Facial attractiveness, symmetry, and cues of good genes. *Proceedings of the Royal Society of London B, 266,* 1913–1917.

Thornhill, R., & Grammer, K. (1999). The body and face of woman: One ornament that signals quality? *Evolution and Human Behavior, 20,* 105–120.

Critical Thinking Questions

1. In addition to facial attractiveness, what other physical qualities might reflect the ability to successfully produce offspring?

2. In addition to the evolutionary sources of our attraction to various qualities of faces, what could be some other sources of our preferences for certain facial qualities?

3. Based on the findings described in this article, and/or any other research results of which you are aware, how and why should physical attractiveness be related to relationship processes and outcomes?

This article has been reprinted as it originally appeared in *Current Directions in Psychological Science*. Citation information for this article as originally published appears above.

The Neurochemistry of Pair Bonding

J. Thomas Curtis[1] and Zuoxin Wang

Department of Psychology and Program in Neuroscience,
Florida State University, Tallahassee, Florida

Abstract

The formation and maintenance of social attachments are fundamental to human biology. Because deficits in the ability to form such attachments are associated with a variety of psychological disorders, an understanding of the neural basis of social attachment may provide insights into the causes of such disorders. Comparative studies using several closely related species of voles that display different social organizations and behaviors have begun to provide important insights into the neurochemical events underlying social attachment. Here we review recent developments in the study of social attachment, focusing on the roles of specific neurochemical systems in pair-bond formation.

Keywords

vasopressin; oxytocin; dopamine; corticosterone; social attachment

Interpersonal interactions, such as parent-child, spousal, and work relationships, all rely to some extent on the ability to form and maintain social ties. Deficits in the ability to form meaningful social bonds are associated with human psychological impairments, such as schizophrenia and autism. Moreover, the loss of a significant relationship can exacerbate depression. Thus, understanding the neural basis of social attachment may provide insights into the causes of some psychological disorders.

THE VOLE MODEL

Only about 3% of mammalian species are typically monogamous, and there appears to be no phylogenetic pattern to explain the distribution of monogamy among mammals. Nonetheless, there is evidence that the neurochemical basis of pair bonding may be similar among mammalian species (Insel & Young, 2000); thus, observations in one species may be applicable to others. The microtine rodents (voles) provide an excellent animal model for comparative studies on the neurochemical bases of social attachment. Although closely related, different vole species display a range of life strategies and social behaviors. Meadow and montane voles are promiscuous and show little in the way of social attachment or paternal care of offspring. In contrast, the prairie and pine voles are monogamous and exhibit strong social attachments. In prairie voles, the more studied of the latter two species, pairs share a common nest even beyond the breeding season, and both sexes provide parental care and display aggression against unfamiliar individuals.

Studying complex behaviors such as pair bonding requires a reliable behavioral index. Mating facilitates pair bonding in monogamous voles and provides a benchmark by which the "beginning" of pair-bond formation may be measured.

Prairie voles display pair bonds after as few as 6 hr of mating, whereas 24 to 48 hr of cohabitation are needed for pair-bond formation in the absence of mating. This difference has been exploited in the development of the *partner-preference test,* a choice test in which an animal has the option of associating either with a familiar partner or with an unfamiliar stranger (Fig. 1). Prairie voles paired for 6 hr without mating are equally likely to associate with either the partner or the stranger, but will show a preference for the partner after manipulations designed to facilitate pair bonding. Conversely, voles that mate repeatedly over 24 hr reliably display a robust preference for the familiar partner, although manipulations designed to interfere with pair bonding disrupt this preference. This behavioral paradigm has been employed widely to study the mechanisms underlying pair bonding.

Here we review recent research examining the neurochemistry of pair bonding using the vole model. We focus on four neurochemicals—vasopressin, oxytocin, dopamine, and the stress hormone corticosterone—and briefly discuss their involvement in pair-bond formation in prairie voles.

NEUROCHEMICAL ACTIVITY

The effects of neurochemicals released within the brain are mediated by specialized proteins known as receptors that are located either on the cell surface or within the cell. Binding of a neurochemical to its receptor initiates an array of responses within the target cell. For many neurochemicals, there are different receptor subtypes that vary in the ability to bind the neurochemical and in the effects produced after binding. The receptor subtype and location within the brain where the receptor is produced are dictated by receptor genes that contain both directions for producing the receptor itself (gene expression) and promoter regions that control where in the brain the receptor is present. In many cases, drugs that mimic (agonists) or block (antagonists) the effects of neurochemicals have been developed. These drugs have allowed detailed analysis of the roles played by neurochemicals in a variety of behaviors, including pair-bond formation.

NEUROCHEMICALS INVOLVED IN PAIR BONDING

Vasopressin

Vasopressin is synthesized in the brain and strongly influences behavior and cognition when released centrally (within the brain). The distribution of vasopressin-synthesizing cells and their fibers in the vole brain shows pronounced sexual dimorphism, as in almost all rodent species that have been examined. Many of the same areas that show sexual dimorphism have been implicated in pair bonding. For example, when male prairie voles are exposed to an individual of the opposite sex, vasopressin appears to be released in the lateral septum, an area that shows sexual dimorphism and is involved in recognition of individuals. The fact that this does not occur in females, or in either sex in promiscuous voles (Bamshad, Novak, & De Vries, 1993), suggests that vasopressin mediates pair bonding in male prairie voles. This hypothesis is supported by studies showing that in male prairie voles, central administration of vasopressin induces pair bonding in the absence of mating, whereas a vasopressin receptor antagonist blocks

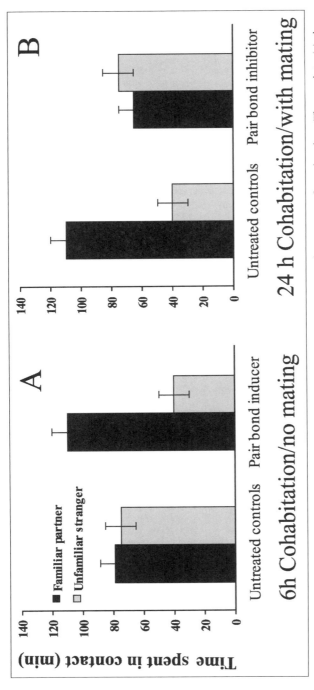

Fig. 1. Typical results for control and experimental conditions in the 3-hr partner-preference test of pair bonding. The graph in (a) shows typical results for unmated pairs housed together for 6 hr. This amount of contact is generally insufficient to yield a preference for the familiar partner (left set of bars), but a partner preference can be induced experimentally (right set of bars). The graph in (b) shows typical results for mated pairs housed together for 24 hr. This amount of contact is usually sufficient to yield a preference for the familiar partner, but the formation of such preferences can be inhibited experimentally.

mating-induced pair bonding (Winslow, Hastings, Carter, Harbaugh, & Insel, 1993). Using markers of neuronal activation, we have recently shown that some vasopressin-containing regions are activated during mating in prairie voles, and that site-specific administration of vasopressin into the lateral septum of male prairie voles induces pair bonding without mating (Liu, Curtis, & Wang, 2001).

In contrast to its effects in monogamous voles, central vasopressin administration does not induce pair bonds in promiscuous voles, suggesting fundamental differences in the vasopressin systems of the two types of voles. How might these species differences be mediated? Comparative studies have shown that throughout postnatal development and into adulthood, monogamous and promiscuous voles differ in the distribution pattern of vasopressin receptors (Wang, Young, Liu, & Insel, 1997). Central vasopressin binds primarily to vasopressin V_{1a} receptors. Prairie and montane voles have almost identical gene sequences for the receptor itself, but differ in the promoter region. Could differences in gene promoters result in species-specific patterns of receptor distribution? Recently, genetically altered mice that express the prairie vole vasopressin receptor gene have been produced. These mice express vasopressin receptors in the brain in a pattern similar to that of monogamous voles, and in fact, show increased affiliative behavior after administration of vasopressin (Young, Nilsen, Waymire, Mac-Gregor, & Insel, 1999).

Oxytocin

Oxytocin also plays an important role in pair-bond formation, and in many ways, the oxytocin system in voles parallels that for vasopressin. The first experiments examining the involvement of oxytocin in pair bonding were based in part on observations that oxytocin facilitated the formation of another type of social bond—that between mother and offspring. Administration of oxytocin into the lateral ventricles (large cavities within the brain; drugs administered in the ventricles may reach nearly any part of the brain) in female prairie voles can indeed induce pair bonding, whereas an antagonist specific to the oxytocin receptor blocks both mating- and oxytocin-induced pair bonding (Williams, Insel, Harbaugh, & Carter, 1994). Similar treatments are ineffective in promiscuous vole species.

Is the species-specific effect of oxytocin, like that of vasopressin, receptor mediated? Comparative studies on the distribution of oxytocin-containing cells and fibers within the brain do show subtle species differences between voles with differing social structures, but no consistent pattern differentiates social and nonsocial species. However, the distribution pattern of oxytocin receptors is most similar among vole species that share similar social structures (Insel & Shapiro, 1992). Again, as we have seen with vasopressin, the species-specific receptor distribution patterns are apparent throughout development and are not the result of different receptor subtypes, because all voles express the same type of oxytocin receptor. Are the species differences in the distribution of oxytocin receptors the result of differences in the promoter region for oxytocin, much as we suggested for vasopressin? The data addressing this question are not conclusive; however, subtle differences in the oxytocin promoter region may be sufficient to drive differential expression. Support for this possibility came when researchers were able to cause a reporter gene (a gene not normally expressed) to be expressed in socially relevant brain regions in mice by linking the reporter gene to the oxytocin promoter from social voles (Young et al., 1997).

Interestingly, after the birth of young, the distribution of oxytocin receptors in the nonsocial montane vole female grows to resemble the distribution seen in social voles (Insel & Shapiro, 1992). This to some extent brings the field full circle, because the original experiments examining a potential role for oxytocin in pair bonding were based on oxytocin's role in maternal bonding. The maternal "circuit" (brain areas associated with maternal behavior) includes most of the neural components implicated in pair bonding. Thus, one possibility for the origin of pair bonding is that pair-bonding species have co-opted the mechanism (or mechanisms) by which maternal bonds are formed. This possibility is further supported by observations that even sexually naive male prairie voles display maternal-type behaviors when exposed to pups, and that prairie vole mothers display considerably more maternal care than do meadow vole mothers.

The data we have presented suggest sex-specific roles for oxytocin and vasopressin: Oxytocin is the "pair-bond hormone" in females, whereas vasopressin performs this function in males. Recent studies, however, have shown that the roles of vasopressin and oxytocin in the regulation of pair bonding may not be quite so straightforward. Central administration of either compound at relatively high doses can induce pair bonding in both sexes. Similarly, pair bonding in both sexes can be blocked by antagonists specific to either type of receptor (Cho, DeVries, Williams, & Carter, 1999). Further, when injected into the lateral septum in male prairie voles, oxytocin, like vasopressin, can induce pair bonding (Liu et al., 2001). These data indicate that both vasopressin and oxytocin are involved in pair bonding in both sexes of prairie voles. Despite these findings, however, there are important sex differences in responses to various doses of these neurochemicals, indicating that the sexes may differ in their relative sensitivities to vasopressin and oxytocin. Further, when sex differences are found, they tend to reinforce the notion that vasopressin is more effective in males than in females, whereas oxytocin is more effective in females than in males. Finally, sex differences may also exist in other systems that interact with vasopressin and oxytocin in regulating pair bonding.

Dopamine

Drugs targeting the dopamine system are frequently used to treat disorders associated with social attachment, such as autism and social phobia. Further, dopamine is strongly implicated in learning and memory, processes likely to be important in pair bonding. The first evidence for dopamine's involvement in pair bonding came from observations that, in female prairie voles, peripheral (outside the brain) administration of apomorphine, a dopamine agonist, induced pair bonding absent mating, whereas haloperidol, a dopamine antagonist, blocked mating-induced pair-bond formation (Wang et al., 1999). The same study found that dopamine acts on the D_2 family of dopamine receptors to regulate pair bonding.

In female prairie voles, dopamine is released in the nucleus accumbens during mating. Blockade of D_2 receptors, but not the D_1 family of receptors, in the nucleus accumbens inhibits mating-induced pair bonding, whereas site-specific administration of D_2, but not D_1, agonists induces pair bonding absent mating (Gingrich, Liu, Cascio, Wang, & Insel, 2000). Recently, we have found that dopamine also is involved in pair bonding in male prairie voles. Interestingly, facilitation of pair bonding requires higher doses of dopamine agonists in female voles than in male voles, indicating a potential sex difference. However, at very high doses, apomorphine becomes ineffective in males. Apomorphine activates primarily D_2 receptors, but at high doses, it may also activate D_1-type receptors. Thus, activation of D_1 receptors may in fact inhibit pair-bond formation (Aragona, Liu, Curtis, Stephan, & Wang, in press).

Corticosterone

Prairie voles have very high basal levels of corticosterone circulating in their blood. When corticosterone levels are reduced after removal of the adrenal glands (adrenalectomy), female prairie voles form pair bonds after as little as 1 hr of non-sexual cohabitation with a male (DeVries, DeVries, Taymans, & Carter, 1996). Stress-induced or artificial elevation of corticosterone in females actually seems to produce an aversion to the familiar partner. Interestingly, the effects of corticosterone on pair bonding are sexually dimorphic: In male prairie voles, adrenalectomy inhibits pair-bond formation, whereas stress-induced or artificial elevation of corticosterone facilitates pair-bond formation. These opposite effects occur despite the fact that stress elevates circulating levels of corticosterone similarly in male and female prairie voles.

Neurochemical Interactions

Although the neurochemicals we have discussed all have been implicated in pair bonding, it is unknown whether they act in concert or independently to regulate behavior. In addition, the nature of their interactions, if any, and the brain circuits in which such interactions occur remain to be determined. Recently we have begun to address these questions. In male prairie voles, vasopressin administration in the lateral septum induces pair bonding, but this effect is blocked by co-administration of either vasopressin or oxytocin receptor antagonists, suggesting that access to both kinds of receptors is essential for vasopressin to induce pair bonding (Liu et al., 2001). Administration of either oxytocin or D_2 agonists in the nucleus accumbens, which contains both oxytocin and D_2 receptors, induces pair bonding in female prairie voles. Interestingly, the abilities of both oxytocin and dopamine to induce pair bonds can be blocked by antagonists to either type of receptor. These results suggest that oxytocin and dopamine act synergistically in the nucleus accumbens to regulate pair bonding.

FUTURE DIRECTIONS

Considerable work is still needed to provide a comprehensive understanding of the neurochemical basis of pair bonding. Very little is known about responses at the cellular level in brain areas that are involved. We recently have begun to examine the control of gene transcription, which may affect learning, in mediating pair-bond formation. In addition, studies examining the role of tissue-specific gene expression in social behavior have begun. Monogamous voles that overexpress the vasopressin receptors in some brain areas display increased affiliative behavior (Pitkow et al., 2001). These results highlight the potential of genetic research in the study of social attachment. Further, recent studies have revealed that new neurons are constantly being produced in adult mammalian brains. We have found that exposure to the opposite sex can significantly increase the number of new neurons in brain areas important for pair-bond formation in prairie voles (Fowler, Liu, Ouimet, & Wang, 2002). The prairie vole, therefore, may provide a model in which to investigate the role of new neurons in social behaviors such as pair-bond formation. Finally, researchers and practitioners must begin to apply the lessons learned in the study of pair bonding to the diagnosis and treatment of human psychological disorders. For example, current methods of treatment for schizophrenia often produce negative side effects, and understanding the neuroanatomy and neurochemistry of social attachment may allow more specifically targeted treatments to be developed.

Recommended Reading

Carter, C.S., & Getz, L.L. (1993). Monogamy and the prairie vole. *Scientific American, 268*, 100–106.
De Vries, G.J., & Boyle, P.A. (1998). Double duty for sex differences in the brain. *Behavioral Brain Research, 92*, 205–213.
Wang, Z., Young, L.J., De Vries, G.J., & Insel, T.R. (1998). Voles and vasopressin: A review of molecular, cellular, and behavioral studies of pair bonding and paternal behaviors. *Progress in Brain Research, 119*, 483–499.
Young, L.J., Wang, Z., & Insel, T.R. (1998). Neuroendocrine bases of monogamy. *Trends in Neuroscience, 21*, 71–75.

Acknowledgments—We would like to thank Y. Liu, C. Fowler, B. Aragona, and J. Stowe for helpful comments. Preparation of this article was partly supported by National Institutes of Health Grants NICHD 40722 (to J.T.C.) and NIMH 54554 and 58616 (to Z.W.).

Note

1. Address correspondence to J. Thomas Curtis, Department of Psychology, Florida State University, 209 Copeland Ave., Tallahassee, FL 32306-1270; e-mail: tcurtis@psy.fsu.edu.

References

Aragona, B.J., Liu, Y., Curtis, J.T., Stephan, F.K., & Wang, Z.X. (in press). A critical role for dopamine in pair bonding in male prairie voles. *Journal of Neuroscience*.
Bamshad, M., Novak, M.A., & De Vries, G.J. (1993). Sex and species differences in the vasopressin innervation of sexually naive and parental prairie voles, *Microtus ochrogaster* and Meadow voles, *Microtus pennsylvanicus*. *Journal of Neuroendocrinology, 5*, 247–255.
Cho, M.M., DeVries, A.C., Williams, J.R., & Carter, C.S. (1999). The effects of oxytocin and vasopressin on partner preferences in male and female prairie voles *(Microtus ochrogaster)*. *Behavioral Neuroscience, 113*, 1071–1079.
DeVries, A.C., DeVries, M.B., Taymans, S.E., & Carter, C.S. (1996). The effects of stress on social preferences are sexually dimorphic in prairie voles. *Proceedings of the National Academy of Sciences, USA, 93*, 11980–11984.

Fowler, C.D., Liu, Y., Ouimet, C., & Wang, Z. (2002). The effects of social environment on adult neurogenesis in the female prairie vole. *Journal of Neurobiology, 51,* 115–128.

Gingrich, B., Liu, Y., Cascio, C., Wang, Z., & Insel, T.R. (2000). Dopamine D2 receptors in the nucleus accumbens are important for social attachment in female prairie voles (*Microtus ochrogaster*). *Behavioral Neuroscience, 114,* 173–183.

Insel, T.R., & Shapiro, L.E. (1992). Oxytocin receptor distribution reflects social organization in monogamous and polygamous voles. *Proceedings of the National Academy of Sciences, USA, 89,* 5981–5985.

Insel, T.R., & Young, L.J. (2000). Neuropeptides and the evolution of social behavior. *Current Opinion in Neurobiology, 10,* 784–789.

Liu, Y., Curtis, J.T., & Wang, Z. (2001). Vasopressin in the lateral septum regulates pair bond formation in male prairie voles (*Microtus ochrogaster*). *Behavioral Neuroscience, 115,* 910–919.

Pitkow, L.J., Sharer, C.A., Ren, X., Insel, T.R., Terwilliger, E.F., & Young, L.J. (2001). Facilitation of affiliation and pair-bond formation by vasopressin receptor gene transfer into the ventral forebrain of a monogamous vole. *Journal of Neuroscience, 21,* 7392–7396.

Wang, Z., Young, L.J., Liu, Y., & Insel, T.R. (1997). Species differences in vasopressin receptor binding are evident early in development: Comparative anatomic studies in prairie and montane voles. *Journal of Comparative Neurology, 378,* 535–546.

Wang, Z., Yu, G., Cascio, C., Liu, Y., Gingrich, B., & Insel, T.R. (1999). Dopamine D2 receptor-mediated regulation of partner preferences in female prairie voles (*Microtus ochrogaster*): A mechanism for pair bonding? *Behavioral Neuroscience, 113,* 602–611.

Williams, J.R., Insel, T.R., Harbaugh, C.R., & Carter, C.S. (1994). Oxytocin administered centrally facilitates formation of a partner preference in female prairie voles (*Microtus ochrogaster*). *Journal of Neuroendocrinology, 6,* 247–250.

Winslow, J.T., Hastings, N., Carter, C.S., Harbaugh, C.R., & Insel, T.R. (1993). A role for central vasopressin in pair bonding in monogamous prairie voles. *Nature, 365,* 545–548.

Young, L.J., Nilsen, R., Waymire, K.G., MacGregor, G.R., & Insel, T.R. (1999). Increased affiliative response to vasopressin in mice expressing the v1a receptor from a monogamous vole. *Nature, 400,* 766–768.

Young, L.J., Waymire, K.G., Nilsen, R., MacGregor, G.R., Wang, Z., & Insel, T.R. (1997). The 5' flanking region of the monogamous prairie vole oxytocin receptor gene directs tissue-specific expression in transgenic mice. *Annals of the New York Academy of Science, 807,* 515–517.

Critical Thinking Questions

1. Can studies of voles advance our understanding of human relationships?

2. How can we examine these issues in humans?

3. According to these studies, what role might biology play in human relationships?

4. Do these studies have any practical implications for human relationships?

This article has been reprinted as it originally appeared in *Current Directions in Psychological Science*. Citation information for this article as originally published appears above.

Section 3: Sex Differences

In this section on male-female differences in sexual behavior and relation-ships, the readings are largely evolutionary based. This is partially because of the dearth of alternative theories in the area of sexuality. Evolutionary psychology provides a neat theoretical basis for the design and interpreta-tion of research. It is also a perspective that has caught the attention of a great many psychologists, and seems to explain a number of otherwise difficult to understand sex differences. Therefore, at the moment, the tenets of this approach are the ones on which much theoretically based research is focused, either in an attempt to support or to weaken the theory.

In the first article, David Bjorklund and Todd Shackelford apply parental investment theory to explain sex differences in sexual behavior. There is differential effort required of males and females in the process of passing their genes along to the next generation—whereas the minimum investment of males is one mating encounter, the minimum investment for females is nine months gestation. Accordingly, Bjorklund and Shackelford argue that different approaches to mating have evolved for the two sexes. They highlight two examples: differential sexual strategies—with females being more selective than males, and differential behavioral inhibition—with females being better able to inhibit sexual responses than males.

Might the sex differences that resulted from men's and women's dif-ferent evolutionary histories also affect relationships by producing conflict between heterosexual partners? The article by David Buss reviews evidence supportive of two theories that suggest it may. *Error management theory* posits that men and women evolved different cognitive biases because those biases helped them resolve their unique evolutionary pressures, such as those encountered in the areas of commitment and sexual interest. *Strategic interference theory* posits that men and women evolved tenden-cies to experience certain emotions (e.g., jealousy) in different situations (e.g., infidelity; sexual rivalry) because those emotions were differentially adaptive in those situations.

The article by Lynn Carol Miller, Anila Putcha-Bhagavatula, and William Pedersen provides a twist to the story by illustrating that there are some-times different ways to collect and interpret the same data. These authors suggest such methodological differences may have implications for some of the findings presumed to support evolutionary theory. Specifically, they take a penetrating look at some of the premises of the application of parental investment theory termed "sexual strategies theory" in order to determine if there are really sex differences in the mating preferences of men and women. They make a convincing case that men and women are far more similar than different in mating preferences and strategies, and further, they conclude that there is little evidence for mechanisms that have evolved in humans to facilitate short-term mating.

Differences in Parental Investment Contribute to Important Differences Between Men and Women

David F. Bjorklund[1] and Todd K. Shackelford

Department of Psychology, Florida Atlantic University, Boca Raton, Florida

Abstract

Parental investment theory addresses sex differences that result from the trade-off between parenting effort and mating effort. For example, relative to men, women spend more time caring for offspring, are more selective in assenting to sexual intercourse, are more upset by a partner's emotional infidelity than by a partner's sexual infidelity, and are better able to inhibit their behaviors in certain situations. These and other sex differences are attributable to evolved mechanisms that work in interaction with the physical and social environments.

Keywords

parental investment theory; evolutionary psychology; sexual strategies

Sex differences in behaviors traditionally have been attributed to "social" factors, because of the presumed flexibility of human behavior. Proposals that evolved mechanisms explain why men and women behave as they do have been regarded warily because of the belief that "biological" causation (including evolutionary causes) implies biological determinism. Modern evolutionary psychological theory, however, makes no such claims, but argues that contrasting "social" with "evolutionary" explanations is a false dichotomy (see Tooby & Cosmides, 1992). From this perspective, human nature includes evolved psychological mechanisms that require input such as social norms and cultural beliefs for their operation, and different behavioral outcomes will result from these evolved mechanisms in different environments. In this article, we apply a theory motivated by such evolutionary psychological logic, parental investment theory (Trivers, 1972), to interpret some well-documented sex differences.

According to an evolutionary psychological perspective (see Buss, 1994), ancestral men and women faced different adaptive problems that threatened their survival and reproduction. As a result, they evolved different psychological mechanisms, and evidence of this ancient heritage is apparent in modern humans (for a review, see Buss, 1994). Parental investment theory accounts for many of these differences. According to this theory, there is a conflict for both males and females in how much time, effort, and resources to invest in mating versus parenting. For many species, including humans, males need to invest substantially less in parenting than females to achieve successful reproduction. In mammals, fertilization and gestation occur within the female, and, after birth, mothers provide the primary nutritional support for their offspring until they are weaned. Male investment in offspring may be as little as the sperm produced during copulation. In humans, paternal investment is not essential for a man's offspring to reach adulthood, and although the amount of time men spend in child care varies across cultures, fathers spend less time interacting with and caring for their children than do mothers in all cultures that have been studied (see Geary, 1998).

Yet human males spend more time caring for their offspring than is typical for male mammals. One factor contributing to this unusually high level of paternal investment is humans' extended childhood. Humans spend more time as juveniles than other primates, needing many years to develop the brain and the knowledge necessary to navigate the complexities of society. This prolonged immaturity requires a supportive environment to which both mothers and fathers ideally contribute. Evidence from many cultures and historical records indicates that the death rate of offspring increases as a function of father's absence, particularly in harsh environments (see Geary, 1998). Thus, whereas mothers opt to invest substantially in their children's care after birth in order to ensure their offsprings' survival, the case is not as clear-cut for fathers, particularly when one considers the number of additional offspring men can have by investing more effort in mating. Women also may choose to invest less in the care of a child and more in mating, but the caloric costs and duration of pregnancy and nursing (in traditional societies today, and surely in our evolutionary past, nursing extends to the age of 3 or 4 years) reduce the number of children a woman can expect to have in her lifetime.

There is evidence that paternal investment influences socialization practices and the amount of parental investment subsequent generations devote to their offspring (Belsky, Steinberg, & Draper, 1991). In environments where fathers are absent or where there is marital discord, the resulting stress produces harsh and inconsistent child care and insecure attachment. Under such situations, children reach puberty early, form short-term and unstable relationships, and invest relatively little in their own offspring. In stressful and uncertain environments, there is a tendency to invest more in mating (for both sexes) than in parenting. The pattern is reversed for children growing up in harmonious homes and homes where the father is present; such children mature later, postpone sexual activity, and display greater investment in the fewer children they produce. In sum, the availability of resources, which is related to paternal investment and spousal harmony, leads to different patterns of socialization, resulting in differential parental investment in the next generation.

The differential investment of males and females in their offspring has resulted in the evolution of different ways of behaving and thinking in men and women. Although these differences are generated by evolved psychological mechanisms, they are more variable than is typical in mammals. Here, we discuss two areas in which men and women behave and think differently, as predicted by parental investment theory: sexual strategies and inhibitory abilities.

SEXUAL STRATEGIES

One class of sex differences that can be understood in terms of parental investment theory is sexual strategies (Buss, 1994). Males in most mammals can achieve tremendous reproductive success by inseminating many females, making males relatively indiscriminate when it comes to choosing a sex partner. Females, in contrast, have much more invested, at least potentially, in a single copulation. The possibility of pregnancy, and the time and energy spent caring for the resulting offspring, favored ancestral females who were selective in mating. Because of the long period of immaturity in humans, ancient women's reproductive interests were often best served by selecting a mate who not only would provide good genes (e.g., as signaled by facial symmetry; Shackelford & Larsen, 1997), but who also would invest in her and her offspring. Over evolutionary time, it was also in men's reproductive interests to see to it that their offspring received the support necessary to survive to reproductive age. But the amount and duration of investment necessary to ensure the survival of offspring was less for men than for women. Thus, although both men and women shared a common reproductive goal (getting their offspring to adulthood), the optimal level of investment to achieve this goal was unequal for the sexes, placing males' and females' reproductive interests in conflict.

Men are not indiscriminate when it comes to selecting a mate, especially when selecting a long-term partner. Men around the world want long-term partners who are attractive, intelligent, and kind. Women also desire attractive, intelligent, and kind men as husbands, but, as predicted by parental investment theory, they rate financial resources as more important in a mate than do men (Buss, 1989). Despite the selectivity that men and women universally display in choosing a long-term partner, and consistent with parental investment theory, women are more selective in granting sex, and men are more eager to have casual sex (see Buss, 1994).

Men and women have evolved different psychological mechanisms as solutions to the adaptive problems unique to their sex. For example, fertilization occurs within the female, and it is the female who gestates and gives birth to the offspring. This greater prenatal investment of the female comes at considerable cost but brings with it certainty of maternity. In contrast, males, who may invest only sperm and the energy necessary to copulate, cannot be certain of paternity. Furthermore, because women conceal ovulation and are potentially sexually receptive throughout their menstrual cycle, it is difficult for a man to know when copulation is likely to result in pregnancy. As a result, being the unwitting social father to another man's genetic offspring is a possibility for men. This in fact occurs in between 2% and 30% of all births; the rate is similar in traditional societies, and there is no reason to believe that it differed substantially for our ancestors (see Baker & Bellis, 1995). Women, of course, cannot so easily be fooled into rearing another woman's child who they believe is their own, although they do risk losing a mate's investment to another woman.

One consequence of this sex difference in the certainty of genetic parenthood can be seen in men's and women's reactions to a long-term partner's infidelity. When asked to imagine that their long-term partner is either (a) having casual sex with another person or (b) developing a close emotional relationship with another person, men and women respond differently. Verbal reports and measures of physiological arousal indicate that women are more upset by a partner's emotional infidelity, which could signal a loss of resources, whereas men are more upset by a partner's sexual infidelity (Buss, Larsen, Westen, & Semmelroth, 1992).

In conclusion, human sex differences in parental investment predict sex differences in sexual strategies. These sex differences include the greater inclination of men to pursue short-term casual sex; the greater selectivity of women in choosing a mate, especially in the context of short-term mating; and the greater distress of men in response to a long-term partner's sexual infidelity and of women in response to a partner's emotional infidelity.

INHIBITORY ABILITIES

Inhibition refers to the withholding of a response in situations in which that response otherwise would be made. The ability to inhibit inappropriate sexual and aggressive responses is important for the success of both men and women in modern (and presumably ancestral) society and may have played a role in the evolution of human intelligence, particularly social intelligence (Bjorklund & Harnishfeger, 1995). However, ancestral women may have needed greater inhibitory abilities than ancestral men in certain contexts, because of their different reproductive strategies (Bjorklund & Kipp, 1996). For example, because of ancestral women's greater investment in the potential consequences of an act of copulation, it might have been in their reproductive interests to have greater control of their sexual arousal and related behaviors in order to more closely evaluate the value of a man before assenting to sex. Ancestral women also may have needed substantial political skill in order to keep sexual interests in other men hidden from a mate. Male response to suspected female infidelity can be violent, and even when adultery does not lead to aggression, it often leads to divorce, which both historically and in contemporary societies is more detrimental to a woman and her offspring than to a man (see Buss, 1994).

Similarly, the bulk of child-care responsibilities falls to women, and these also may require enhanced inhibitory abilities. For example, parents often must put the needs of their infants ahead of their own, delaying gratification of their own desires and resisting distractions that would take them away from their infants. They also must inhibit aggression toward infants or young children who may cry continuously, disobey, and damage personal property.

In support of these hypotheses, research has shown that women are better able to control the expression of their emotions than are men, despite the fact that women are more emotionally expressive than men. In studies in which people are asked to display a positive emotion after a negative experience (e.g., pretending that a foul-tasting drink tastes good) or vice versa, females (from the age of 4 years and up) are better able to control their emotional expressions (i.e., fool a judge watching their reactions) than are males (e.g., Cole, 1986). In other research, there is evidence that females are better than males on tasks that involve resisting temptation and delaying gratification (e.g., Kochanska, Murray, Jacques, Koenig, & Vandegeest, 1996), precisely the pattern one would predict if selection pressures associated with child care were greater on ancestral females than on ancestral males. And there is limited evidence that women are better able to inhibit sexual arousal than are men (Cerny, 1978; Rosen, 1973). In contrast, there is no female advantage in inhibitory abilities for cognitive tasks such as selective attention, suggesting that the sex differences are relatively domain-specific, restricted to abilities related to sexual and parenting contexts, as predicted by parental investment theory.

CONCLUSIONS

Different psychological mechanisms in men and women, attributable to sex differences in minimum parental investment over evolutionary history, provide the skeletal features for adapted behaviors. They represent biases that, in the distant past, served men's and women's reproductive fitness well. However, humans exert greater intentional control over sexual behavior than any other animal, and the evolved sexual and child-care strategies of men and women are not invariantly manifested, but instead are responsive to physical and social environments over the course of development. From this perspective, nature and nurture are not alternative explanations, but instead are two sides of the same explanatory coin.

Recommended Reading

Bjorklund, D.F., & Kipp, K. (1996). (See References)
Buss, D.M. (1994). (See References)
Buss, D.M. (1999). *Evolutionary psychology: The new science of the mind.* Needham Heights, MA: Allyn & Bacon.
Geary, D.C. (1998). (See References)
Trivers, R. (1972). (See References)

Acknowledgments—We would like to thank David Buss, David Geary, Erika Hoff-Ginsberg, Martha Hubertz, Gregg LeBlanc, Santo Tarantino, Robin Vallacher, and Viviana Weekes, who provided helpful comments and suggestions that improved this article.

Note

1. Address correspondence to either David F. Bjorklund, Department of Psychology, Florida Atlantic University, Boca Raton, FL 33431, e-mail: dbjorklund@fau.edu, or Todd K. Shackelford, Division of Science—Psychology, Florida Atlantic University, 2912 College Ave., Davie, FL 33314, e-mail: tshackel@fau.edu.

References

Baker, R.R., & Bellis, M.A. (1995). *Human sperm competition.* London: Chapman & Hall.
Belsky, J., Steinberg, L., & Draper, P. (1991). Childhood experience, interpersonal development, and reproductive strategy: An evolutionary theory of socialization. *Child Development, 62,* 647–670.
Bjorklund, D.F., & Harnishfeger, K.K. (1995). The role of inhibition mechanisms in the evolution of human cognition. In F.N. Dempster & C.J. Brainerd (Eds.), *New perspectives on interference and inhibition in cognition* (pp. 141–173). New York: Academic Press.
Bjorklund, D.F., & Kipp, K. (1996). Parental investment theory and gender differences in the evolution of inhibition mechanisms. *Psychological Bulletin, 120,* 163–188.
Buss, D.M. (1989). Sex differences in human mate preferences: Evolutionary hypotheses tested in 37 cultures. *Behavioral and Brain Sciences, 12,* 1–49.
Buss, D.M. (1994). *The evolution of desire.* New York: Basic Books.
Buss, D.M., Larsen, R.J., Westen, D., & Semmelroth, J. (1992). Sex differences in jealousy: Evolution, physiology, and psychology. *Psychological Science, 3,* 251–255.
Cerny, J.A. (1978). Biofeedback and the voluntary control of sexual arousal in women. *Behavior Therapy, 9,* 847–855.

Cole, P.M. (1986). Children's spontaneous control of facial expression. *Child Development, 57,* 1309–1321.

Geary, D.C. (1998). *Male, female: The evolution of human sex differences.* Washington, DC: American Psychological Association.

Kochanska, G., Murray, K., Jacques, J.Y., Koenig, A.L., & Vandegeest, K.A. (1996). Inhibitory control in young children and its role in emerging internalization. *Child Development, 67,* 490–507.

Rosen, R.C. (1973). Suppression of penile tumescence by instrumental conditioning. *Psychometric Medicine, 35,* 509–514.

Shackelford, T.K., & Larsen, R.J. (1997). Facial asymmetry as an indicator of psychological, emotional, and physiological distress. *Journal of Personality and Social Psychology, 72,* 456–466.

Tooby, J., & Cosmides, L. (1992). The psychological foundations of culture. In J. Barkow, L. Cosmides, & J. Tooby (Eds.), *The adapted mind* (pp. 19–136). New York: Oxford University Press.

Trivers, R. (1972). Parental investment and sexual selection. In B. Campbell (Ed.), *Sexual selection and the descent of man* (pp. 136–179). New York: Aldine de Gruyter.

Critical Thinking Questions

1. Can you make additional predictions based on parental investment theory?

2. Bjorklund and Shackelford make a strong evolutionary-based case that in the past, women, more so than men, may have needed to be able to inhibit their behavior. Alternatively, can you come up with any reasons that ancestral men may have needed greater inhibitory abilities than ancestral women?

This article has been reprinted as it originally appeared in *Current Directions in Psychological Science*. Citation information for this article as originally published appears above.

Men's and Women's Mating Preferences: Distinct Evolutionary Mechanisms?

Lynn Carol Miller,[1] Anila Putcha-Bhagavatula, and William C. Pedersen

Annenberg School for Communication, University of Southern California, Los Angeles, California

Abstract

Have men and women evolved sex-distinct mating preferences for short-term and long-term mating, as postulated by some evolutionary theorists? Direct tests of assumptions, consideration of confounds with gender, and examination of the same variables for both sexes suggest men and women are remarkably similar. Furthermore, cross-species comparisons indicate that humans do not evidence mating mechanisms indicative of short-term mating (e.g., large female sexual skins, large testicles). Understanding human variability in mating preferences is apt to involve more detailed knowledge of the links between these preferences and biological and chemical mechanisms associated with sexual motivation, sexual arousal, and sexual functioning.

Keywords

sex; mating strategies; evolution

For Darwin, evolution via sexual selection occurred when characteristics afforded individuals a reproductive advantage over their rivals, either in competing directly against same-sex competitors (e.g., better weaponry) or in having characteristics that opposite-sex mates preferred (e.g., greater attractiveness). Trivers (1972), in his parental investment theory, argued that an important factor guiding sexual selection is the relative amount of parental investment that males and females devote to offspring. The sex that invests less in offspring (typically males, who minimally invest sperm, compared with females, who minimally invest eggs, gestation, lactation, and other care) should devote proportionately more mating effort to short-term couplings and less to parental investment. The sex that invests less should also be less choosy in its mate-selection criteria and more apt to engage in same-sex competition for mates. Sexual asymmetries in parental investment, according to this approach, should predict sex-differentiated mating preferences and more competition between members of the less-investing sex.

Among psychologists, there are those who have applied parental investment theory to humans (e.g., Buss & Schmitt, 1993; Geary, 2000). Buss and his colleagues, for example, have argued that because men minimally invest sperm, short-term mating is reproductively more advantageous for men than for women. The claim that men and women have evolved sex-distinct sexual strategies (e.g., such that men spend proportionately more of their mating effort in short-term mating than do women) seems to have permeated the popular culture, as well as the professional literature. However, other psychologists dispute these claims, citing evidence from psychology, primatology, cross-cultural analyses, and neurobiology. In this article, we discuss some recent evidence in this debate.

Part of Buss and Schmitt's (1993) argument is that men and women evolved distinct mechanisms for both short-term and long-term mating. We begin by reviewing relevant evidence from primatology, where similar distinctions between long-term and short-term mating are made.

HUMANS ARE PRIMATES

Are Humans Designed to Be Short-Term Maters?

Among primates (Dixson, 1998), there are those with short-term and those with long-term mating systems.[2] Two long-term systems are monogamy (one male mates long term with one female; e.g., gibbon, siamang) and polygyny (one male mates long term with two or more females; e.g., gorilla). In both long-term and short-term mating, males and females attract (and sometimes retain) mates by having desirable characteristics. In addition, characteristics that enhance one's competitive advantage among members of the same gender may afford reproductive advantage. In long-term mating, the male is often able to restrict competitors by maintaining proximity to his female mate (or mates) and by physically defending her (their) territory.

Some evolved mating mechanisms (e.g., large female sexual skins, large testicles) indicate that short-term mating played a significant role in a species' evolved mating strategies. For example, among common chimpanzee and bonobo, large female sexual skins attract so many male competitors when a female is fertile that long-term male defense strategies are inadequate (e.g., to ensure that a given male is the biological father of his mate's offspring). Instead, evolution favors the reproductive success of males who can better compete via mechanisms for enhancing the probability that their sperm, and not that of their competitors, will impregnate the female. Thus, when females have large sexual skins when fertile, males who have more sperm (i.e., larger testicles) or produce sperm plugs (e.g., that might reduce sperm displacement by the next partner) increase their chances of fathering offspring. As indicated in Table 1, chimpanzee females exhibit large sexual skins and chimpanzee males exhibit sperm-competition mechanisms. But humans, and other long-term maters among apes, do not possess such mechanisms.

Table 1. *Mating-system variables: Comparisons of humans and other apes*

Variable	Humans	Gibbons/siamangs (monogamous)	Orangutans (polygynous)	Gorillas (polygynous)	Chimpanzees (promiscuous)
		Long-term maters			Short-term maters
Testicle weight (g)/ body weight (kg)	0.79	0.83–1.00	0.33–0.74	0.09–0.18	2.68–2.83
Copulatory plugs	No	No (4 species)	Unknown	Unknown	Yes
Sexual skin	No visible swelling or skin (concealed ovulation)	Very small sexual skins (gibbon) (unknown if siamang females have sexual skins)	No visible swelling or skin (concealed ovulation)	Sexual swelling at midcycle, visible on close inspection; no sexual skin	Very large sexual skins, visible at a considerable distance, that attract multiple males

Note. All data are from Dixson (1998).

Researchers suggesting that humans have evolved short-term mating mechanisms have pointed to arguments that there are kamikaze sperm that are designed to kill the sperm of human male competitors. But *in vitro* analyses of spermatozoa from multiple human males (Moore, Martin, & Birkhead, 1999) do not support this claim. Overall, human mating characteristics, discussed here and elsewhere, fit the pattern of primates whose primary or secondary mating systems are long-term and not short-term ones (Dixson, 1998).

Parenting and Mating-System Differences

Primatologists have argued that Trivers's theory does not apply well to primates. One reason may be that "traditional examination of male mating and parental investment has overlooked the wide and costly array of physiological and social mechanisms" that are involved in male primate investment, including the defense of troop members and territory (Fuentes, 2000, p. 602). Including these additional mechanisms in conceptualizations of parental investment would suggest much less sexual asymmetry in investment among primates than among other mammals.

There are many primate species in which males do not typically provide direct care of offspring. Nevertheless, males among some of these species can and will do so. For example, gorilla males, who are polygynous, will assume primary parental caregiving (e.g., nurturing and rearing the infant themselves) when a mate or sister has been killed. That is, the underlying evolved mechanisms for directly providing parental care are present. In any event, with more symmetry in parental investment, the sexes might be expected to have more similar mate preferences.

EVOLVED SEX-DISTINCT MATING PREFERENCES?

Trivers's argument concerning the role of male and female asymmetries in parental investment leads some psychologists (e.g., Buss & Schmitt, 1993) to argue (e.g., sexual strategies theory) for a variety of sex-distinct mating preferences for men and women. Other psychologists, influenced by attachment theory (e.g., Miller & Fishkin, 1997; Miller, Pedersen, & Putcha, 2002) or positing the influence of cultural factors (Eagly & Wood, 1999), argue for relatively few, less pronounced, or no sex-distinct evolved mating preferences in humans. What is the evidence?

Sex Differences in Jealousy

According to Buss and Schmitt (1993), because men need to guard against cuckoldry (investing in nonbiological offspring) and women need to guard against losing a mate's resources, men should focus more on signs of *sexual* infidelity in their partner, whereas women should react more strongly to cues that signal *emotional* infidelity. This prediction was tested and supported by Buss and his colleagues. But both Harris and Christenfeld (1996) and DeSteno and Salovey (1996) suggested that the two types of infidelity are equally upsetting to men and women, and that the sex difference is the result of an artifact (i.e., a sex difference in which type of infidelity more strongly signals the other). They separately found that once this artifact is controlled for, there is not a sex difference.

Sex Differences in Preferences for Mate Resources

Buss and Schmitt (1993) also argued that there are evolved sex differences in men's and women's desire for a mate who has or appears able to procure resources. For example, they argued that in choosing a long-term mate, women—more than men—should value ambition, good earning capacity, professional degrees, and wealth. Across 37 cultures, Buss found that women, more so than men, desired such resource-acquisition cues in long-term mates. But might cultural factors explain these effects? Eagly and Wood (1999) assessed a variety of indicators of women's power, such as access to educational and financial equality, across these 37 cultures. They found that in those cultures where women enjoyed less power, there were stronger sex differences in preferences for these resource cues.

Even in hunter-gatherer societies, women's economic power (e.g., role in hunting and procuring meat and fish) may historically have differentiated cultures where men and women had comparable authority[3] from those where they did not (Boehm, 1999). But in band living, men are equals, meat is shared, and individual hunting ability is obscured. With little if any variability in men's resources within the band, resource cues among males are unlikely to have become the basis for an evolved mating preference in females. With the advent of agriculture less than 10,000 years ago, however, more widespread and larger resource differentials among men were created. Understanding how societal structures and dynamics affect sex-based resource differentials and resultant mating preferences remains an important issue demanding further research.

Testing Theoretical Assumptions

Buss and Schmitt (1993) did not directly test many of sexual strategies theory's assumptions. We consider two examples. First, Buss and Schmitt argued that men should seek more short-term sexual partners than women. But when they asked men and women how many partners they ideally desired over various time periods, they did not ask their participants how many of these were short-term, intermediate-term, or long-term sexual partners. When we (Pedersen, Miller, Putcha-Bhagavatula, & Yang, 2002) directly examined desires for all three types of relationships,[4] we found that virtually all men (98.9%) and all women (99.2%) wanted to eventually settle down in a long-term mutually exclusive sexual relationship, typically within 5 years into the future. Moreover, over this 5-year period, the typical man and woman each desired no short-term partners.

Second, according to sexual strategies theory, "because of a fundamental asymmetry between the sexes in minimum levels of parental investment, men devote a larger proportion of their total mating effort to short-term mating than do women" (Buss & Schmitt, 1993, p. 205). But Buss and Schmitt did not directly test this critical proportional assumption. When we did, we found that men and women did not differ either in the proportion of time or in the proportion of money they expended in short-term mating relative to their total mating effort (Miller et al., 2002).

In addition, Buss and Schmitt (1993) pointed to mean differences between men and women in the desirability of characteristics for a short-term versus a long-term mate as another example of sex-distinct mating mechanisms. But a closer look at the 30 variables (covering 17 of 22 predictions) Buss and Schmitt reported shows that they compared short-term versus long-term preferences on different variables for men than for women (see Table 2). How can one tell if a mean difference in preferences between short-term and long-term contexts among men supports the argument that men and women have distinct mating mechanisms if the same data are not consistently reported for women?

To address this issue, we (Miller et al., 2002) collected new data on nearly all of these preference items for both men and women. With few exceptions, if there was a significant difference between preferences in the short-term and long-term contexts for one gender, there was a significant difference in the same direction for the other gender. In fact, across the data, what men desired most in a mate women also desired most in a mate. What men found most undesirable in a mate women also found most undesirable in a mate. This yielded extraordinarily high correlations between men's and women's ratings for both short-term and long-term sexual partners. Furthermore, we and other researchers have identified a variety of confounds with gender in predicting mating preferences, including

Table 2. *Variables for which Buss and Schmitt (1993) reported means and t tests in their study of college men's and women's preferences for short-term and long-term mates*

Preference items provided by Buss and Schmitt (1993)	Means reported				t tests reported			
	Men		Women		Short vs. long term		Men vs. women	
	Short term	Long term	Short term	Long term	Men	Women	Short term	Long term
Already in a relationship	X		X				X	
Promiscuous	X	X	X	X	X		X	
Physically attractive[a]	X	X	X	X	X			
Good looking	X	X	X	X	X			
Physically unattractive	X	X	X	X	X			
Sexually experienced	X	X			X			
Sex appeal	X	X			X			
Prudishness	X	X			X			
Sexual inexperience	X	X			X			
Low sex drive	X	X			X			
Wants a commitment[b]	X	X			X			
Faithfulness	X	X			X			
Sexual loyalty	X	X			X			
Chastity[a,c]	X	X			X		?	
Unfaithful[c]	X	X			X		?	
Sleeps around a lot[c]	X	X			X		?	
Spends a lot . . . early on			X	X		X		
Gives gifts early on			X	X		X		
Has . . . extravagant lifestyle			X	X		X		
Stingy early on			X	X		X		
Physical strength						X	X	X
Good financial prospects[d]			X	X		X		?
Promising career[d,e]			X	X		X		?
Likely to succeed . . . [d,e]			X	X		X		?
Likely to earn . . . [d,e]			X	X		X		?
Has reliable . . . career[d,e]			X	X		X		?
Unable to support you . . . [d]			X	X		X		
Financially poor[c]			X	X		X	?	?
Lacks ambition[c]			X	X		X	?	?
Uneducated[c]			X	X		X	?	?

Note. Xs indicate results that were reported, and ?s indicate that differences were mentioned or implied but not presented. Empty cells indicate no results were mentioned.

[a]Buss and Schmitt (1993) alluded to earlier work in which *t*-test comparisons between men and women in long-term relationships but not short-term relationships were reported for other (e.g., cross-cultural) samples.

[b]Buss and Schmitt (1993) noted that a "context difference was also found but was not nearly as strong [for women]" (p. 213, material in brackets added). But they provided no *t* tests for women nor a test of the Context × Sex interaction alluded to. That is, Buss and Schmitt must have collected data on this variable for women as well as for men, but it is not clear from their description if this difference was significant for women and more significant for men than women.

[c]No *t* tests were provided for men versus women, but Buss and Schmitt (1993) noted in the text that there were significant sex differences for these preferences.

[d]Men and women did not provide personal assessments on these preferences, but made stereotype judgments about men and women (e.g., indicating "how desirable the 'average male' or 'average female' would find each attribute in short-term and long-term mating contexts"; Buss & Schmitt, 1993, p. 223).

[e]Buss and Schmitt (1993) did not provide *t* tests of sex differences but claimed that they performed the tests and found sex differences.

age, ethnicity, relationship status, sexual experience, and perceptions of the quality of care provided by one's parents.

Note that typically, in our own work and the work of other scientists, the findings reported by Buss and his colleagues were replicated. By collecting additional data and conducting new analyses of data that went beyond those provided by Buss and his colleagues, however, we and other scientists have been able to develop a fuller and different overall story than that provided by sexual strategies theory. For example, in contrast to Buss and his colleagues, we did not find overall support for sexual strategies theory when we collected and examined data on the same variables for both genders.

In short, comparative analyses with other primates provide little evidence for biological mechanisms uniquely designed for short-term mating for humans. Emerging reviews and psychological evidence also challenge the claim that there are sex-distinct evolved mating mechanisms involving mating preferences.

FUTURE DIRECTIONS

Understanding evolutionary design, as part of and apart from the effects of cultural diffusion and innovation, is one of the biggest challenges for evolutionary approaches. Social constraint and culture-developing mechanisms are part of the evolutionary design of larger-brained primates. But these mechanisms produce cultural products that can bias mating or sex differences in behavior. For example, alcohol is often used to reduce sexual inhibitions in short-term mating. But alcohol was not produced in the Pleistocene.[5] An important methodological challenge is to not confound cultural products and evolved design, yet understand cultural mechanisms, and adaptation to environmental change, as part of that evolved design. It also behooves researchers to guard against sexual stereotypes and confounds. Even scientists can wear cultural blinders that can bias the collection, presentation, and interpretation of data.

Another challenge is to better specify psychological mechanisms and, where possible, tie them to related brain structures and biological and chemical processes. Researchers also need to better delineate the processes by which these mechanisms predict outcomes (e.g., preferences, decisions, behaviors). For example, primates may provide higher levels of paternal care and investment than most other mammals. Is this related to the greater sex-related plasticity found in primate brains (Dixson, 1998)? In nonprimate mammals, monogamous species have greater overlap in underlying biological and chemical mechanisms for males and females than do promiscuous species, with the former also providing higher levels of paternal care (Insel, 1997). However, in a variety of species, including humans, the brain shows sex differences (e.g., differences in the size of various portions of the brain) that might affect sex-related behaviors. Whether and how these sex differences influence or are influenced by behavior, or might interact with hormones, remains unclear.

Hormonal patterns, however, are more clearly related to some sexual behaviors. For example, hormonal fluctuations throughout the monthly human female cycle seem related to the timing of male and female sexual initiation (proceptivity) or sexual motivation. Such sex differences are similar to those found across many primate species with diverse mating systems, varying from short-term to long-term ones (Dixson, 1998). For example, in all nonsimian primates, unlike other mammals, females are receptive to sex throughout their cycles, but actively seek sex just prior to ovulation, when levels of testosterone and estradiol surge. Because similar sex differences are found across primates with varying mating systems, these sex differences are unlikely to shed much light on differences in mating systems.

But exploring how hormonal fluctuations covary with mating preferences for both men and women might provide exciting insight into variability both within and between individuals. In such investigations, however, scientists should not consider men's and women's preferences and behaviors in isolation. Emerging research, for example, suggests that mutual influence between men and women, hormonally and pheromonally, affects sexual outcomes (Miller & Fishkin, 1997).

Spurred on by the development of Viagra, scientists have undertaken considerable work on humans' sexual dysfunction and sexual arousal. This work suggests that the sexual circuitry system—and the biological and chemical processes affecting sexual functioning and enjoyment—is surprisingly similar in men and women (Goldstein, 2000). The balance of serotonin (which plays a role in inhibiting sexual arousal) to oxytocin (which serves as the sexual-excitation neurotransmitter) is critical to sexual function and affects sexual enjoyment. Psychological factors (e.g., anxiety, anger, comfort, liking, attraction, love), for both men and women, impact the biological and chemical processes affecting inhibition and excitation. Thus, higher levels of emotional bonding are associated with higher levels of sexual enjoyment (Miller & Fishkin, 1997), and anxiety is predictive of reduced sexual enjoyment and functioning. Psychological factors that influence sexual functioning may be key to understanding fluctuations in mating preferences within and between individuals (Miller et al., 2002). Given the observed similarities between men's and women's patterns of mating preferences, sexual circuitry, and sexual enjoyment, however, sex-distinct mating preferences related to sexual arousal and functioning do not seem promising. But, because the wiring of the sexual circuitry system may be species-specific (Insel, 1997), differences across species in these evolved biological, chemical, and psychological systems might shed light on differences in expressed mating preferences and behaviors.

In all this complexity, one thing is clear: Scientists studying mating systems, and sex differences within them, have to more carefully consider the systems of relevant mechanisms (both shared across species and unique to humans) and how these, in combination, interact with environments to affect mating preferences and behaviors.

Recommended Reading

Dixson, A.F. (1998). (See References)
Pedersen, W.C., Miller, L.C., Putcha-Bhagavatula, A.D., & Yang, Y. (2002). (See References)

Notes

1. Address correspondence to Lynn Carol Miller, Annenberg School for Communication, University of Southern California, Los Angeles, CA 90089-0281; e-mail: Lmiller@rcf.usc.edu.

2. Mating systems are not absolute. Rather, each is composed of a set of mechanisms that increase the probability of particular mating outcomes. Primatologists classify primates as having primary, and sometimes secondary, mating systems. Thus, the occurrence of occasional extrapair mating, by itself, does not alter the species' mating classification (e.g., as primarily long-term maters).

3. For example, where females and males hunt boar with dogs (e.g., the Agta of the Philippines), the sexes have economic and political parity (Boehm, 1999).

4. In our study, we employed the same terminology used by Buss and Schmitt (1993) to define these three types of relationships to subjects. Specifically, short-term relationships were defined as "a 1-night stand, brief affair, etc." (p. 210). Intermediate-term relationships were defined as "dating, going steady, brief marriages, or intermediate-length affairs" (p. 204). Long-term mates were defined as "a marriage partner" (p. 210).

5. Mating preferences are fundamental facets of evolutionary processes. Changing them might take tens of thousands of years or more. That is why when scientists search for evolutionary adaptations, they typically consider what humans were like during the Pleistocene era, which ended more than 10,000 years ago. At that point in time, and for most of human evolution, *Homo sapiens* were nomadic hunter-gatherers.

References

Boehm, C. (1999). *Hierarchy in the forest: The evolution of egalitarian behavior*. Cambridge, MA: Harvard University Press.

Buss, D.M., & Schmitt, D.P. (1993). Sexual Strategies Theory: An evolutionary perspective on human mating. *Psychological Review, 100,* 204–232.

DeSteno, D.A., & Salovey, P. (1996). Evolutionary origins of sex differences in jealousy? Questioning the "fitness" of the model. *Psychological Science, 7,* 367–372.

Dixson, A.F. (1998). *Primate sexuality: Comparative studies of the prosimians, monkeys, apes, and human beings*. Oxford, England: Oxford University Press.

Eagly, A.H., & Wood, W. (1999). The origins of sex differences in human behavior: Evolved dispositions versus social roles. *American Psychologist, 54,* 408–423.

Fuentes, A. (2000). Human mating models can benefit from comparative primatology and careful methodology. *Behavioral and Brain Sciences, 23,* 602–603.

Geary, D.C. (2000). Evolution and proximate expression of human paternal investment. *Psychological Bulletin, 126,* 55–77.

Goldstein, I. (2000). Male sexual circuitry. *Scientific American, 283,* 70–75.

Harris, C.R., & Christenfeld, N. (1996). Gender, jealousy, and reason. *Psychological Science, 7,* 364–366.

Insel, T.R. (1997). A neurobiological basis of social attachment. *American Journal of Psychiatry, 154,* 726–735.

Miller, L.C., & Fishkin, S.A. (1997). On the dynamics of human bonding and reproductive success: Seeking "windows" on the "adapted-for" human-environmental interface. In J.A. Simpson & D.T. Kenrick (Eds.), *Evolutionary social psychology* (pp. 197–235). Mahwah, NJ: Erlbaum.

Miller, L.C., Pedersen, W.C., & Putcha, A.D. (2002). *Mating mechanisms for men and women: From smoke, mirrors, and leaps of faith . . . toward a mindful evolutionary dynamics*. Unpublished manuscript, University of Southern California, Los Angeles.

Moore, H.D.M., Martin, M., & Birkhead, T.R. (1999). No evidence for killer sperm or other selective interactions between human spermatozoa in ejaculates of different males in vitro. *Proceedings of the Royal Society of London B, 266,* 2343–2350.

Pedersen, W.C., Miller, L.C., Putcha-Bhagavatula, A.D., & Yang, Y. (2002). Evolved sex differences in the number of partners desired? The long and the short of it. *Psychological Science, 13,* 157–161.

Trivers, R. (1972). Parental investment and sexual selection. In B. Campbell (Ed.), *Sexual selection and the descent of man 1871–1971* (pp. 136–179). Chicago: Aldine-Atherton.

Critical Thinking Questions

1. Miller et al. discuss research on infidelity, in which some researchers argue that men react more negatively to sexual infidelity in their mates and women react more negatively to emotional infidelity in their mates. There are other studies, however, that suggest this is only an illusory sex difference, because a man is likely to assume that sexual infidelity in his partner indicates that there is also an emotional relationship, whereas a woman is more likely to assume that an emotional breach implies sexual infidelity as well. How might you go about testing this idea?

2. How can you account for the difference in findings between Buss and Schmitt, who found that men desire more sexual partners than do women, and Pedersen, Miller, Putcha-Bhagavatula, and Yang, who found that almost all men and women reported the wish to have one long-term, committed relationship within the next five years?

This article has been reprinted as it originally appeared in *Current Directions in Psychological Science*. Citation information for this article as originally published appears above.

Cognitive Biases and Emotional Wisdom in the Evolution of Conflict Between the Sexes

David M. Buss[1]

Department of Psychology, University of Texas, Austin, Texas

Abstract

Two recent theories within evolutionary psychology have produced novel insights into conflict between the sexes. According to *error management theory* (EMT), asymmetries over evolutionary time in the cost-benefit consequences of specific social inferences have produced predictable cognitive biases. Women, for example, appear to underinfer commitment in response to signals of resource display. Men often overinfer a woman's sexual desire when she merely smiles at or casually touches them. These inferential biases, according to EMT, represent functional adaptations rather than markers of irrationality in information processing. According to *strategic interference theory,* certain "negative emotions" function to motivate action to reduce conflict produced by impediments to preferred social strategies. Emotions such as jealousy and anger, rather than reducing rationality, may embody inherited ancestral wisdom functional in dealing with interference inflicted by other individuals. These evolution-based theories have produced novel empirical discoveries and challenge traditional theories anchored in the premise that cognitive biases and negative emotions necessarily lead to irrationality.

Keywords

conflict; cognitive bias; negative emotions; sex differences; sexuality; evolutionary psychology

In mating and sexuality more than in any other domain, women and men have confronted different adaptive challenges over the long course of human evolutionary history. Women have been required to make a 9-month investment to produce a child. Men have not. Because fertilization occurs within women, men have faced the problem of uncertainty that they are the genetic parents. Women have not. It would be astonishing if men and women had not evolved somewhat different mating strategies to grapple with their differing adaptive challenges (Buss & Schmitt, 1993). Predictions generated by evolutionary models about sex differences in mate preferences, sexual desires, and elicitors of romantic jealousy, for example, have all been robustly documented across a variety of cultures (Buss, 1999). What has been less well appreciated is how sex differences in mating strategies produce specific forms of sexual conflict when they are expressed in behavior (see Buss & Malamuth, 1996).

Recent evolutionary work has inspired subtle hypotheses about the ways in which women and men clash, ranging from the erroneous inferences they make about the other sex to the emotions they experience when preferred mating strategies are thwarted. This article highlights two of these evolutionarily inspired research programs, one dealing with cognitive biases and one dealing with emotions as tracking devices.

ERROR MANAGEMENT THEORY: ADAPTIVE COGNITIVE ERRORS AND CONFLICT BETWEEN THE SEXES

Humans live in an uncertain social world. We must make inferences about others' intentions and emotional states. How attracted is he to her? How committed is she to him? Was that bump in the hall-way an accident, or does it reveal hostile intentions? Some deeds, such as sexual infidelity and murder, are intentionally concealed, rendering uncertainty greater and inferences more tortuous. We are forced to make inferences about intentions and concealed deeds using a chaos of cues that are only probabilistically related to the deeds' occurrence. An unexplained scent on one's romantic partner, for example, could signal an extra-marital affair or innocuous olfactory acquisition from a casual conversation.

Just as there are two types of correct inferences (true positives, true negatives), there are two types of inferential errors. One can falsely infer an intention or deed that is not there. Or one can fail to infer an intention or deed that is there. A spouse might falsely suspect a partner of sexual treachery, for example, or fail to infer an extant infidelity. Both errors cannot simultaneously be minimized. Setting a low threshold for inferring infidelity, for example, minimizes missed detections, but simultaneously increases false accusations. Setting a higher threshold for inferring infidelity minimizes false accusations, but simultaneously increases missed detections.

According to *error management theory* (EMT; Haselton & Buss, 2000), it would be exceedingly unlikely that the cost-benefit consequences of the two types of errors would be identical across their many occurrences. We intuitively understand this in the context of smoke alarms, which are typically set sensitively. The costs of the occasional false alarm are trivial compared with the catastrophic costs of failing to detect a real house fire. EMT extends this logic to cost-benefit consequences in evolutionary fitness.

According to one EMT hypothesis, the recurrent fitness costs of failing to detect spousal infidelities typically would have been greater than the costs of occasional false suspicions (Buss, 2000a). An unknowingly cuckolded man, for example, would have risked investing in a rival's children in the mistaken belief that they were his. An unknowingly betrayed woman would have risked the diversion of her partner's resources and commitments to another woman and her children, producing cascading costs for her own children.

Cognitive Biases

According to EMT, asymmetries in the cost-benefit consequences of social inferences, if they recur over evolutionary time, create selection pressures that produce predictable *cognitive biases*. Just as smoke alarms are biased to produce more false positives than false negatives, EMT predicts that evolved information processing procedures will be biased to produce more of one type of inferential error than another. The direction and degree of bias, of course, greatly depend on such factors as context and gender. Inferences about the sexual intentions of a potential romantic partner, for example, carry a different cost-benefit calculus than inferences about the level of commitment in a current romantic partner. The cost-benefit consequences of particular types of inferential errors differed for men and women, according to EMT, producing different inferential biases in men and women. No prior psychological theory of cognitive biases predicts these sex differences. Nor do prior theories hypothesize different sex-linked inferential biases depending on domain.

Sexual Overperception and Commitment Skepticism

Empirical research has confirmed several hypotheses derived from specific applications of EMT (Haselton & Buss, 2000). It has been used to explain the sex-linked *sexual overperception bias,* whereby men are hypothesized to possess mind-reading biases designed to minimize the costs of missed sexual opportunities. EMT provides a cogent explanation, for example, of why men appear to falsely infer that a woman is sexually interested merely when she smiles or touches a man's arm. Furthermore, this EMT-based hypothesis predicts specific contexts in which the bias will disappear, such as when the target woman is genetically related to the man in question or low in reproductive value.

Another application of EMT has predicted an opposite sort of cognitive bias in women, the *commitment-skepticism bias.* According to this hypothesis, women have evolved an inferential bias designed to underestimate men's actual level of commitment early in courtship in order to minimize the costs of being sexually deceived by men who feign commitment (Haselton & Buss, 2000). If men give flowers or gifts to women, for example, third-party observers infer that the men are signaling greater commitment than do the women who are the recipients of these displays, who show greater skepticism about the depth of the men's feelings.

EMT also predicts cognitive biases linked with sexual jealousy that lead to false inferences of a partner's sexual infidelity (Buss, 2000a). Men and women, in very predictable contexts, sometimes have false beliefs that a partner is unfaithful when he or she has in fact remained loyal. This bias appears to get especially activated in social contexts that historically have tended to be linked with infidelity, even if the target person has never been betrayed. A partner's sexual dissatisfaction, a sudden decline in sexual desire, and an increasing gap in desirability between the two partners, for example, all trigger suspicions of infidelity. Modern humans appear to have inherited ancestral tracking devices that signal circumstances indicating a statistical likelihood of infidelity, even if these procedures produce false positive errors (Buss, 2000a).

EMT offers a fresh perspective on cognitive biases by suggesting that certain types of inferential errors represent adaptive errors rather than design flaws in the psychological machinery (Haselton & Buss, 2000). It has provided new insights into why men and women get into certain types of conflict—for example, men's sexual overperception bias can lead to unwanted sexual overtures. Although extant empirical tests of EMT have borne fruit, only future work can determine whether this theory will provide a more general theory of cognitive biases.

Nonetheless, EMT has been a source of inspiration for novel hypotheses about cognitive biases (e.g., commitment-skepticism bias), raised suspicions of some traditional explanations (e.g., that errors necessarily represent design flaws in human cognition), and suggested novel predictions about when biases occur (e.g., contexts in which false accusations of infidelity will occur).

STRATEGIC INTERFERENCE THEORY: "NEGATIVE" EMOTIONS AND CONFLICT BETWEEN THE SEXES

Conflict between the sexes is not produced solely from passionless cognitive biases. *Strategic interference theory* posits that emotions are psychological mechanisms that evolved in part to grapple with particular forms of conflict (Buss, 1989, 2000a). In the scientific history of emotions research, many theorists have contrasted "emotionality" with "rationality" (see Frank, 1988). According to this view, rationality is what causes humans to make sensible decisions. When faced with a problem, we use reason and logic to reach rational solutions. Emotions, according to this view, only get in the way—anger addles the brain; fear distorts reason; jealousy clouds the mind. Emotions are presumed by some theorists to be unfortunate relics from an ancient time in which human ancestors acted more from instinct than from logic. Psychologists have labeled anger, fear, and jealousy the "negative" emotions, presumably because they need to be controlled, reigned in, and subdued so that they do not impede rational action.

Negative Emotions as Functional

According to strategic interference theory, these emotions are adaptively designed to solve problems of strategic interference (Buss, 1989). Strategic interference occurs whenever something or someone impedes or blocks a preferred strategy or set of goal-directed actions. It is hypothesized that the negative emotions have been (and perhaps continue to be) beneficial, serving several related functions. First, they focus attention on the source of strategic interference, temporarily screening out other information less relevant to the adaptive problem. Second, they prompt storage of the relevant information in memory so that it is available for subsequent retrieval under appropriate circumstances. Third, they motivate action designed to eliminate or reduce strategic interference. And fourth, they motivate action designed to avoid future episodes of strategic interference.

Because men and women have evolved somewhat different sexual strategies, the events that cause strategic interference are predicted to differ for the sexes. Therefore, the events that trigger emotions such as anger, jealousy, and subjective distress should differ for the sexes. This theory has heuristic value in guiding researchers to phenomena not predicted by other theories. No other theory of emotions, for example, predicts fundamental sex differences in the events that elicit these emotions.

Strategic interference theory has been tested empirically in several domains. In the domain of sexual strategies, research has shown that the patterns of men's and women's anger correspond precisely to their respective sources of strategic interference (Buss, 1999). Women, far more than men, become angry and upset by individuals who seek sex with them sooner, more frequently, and more persistently than they want. Men, far more than women, become angry and upset by individuals who delay sex or thwart their sexual advances.

Jealousy and Sexual Rivalry

More subtle tests of strategic interference theory have taken place in the domains of jealousy and same-sex rivalry. One series of studies conducted in Korea, Japan, and the United States discovered large and cross-culturally consistent sex differences in whether sexual or emotional betrayal by a partner was more distressing (Buss et al., 1999). These sex-linked emotional reactions were precisely predicted from the premise that sexual infidelity by a man's partner interferes with his strategy of monopolizing her reproductive capacities, producing paternity uncertainty. Emotional infidelity by a woman's partner interferes with her strategy of monopolizing a man's commitments and resources, which could get diverted to a rival woman and her children as a consequence of a man's emotional involvement.

Another domain in which strategic interference theory has been tested pertains to the specific qualities of mating rivals that evoke distress. Because women and men have evolved somewhat different mate preferences, the qualities of intrasexual rivals that will be alluring to one's partner should differ for the sexes (Buss & Schmitt, 1993). Interested rivals inflict strategic interference when they possess these desirable qualities. Partners inflict strategic interference when they are attracted to desirable rivals.

Parallel studies conducted in the Netherlands, the United States, and Korea documented these sex differences (Buss, Shackelford, Choe, Buunk, & Dijkstra, 2000). Dutch, American, and Korean men, more than their female counter-parts, reported particular emotional distress when a rival surpassed them on financial prospects, job prospects, and physical strength. Dutch, American, and Korean women, in contrast, reported greater distress when a rival surpassed them on facial attractiveness and body attractiveness. Although the cultures differed in some respects, and the sexes were similarly distressed by rivals who exceeded them on qualities such as kindness and sense of humor, the study demonstrated sex differences in emotional distress precisely for those rival characteristics predicted by strategic interference theory.

The so-called negative emotions, in short, may represent ancestral wisdom, inherited from a long line of successful ancestors who acted to minimize strategic interference. Emotions, far from distorting reason, may alert us to particular ways in which others may be impeding our preferred strategies. Emotions motivate efforts to reduce impedance. Strategic interference theory has inspired several novel hypotheses, raised suspicion of the common view that negative emotions interfere with reason, and led to the discovery of important sex differences in emotional experience that prior approaches had not uncovered.

CONCLUSIONS

Conflict between the sexes and conflict surrounding sex are ubiquitous phenomena in group-living species. The proposal that humans have evolved psychological mechanisms to deal with cross-sex interactions does not imply that what was ancestrally adaptive is necessarily currently functional in modern environments. Nor does it provide a panacea for reducing conflict between the sexes. In fact, it highlights some important obstacles to personal happiness and social harmony—emotions designed to produce subjective distress, inferential biases designed to produce errors, and mechanisms that benefit one person at the expense of others (Buss, 2000b).

Cautious skepticism is appropriate when evaluating new psychological approaches, and many critical issues remain unresolved. Will EMT lead to the discovery of additional cognitive biases beyond those discussed here, such as functional overestimates of other people's homicidal intentions (Buss & Duntley, 2001)? Will EMT prove capable of explaining well-documented cognitive biases, such as the tendency for people to overestimate their likelihood of success at certain tasks? Will EMT furnish a more powerful explanation than traditional treatments of cognitive biases, which typically invoke limited cognitive capacity, simplifying heuristics, and information processing shortcuts?

Similar unresolved issues remain for strategic interference theory. Will it continue to lead to the discovery of new phenomena that must be explained by any comprehensive theory of emotions, such as the connection between specific forms of cross-sex deception and sex-linked anger (Haselton & Buss, 2001) and the difficulty men and women often have in being "just friends" (Bleske & Buss, 2000)? How will strategic interference theory be integrated into a more comprehensive theory that includes both positively and negatively valenced emotions?

Psychology during the past few decades has delighted in demonstrating that humans are irrational information processors—cognitive heuristics produce bias, emotions cloud reason. But what is properly regarded as rational or irrational must be evaluated by the criterion of what problems particular mechanisms are designed to solve. Smoke alarms are biased—they produce many false positives. But they are not "irrational." Humans are designed to solve social adaptive problems. These include grappling with strategic interference. They also include making inferences about the differently constituted minds of the opposite sex. Within these and perhaps other domains, emotions may be rational and cognitive biases functional.

Recommended Reading

Barkow, J., Cosmides, L., & Tooby, J. (Eds.). (1992). *The adapted mind: Evolutionary psychology and the generation of culture.* New York: Oxford University Press.
Buss, D.M. (1999). (See References)
Buss, D.M. (2000a). (See References)
Geary, D. (1999). *Male, female: The evolution of human sex differences.* Washington, DC: American Psychological Association.
Mealy, L. (2000). *Sex differences: Developmental and evolutionary strategies.* New York: Academic Press.

Acknowledgments—I thank Martie Haselton and Art Markman for helpful comments.

Note

1. Address correspondence to David M. Buss, Department of Psychology, University of Texas, Austin, TX 78712; e-mail: dbuss@psy.utexas.edu.

References

Bleske, A., & Buss, D.M. (2000). Can men and women just be friends? *Personal Relationships, 7,* 131–151.

Buss, D.M. (1989). Conflict between the sexes: Strategic interference and the evocation of anger and upset. *Journal of Personality and Social Psychology, 56,* 735–747.

Buss, D.M. (1999). *Evolutionary psychology: The new science of the mind.* Boston: Allyn & Bacon.

Buss, D.M. (2000a). *The dangerous passion: Why jealousy is as necessary as love and sex.* New York: Free Press.

Buss, D.M. (2000b). The evolution of happiness. *American Psychologist, 55,* 15–23.

Buss, D.M., & Duntley, J.D. (2001). *Murder by design: The evolution of homicide.* Manuscript submitted for publication.

Buss, D.M., & Malamuth, N. (1996). *Sex, power, conflict: Evolutionary and feminist perspectives.* New York: Oxford University Press.

Buss, D.M., & Schmitt, D.P. (1993). Sexual Strategies Theory: An evolutionary perspective on human mating. *Psychological Review, 100,* 204–232.

Buss, D.M., Shackelford, T.K., Choe, J., Buunk, B.P., & Dijkstra, P. (2000). Distress about mating rivals. *Personal Relationships, 7,* 235–243.

Buss, D.M., Shackelford, T.K., Kirkpatrick, L.A., Choe, J.C., Lim, H.K., Hasegawa, M., Hasegawa, T., & Bennett, K. (1999). Jealousy and the nature of beliefs about infidelity: Tests of competing hypotheses about sex differences in the United States, Korea, and Japan. *Personal Relationships, 6,* 125–150.

Frank, R. (1988). *Passions within reason.* New York: Norton.

Haselton, M.G., & Buss, D.M. (2000). Error management theory: A new perspective on biases in cross-sex mind reading. *Journal of Personality and Social Psychology, 78,* 81–91.

Haselton, M.G., & Buss, D.M. (2001). *Sex, lies, and strategic interference: The psychology of deception between the sexes.* Manuscript submitted for publication.

Critical Thinking Questions

1. How could the findings described by Buss be used to improve the functioning of romantic relationships?

2. Based on evolutionary psychology, would you expect to find sex differences in any other negative emotions? What about in positive emotions?

3. What are some alternative reasons the sexes might demonstrate the emotional differences described here?

4. What are additional ways to test the theories described here?

This article has been reprinted as it originally appeared in *Current Directions in Psychological Science.* Citation information for this article as originally published appears above.

Section 4: Sexual Orientation

Perhaps no topic in this book is as divisive and misunderstood by the general public as that of sexual orientation. Although numerous questions remain, scientists do know that sexual orientation is more complex than is commonly assumed. Researchers disagree, however, on numerous issues, such as the dichotomous versus continuous nature of homosexuality, and the concept of bisexuality in particular. Some of the reasons for these controversies include the fact that self-identified sexual orientation may change during a lifetime, particularly in women; that some people experience no sexual attraction to either sex; and that humans persist in our need to categorize.

In the opening article of this section, Ritch Savin-Williams explores the question of how to define homosexuality. Specifically, his analysis highlights why defining homosexuality is quite complicated: There is often little correlation between the sex to which one is sexually or romantically attracted, the sex with whom one has had sexual interactions, and one's self-selected sexual identity. Nevertheless, researchers have tended to rely on self-identification, which, Savin-Williams argues, is only part of the picture and may lead to skewed estimates of the prevalence of homosexuality as well as misleading implications.

In the second article, Brian Gladue reviews the biopsychological factors involved in sexual orientation. Although it is less recent than some of the other articles in this reader, it still makes a valuable contribution by highlighting the more promising and less promising biopsychological factors involved in sexual orientation. Since the publication of this article, researchers are not much closer to fully identifying the mechanisms of sexual orientation. Although there is greater and greater consensus among scientists that there are biological-based determinants of the direction taken by sexual attraction, the search continues for a consistent and definitive answer. It is becoming clear that there are different underlying mechanisms for gay men (who have been studied much more) than for lesbians, so getting closer to an understanding of male sexual orientation does not necessarily get us any closer to an understanding of female sexual orientation.

Many people presume that same-sex couples are more unstable and very different in nature than mixed-sex couples. Lawrence Kurdek provides an overview of research on gay and lesbian couples, examining issues such as relationship satisfaction and stability, conflict, and division of household labor. For most factors that have been studied, heterosexual and homosexual couples are largely similar. Notable exceptions include the resolution of conflict, which tends to be more positive in gay and lesbian couples, and the division of household labor, which appears to be more equitable among gay and lesbian couples. Gay and lesbian couples do face one significant disadvantage compared to heterosexual couples, however: A perceived lack of social support by family.

For many, the controversy over sexual orientation revolves around defending traditional views of the family. Are the families of gay and lesbian couples different from the families of heterosexual couples? According to Charlotte Patterson's review, there are many more similarities than differences between homosexual and heterosexual couples in terms of their relationships with families of origin, their chosen families (partners and friends), and their children. Considering the evidence reviewed by Patterson and by Kurdek, it is becoming clear that *who* one loves does not change *how* one loves.

In most of the articles in this section, lack of social acceptance from the family is mentioned as playing a role in the adjustment of lesbians and gay men. Frequently, the lack of support stems from negative attitudes toward homosexuality. Gregory Herek provides a brief examination of the history and implications of various terms used to describe those attitudes. He concludes that the term "sexual prejudice" is the most useful such term because it is non-judgmental, relates to the already familiar psychological concept of prejudice, and can also be used to apply to negative attitudes toward other sexual orientations. Herek goes on to review what we know about sexual prejudice (its prevalence, who possesses it, what predicts it) and then discusses what we don't know (its underlying cognitive processes and motivations, the effectiveness of intervention strategies, and developmental patterns).

By the end of this section, the reader should have a more complete understanding of research-related and practical issues surrounding sexual orientation.

Who's Gay? Does It Matter?

Ritch C. Savin-Williams[1]

Cornell University

Abstract

To answer the question "Who's gay?"—and its logical follow-up, "Does it matter?"—researchers usually define homosexuality with reference to one of three components or expressions of sexual orientation: sexual/romantic attraction or arousal, sexual behavior, and sexual identity. Yet, the three components are imperfectly correlated and inconsistently predictive of each other, resulting in dissimilar conclusions regarding the number and nature of homosexual populations. Depending on which component is assessed, the prevalence rate of homosexuality in the general population ranges from 1 to 21%. When investigators define the homosexual population based on same-sex behavior or identity, they enhance the possibility of finding a biological basis for homosexuality and a compromised mental health (suicidality).

Keywords

gay; sexual orientation; sexual behavior; sexual identity; sexual/romantic attraction

Calculating the number and characteristics of homosexual individuals has become a frequent scientific enterprise, with political, clinical, and scientific ramifications. Historically considered a rare phenomenon and a type of mental and moral deviance, homosexuality presents a unique opportunity for modern investigators to broadly explore biological, clinical, and social influences on developmental aspects of sexuality and gender. The ensuing research, however, has generally ignored one fundamental issue—how homosexuality is defined can determine empirical findings. Here I focus on three possible consequences: the prevalence of homosexuality in the general population, the biological basis of homosexuality, and clinical characteristics attributed to homosexual individuals.

SEXUAL-ORIENTATION COMPONENTS

The question of who belongs in which sexual population group, and on what basis, is central for any viable paradigm for research on sexual orientation (Diamond, 2003a; Savin-Williams, 2005). Yet, few definitive answers regarding the appropriate theoretical basis or empirical means of defining sexual orientation have been provided, resulting in little consensus about what constitutes "a homosexual" and, consequently, reservations about the generalizability of past research findings. Three components or expressions of sexual orientation have been proposed: sexual/romantic attraction, sexual behavior, and sexual identity (see Table 1 for definitions and measures).

When researchers assess the number or characteristics of homosexual individuals, they base their findings on a single sexual-orientation component—usually identity. This approach, however, excludes many same-sex-oriented individuals and misidentifies some heterosexuals as homosexual. Those who

Table 1. *Components of sexual orientation* and example questions for assessment*

Component	Definition	Questions
Sexual/romantic attraction	Attraction toward one sex or the desire to have sexual relations or to be in a primary loving, sexual relationship with one or both sexes	"On a scale of 1 to 4, where 1 is very appealing and 4 is not at all appealing, how would you rate each of these activities: . . . having sex with someone of the same sex?" (Laumann, Gagnon, Michael, & Michaels, 1994, p. 293) "Have you ever had a romantic attraction to a male? Have you ever had a romantic attraction to a female?" (Udry & Chantala, 2005, p. 484)
Sexual behavior	"Any mutually voluntary activity with another person that involves genital contact and sexual excitement or arousal, that is, feeling really turned on, even if intercourse or orgasm did not occur" (Laumann et al., 1994, p. 67)	"Have you ever had a relationship with someone of your own sex which resulted in sexual orgasm?" (Eskin, Kaynak-Demir, & Demir, 2005, p. 188)
Sexual identity	Personally selected, socially and historically bound labels attached to the perceptions and meanings individuals have about their sexuality	"Pick from these six options: gay or lesbian; bisexual, but mostly gay or lesbian; bisexual, equally gay/lesbian and heterosexual; bisexual, but mostly heterosexual; heterosexual; and uncertain, don't know for sure." (D'Augelli, Hershberger, & Pilkington, 2001, p. 252) "Do you think of yourself as heterosexual, homosexual, bisexual, or something else?" (Laumann et al., 1994, p. 293)

Note. *Sexual Orientation is the preponderance of erotic arousals, feelings, fantasies, and behaviors one has for males, females, or both.

self-ascribe a gay/lesbian label are neither exhaustive nor representative of those with a same-sex orientation. If homosexual is assessed by same-sex attraction, there is no consensus about what proportion of an individual's attractions must be directed toward same-sex others, or how strong the attractions must be, in order to count as homosexual. If homosexual is defined by same-sex behavior, gay virgins are omitted, heterosexuals engaging in same-sex behavior for reasons other than preferred sexual arousal are miscounted, and those with same-sex attraction who only have opposite-sex relations are excluded. If, however, homosexual is defined by an identity label, those who experience same-sex arousal or engage in same-sex behavior but who do not identify as gay or lesbian are omitted.

In the biological and health sciences, sexual orientation is usually inferred based on sexual behavior during the past year or since puberty. A single instance of same-sex behavior places an individual in the homosexual category—with little regard for the sexual context, what constitutes sex, the desirability or enjoyment of sex, or the frequency of sex. By contrast, in the psychological and social sciences, sexual orientation is usually determined by sexual identity (gay, lesbian, bisexual, heterosexual). What these terms mean or whether the identity label reflects sexual arousal, behavior, or attraction is seldom explored.

Research findings provide few answers regarding which component is most essential to determine sexual orientation, in part because empirical distinctions among them are seldom made. Consumers of research are left uncertain as to whether components are measuring the same or different constructs and whether these distinctions matter.

PREVALENCE OF HOMOSEXUALITY

Across multiple cultures, age groups, and sexes, rates of homosexuality vary based on which sexual-orientation component is assessed (Table 2). In general, requesting information about attraction elicits the greatest prevalence of homosexuality, occasionally doubling or tripling the proportion of individuals that report same-sex behavior or identify as gay/lesbian/bisexual. In turn, reports of same-sex behavior usually exceed those of homosexual identification. The majority of individuals attracted to their own sex or engaging in same-sex sexual behavior do not identify as homosexual (Laumann, Gagnon, Michael, & Michaels, 1994).

Table 2. *Prevalence of homosexuality among females and males in four countries, separated by sexual-orientation component*

	Attraction		Behavior		Identity	
Country	Female	Male	Female	Male	Female	Male
United States:						
Youth[a]	6%	3%	11%	5%	8%	3%
Young adults[b]	13%	5%	4%	3%	4%	3%
Adults[c]	8%	8%	4%	9%	1%	2%
Australia: Adults[d]	17%	15%	8%	16%	4%	7%
Turkey: Young adults[e]	7%	6%	4%	5%	2%	2%
Norway: Adolescents[f]	21%	9%	7%	6%	5%	5%

Note. [a]Mosher, Chandra, & Jones, 2005; [b]Savin-Williams, 2005; [c]Laumann, Gagnon, Michael, & Michaels, 1994; [d]Dunne, Bailey, Kirk, & Martin, 2000; [e]Eskin, Kaynak-Demir, & Demir, 2005; [f]Wichstrøm & Hegna, 2003

This dissimilarity in prevalence rates is further reflected in people's inconsistent responses to the different components within a study and the instability of their responses over time. Several studies assessed more than one dimension; the resulting correlations ranged from extremely low (0.10) to high (0.79; e.g., Eskin, Kaynak-Demir, & Demir, 2005). Among U.S. adults, just 20% of those who were homosexual on one dimension were homosexual on the other two dimensions; 70% responded in a manner consistent with homosexuality on only one of the three dimensions (Laumann et al., 1994). Diamond's (2003b) research highlights the instability problem. Over 7 years, nearly two thirds of women changed their sexual identity at least once, often because the label did not adequately capture the diversity of their sexual and romantic feelings. In the data set of the longitudinal Add Health study, of the Wave I boys who indicated that they had exclusive same-sex romantic attraction, only 11% reported exclusive same-sex attraction 1 year later; 48% reported only opposite-sex attraction, 35% reported no attraction to either sex, and 6% reported attraction to both sexes (Udry & Chantala, 2005).

Thus, individuals classified as homosexual in one study might not be so designated in another, giving rise to the possibility of discrepant findings across investigations, including divergent conclusions about the biological basis of homosexuality.

BIOLOGY OF HOMOSEXUALITY

Biological theories of homosexuality frequently note its association with gender-atypical behavioral and personality characteristics—"sissy boys" and "tomboy girls." In particular, neuroendocrine theories posit that homosexuality is due to the atypical gendering of relevant brain structures in utero and that prenatal hormones affect the direction both of one's sexuality and of one's gender expression. In their review, Bailey and Zucker (1995) concluded that the association (effect size) between homosexuality and gender nonconformity is one of the largest found in the psychological literature (less so among females). "Sissy boys" are nearly always gay and "tomboy girls" are disproportionately lesbian. Though the potential confounding factors in the association between homosexuality and gender nonconformity (reporting expectations, psychometric properties of gender-atypical scales) were discussed, not considered was whether gender expression varied based on the sexual-orientation dimension assessed.

A later study explicitly explored the relationship between homosexuality and gender nonconformity in a national sample of Australian twins (Dunne, Bailey, Kirk, & Martin, 2000). As expected, gender atypicality was highest among gay-identified individuals and lowest among individuals who identified as heterosexual. More interesting, among heterosexual-identified individuals, those who reported some degree of same-sex attraction were more gender atypical than those who reported engaging in occasional same-sex behavior, and those with both some same-sex attraction and some same-sex behavior were more gender atypical than were those who reported only one of these two. Because nearly all individuals who identified as gay also reported same-sex attraction and behavior, one implication is that these "true gays" have a neuroendocrine basis for their sexual orientation, which is manifested in their gender nonconformity. From this perspective, heterosexually identified individuals with same-sex attraction and/or behavior are not "false gays" but "less gay," occupying various points along the homosexuality–heterosexuality spectrum. These individuals might be less likely to be biologically programmed in their sexuality (or feel same-sex attraction as strongly) than are those who are gay-identified. Alternatively, they may be equally homosexual but get there by a different route. For example, biological factors not involved in gender expression could affect their sexuality or biological factors directing homosexuality may miss the critical window of time necessary to affect gender expression. The association between homosexuality and gender nonconformity might also have a cultural component: Those who are most gender variant identify as gay because of cultural expectations that sissies and tomboys must be gay. Alternatively, such individuals are so biologically driven in their same-sex sexuality that culture is merely correctly reading the gender-expressive cues.

Thus, research linking homosexuality to biological influences might be stacking the deck by only recruiting gay-identifying or behaving subjects—those who are most likely to manifest high levels of gender atypicality (indicative of a biological cause). Which sexual-orientation component is assessed might also shape perceptions about the mental health status of homosexual individuals.

MENTAL HEALTH OF HOMOSEXUAL INDIVIDUALS

Investigators over the past 30 years have documented the considerable empirical support linking homosexual populations with clinical diagnoses such as depression, anxiety, substance abuse, and suicidality (Meyer, 2003). With suicidal-attempt rates that often triple those of heterosexuals, homosexual individuals purportedly experience a lifetime spiral of personal victimization, social discrimination, and cultural stigmatization without sources of support—all of which reach their critical developmental peak during adolescence. The result is "minority stress" and, ultimately, mental health problems. Although empirical support for this causal pathway is more circumstantial than conclusive, most investigators define their homosexual population based on gay identification or engagement in same-sex behavior. Because nearly all self-identified gays engage in same-sex behavior but most individuals who engage in same-sex behavior do not identify as gay, one hypothesis is that the critical risk factor driving the relationship between homosexuality and mental health is not sexual identification but sexual behavior—consistent with what is known about risk factors among heterosexual adolescents (Savin-Williams & Diamond, 2004). For example, among a representative sample of U.S. youth (Youth Risk Behavior Survey), high-risk sexual behavior (without regard for gender of partner: sex before age 14, at least four partners, unsafe sex) was a better predictor of suicide attempts than other factors such as violent behavior, drug use, disturbed eating, binge drinking, and tobacco smoking—with an odds ratio (5.0) double that of the next highest factor for medically treated suicide attempts (Miller & Taylor, 2005). The relationship between psychopathology and the third component, sexual/romantic attraction and arousal, has generally been ignored.

Consistent with this portrayal of the risky nature of child/adolescent sexual behavior, it was found that in a representative sample of Norwegian youth, those who engaged in same-sex behavior were four times more likely than heterosexual youth to attempt suicide (15% vs. 4%). Adolescents with same-sex attraction and identity (9% each) were also more likely to attempt suicide, but less dramatically so. The correlation between attraction and identity was double the correlation between either and same-sex behavior, and when all three were used to predict suicide attempts, only sexual contact was significant (Wichstrøm & Hegna, 2003). Another study, however, demonstrated that it was not same-sex behavior per se that was related to elevated suicidality but an early age of sexual initiation, a large number of sex partners, and permissive attitudes or behaviors regarding unsafe sex (Savin-Williams & Ream, 2003). Although reasons for the risky nature of early, frequent, and unsafe same-sex activities remain speculative, they may be hazardous in the same way that sexual behavior is for heterosexuals: as an expression of a more general clinical syndrome characterized by acting-out behavior, rebellion, and impulsivity.

Thus, distinguishing among sexual-orientation components offers an alternative perspective to the position that homosexuality is inherently pathological or that society's reaction to same-sex sexuality drives young gays and lesbians to attempt suicide. Previous investigators likely oversampled those youth who were most at risk—adolescents engaging in hazardous same-sex behavior.

IMPLICATIONS

Depending on which sexual-orientation component is referenced, different conclusions can be drawn about the prevalence rate, etiology, and mental health profile of homosexual populations. The prevalence rate for homosexuality varies immensely, biological influences on homosexuality need further refinement, and the mental health profiles of homosexual populations may be no different from those of heterosexuals.

These conclusions have real-world consequences. If homosexual individuals constitute only 1% of the general population, it is politically easier to ignore or dismiss them than if they are known to be a constituency that surpasses most ethnic and minority groups. If the number is relatively minor and inconsequential, then it is difficult to argue for community-based same-sex programs and services, mass-media inclusion of gay role models, or Gay/Straight Alliances in public schools. Furthermore, believing that homosexuality is a chosen (nonbiological) condition, moral conservatives eagerly embrace research documenting the negative clinical profile of gays as evidence of homosexuality's intrinsic pathology and mercifully advocate changing homosexual individuals through conversion or reparative therapy, creating "ex-gays." Although sexual behavior and identity are indeed susceptible to alteration by aversive stimuli and religious commitment, there is no scientifically reliable data that same-sex arousal and attraction can be permanently altered through relearning therapies.

What are researchers to do? Until conceptually well-positioned and psychometrically sound and tested definitions are used, it is unlikely that research can possibly or reliably identify the prevalence, causes, and consequences of homosexuality. Although multiple components of sexual orientation can be assessed, little is known about their stability over time, their consistency with each other, or their predictive power for various characteristics of homosexual populations.

Scientifically, two approaches are warranted. First, researchers are better assured of a same-sex oriented sample if they include only those individuals who consistently and reliably report multiple components of sexual orientation. I believe a higher priority should be given to sexual arousal/attraction over behavior and identity, primarily because the latter two are clearly prone to self- and other-deception, social conditions, and variable meanings. To avoid these shortcomings, biological measures of sexual attraction/arousal should be developed and used. Though not generally recognized by social scientists, sexual orientation can be measured by genital arousal in response to erotic stimuli or, less intrusively, through brain scans, eye tracking or pupil dilation in response to visual stimuli, body-odor preference (pheromones preference), and anatomical variations, such as digit-length ratio, right or left handedness, auditory characteristics (e.g., hearing sensitivity), and sex-role motor behavior (e.g., movement of hips while walking, crossing of legs while sitting).

A second approach is to forsake the general notion of sexual orientation altogether and assess only those components that are relevant for the research question being investigated. Examples include the following:

- To assess STDs or HIV transmission, measure sexual behavior
- To assess interpersonal attachments, measure sexual/romantic attraction
- To assess political ideology, measure sexual identity

Until the definition issue is resolved and more refined approaches are taken, caution is advised in estimating the prevalence of homosexuality, the origins and causes of sexual orientation, and the extent to which homosexual individuals are vulnerable for mental health problems.

Recommended Reading

Chivers, M.L., Rieger, G., Latty, E., & Bailey, J.M. (2004). A sex difference in the specificity of sexual arousal. *Psychological Science, 15,* 736–744.

Diamond, L.M. (2003). What does sexual orientation orient? A biobehavioral model distinguishing romantic love and sexual desire. *Psychological Review, 110,* 173–192.

McConaghy, N. (1999). Unresolved issues in scientific sexology. *Archives of Sexual Behavior, 28,* 285–318.

Mustanski, B.S., Chivers, M.L., & Bailey, J.M. (2002). A critical review of recent biological research on human sexual orientation. *Annual Review of Sex Research, 13,* 89–140.

Savin-Williams, R.C. (2005). (See References)

Acknowledgments—I thank my colleagues Steven Ceci and Charles Brainerd for their encouragement. For careful edits and challenges to my ideas, I thank Kenneth Cohen.

Note

1. Address correspondence to Ritch C. Savin-Williams, Human Development, Cornell University, Ithaca, New York 14853; e-mail: res15@cornell.edu.

References

Bailey, J.M., & Zucker, K.J. (1995). Childhood sex-typed behavior and sexual orientation: A conceptual analysis and quantitative review. *Developmental Psychology, 31,* 43–55.

D'Augelli, A.R., Hershberger, S.L., & Pilkington, N.W. (2001). Suicidality patterns and sexual orientation-related factors among lesbian, gay, and bisexual youths. *Suicide and Life-Threatening Behavior, 31,* 250–264.

Diamond, L.M. (2003a). New paradigms for research on heterosexual and sexual-minority development. *Journal of Clinical Child and Adolescent Psychology, 32,* 490–498.

Diamond, L.M. (2003b). Was it a phase? Young women's relinquishment of lesbian/bisexual identities over a 5-year period. *Journal of Personality and Social Psychology, 84,* 352–364.

Dunne, M.P., Bailey, J.M., Kirk, K.M., & Martin, N.G. (2000). The subtlety of sex-atypicality. *Archives of Sexual Behavior, 29,* 549–565.

Eskin, M., Kaynak-Demir, H., & Demir, S. (2005). Same-sex sexual orientation, childhood sexual abuse, and suicidal behavior in university students in Turkey. *Archives of Sexual Behavior, 34,* 185–195.

Laumann, E.O., Gagnon, J., Michael, R.T., & Michaels, S. (1994). *The social organization of sexuality: Sexual practices in the United States.* Chicago: University of Chicago Press.

Meyer, I.H. (2003). Prejudice, social stress, and mental health in lesbian, gay, and bisexual populations: Conceptual issues and research evidence. *Psychological Bulletin, 129,* 674–697.

Miller, T.R., & Taylor, D.M. (2005). Adolescent suicidality: Who will ideate, who will act? *Suicide and Life-Threatening Behavior, 35,* 425–435.

Mosher, W.D., Chandra, A., & Jones, J. (2005). Sexual behavior and selected health measures: Men and women 15–44 years of age, United States, 2002. *Advance Data from Vital and Health Statistics* (no. 362). Hyattsville, MD: National Center for Health Statistics.

Savin-Williams, R.C. (2005). *The new gay teenager.* Cambridge, MA: Harvard University Press.

Savin-Williams, R.C., & Diamond, L.M. (2004). Sex. In R.M. Lerner & L. Steinberg (Eds.), *Handbook of adolescent psychology* (2nd ed., pp. 189–231). New York: John Wiley & Sons.

Savin-Williams, R.C., & Ream, G.L. (2003). Suicide attempts among sexual-minority male youth. *Journal of Clinical Child and Adolescent Psychology, 32,* 509–522.

Udry, J.R., & Chantala, K. (2005). Risk factors differ according to same-sex and opposite-sex interest. *Journal of Biosocial Science, 37,* 481–497.

Wichstrøm, L., & Hegna, K. (2003). Sexual orientation and suicide attempt: A longitudinal study of the general Norwegian adolescent population. *Journal of Abnormal Psychology, 112,* 144–151.

Critical Thinking Questions

1. Savin-Williams presents three different ways of defining sexual orientation (sexual/romantic attraction, sexual behavior, and sexual identity) and points out that there is often inconsistency among these three considerations. What are the implications of this inconsistency for our understanding of the origins of sexual orientation?

2. If you were a researcher with the need to categorize your research participants with regard to their sexual orientation, how would you choose to define their orientation? Why? What method(s) would you use to assess orientation?

This article has been reprinted as it originally appeared in *Current Directions in Psychological Science*. Citation information for this article as originally published appears above.

The Biopsychology of Sexual Orientation

Brian A. Gladue[1]
North Dakota State University (Fargo).

The origins of homosexuality and lesbianism have been deliberated by scholars and scientists for nearly a century. In scholarly journals as well as in popular media, the debate center around whether one's sexual partner preference (man or woman) can be understood by natural science or is a function of social opportunities, circumstances, and outright choice. In its simplest distillation, the question has been phrased: "Are homosexuals born or made?" Until recently, support for the biological side of this "nature-nurture" argument was limited and controversial; some early research and the underlying assumption that, surely, all behavior must have some biological bases kept alive a search for biological determinants of sexual orientation. But now, a remarkable set of findings from the past decade strongly suggests the influence of fundamental biological processes in the development of homosexuality. These findings, combined with new working hypotheses about psychosexual development, have led to the newly emerging viewpoint that sexual orientation is a complex interplay of genetics, neuroanatomy, neuroendocrinology, and environmental factors.

GENETIC EVIDENCE

An early inquiry into heritable components of sexual orientation compared concordance (i.e., agreement between both members of a pair) rates for homosexuality in identical, or monozygotic (MZ), and fraternal, or dizygotic (DZ), twin pairs. The remarkably high (100%) concordance rate in 37 male MZ pairs contrasted with a concordance rate of 15% in 26 DZ pairs. However, concerns about the method of subject selection, zygosity diagnosis, and other methodological issues led some observers to question the high MZ concordance rate. Recent studies using more sophisticated techniques suggest that although the true MZ concordance rate is substantially lower than 100%, sexual orientation has a significant degree of heritability.

The first contemporary family-genetic study of sexual orientation using more sophisticated methodology (blind recruitment of the homosexuals initially selected for study and direct confirmation of siblings' sexual orientation) showed that male homosexuality is familial: Twenty percent of brothers of male homosexuals were also homosexual, compared with only 4% of brothers of heterosexuals. Because family studies cannot distinguish between genetic and shared environmental factors, however, twin and adoption studies are essential. In the most compelling set of genetic studies to date, Bailey and Pillard found that 52% (29/56) of the identical twins of gay males were also gay. (Homosexuals were recruited through advertisements in local media and by word of mouth. Relatives' sexual orientation was directly confirmed in most cases.) In contrast, only 22% (12/54) of DZ twins of gay males were gay, and a mere 11% of 57 adoptive brothers of gay men were also gay.

Using similar recruiting and assessment techniques in a study of lesbian heritability, Bailey and colleagues found comparable concordance rates (48% for MZ co-twins, 16% for DZ co-twins, and 6% for adoptive sisters). Statistical models and various analytical techniques allowed the authors to conclude that approximately 30% to 70% of the behavioral manifestation (so-called phenotypic variance) of sexual orientation diversity in both sexes can be accounted for genetically. Similarly, Whitam and colleagues found recently that 65% (22/34) of MZ twin pairs were concordant for homosexuality, compared with only 29% (4/14) of DZ twin pairs. Finally, tantalizing evidence for a genetic marker for homosexuality in men has been reported. A pedigree analysis of 114 families of homosexual men, coupled with a DNA and chromosomal analysis of a selected group of 40 families in each of which there were two gay brothers, led researchers to conclude that a genetic influence on the development of male sexual orientation was highly probable. Thus, recent studies involving twin pairs, family pedigrees, and molecular genetic analyses generally support the possibility that homosexuality has a substantial biological (i.e., genetic) component.

NEUROHORMONAL THEORY OF SEXUAL DEVELOPMENT

Although genetic influences on sexual development seem more likely than ever, questions still remain regarding how heritable factors might influence the anatomy and physiology of an organism to develop along a certain psychosexual pathway. Much of the thinking in this area has been shaped by research on sexual dimorphisms in animals and humans. The main explanatory model, a theory of neurohormonal sexual differentiation, holds that the developing brain is "masculinized" by exposure to androgens during critical periods of development, usually prenatally or early in postnatal life. The absence of these key hormones at critical times often results in a "feminized" brain. Thus, hormonal exposure at key developmental stages organizes the brain in a lasting manner, predisposing the organism toward certain anatomical, physiological, and behavioral paths. Neuroscientists in the past decade have uncovered a remarkable body of evidence for sex differences in human psychoendocrinology, brain anatomy, and neural functioning related to behavior, much of this evidence fitting into the neurohormonal theory of sexual differentiation. Using these sex differences as a starting point, investigators have gone on to look for corresponding within-sex differences associated with sexual orientation.

HORMONAL AND NEUROENDOCRINE EVIDENCE

We know that levels of testosterone are not markers for homosexuality or heterosexuality, because such hormone levels vary considerably among men, and reflect assorted current situations in men (diet, exercise patterns, drug usage, health status, etc.). There are no differences in circulating hormone levels between adult homosexual and heterosexual men. However, it is possible that specific endocrine interactions with brain tissue during critical periods can organize brain tissue and subsequent behavior toward particular directions, patterns, and developmental pathways.

A series of influential and controversial studies in the 1970s argued that homosexual, but not heterosexual, men have neuroendocrine response patterns that possibly reflect a predominantly "female-differentiated" brain, suggesting a neural predisposition toward femalelike behavior, specifically, an erotic attraction toward men. In this scheme, there is a sex difference in how the hypothalamic-pituitary-gonadal axis responds to steroids, in particular, the hormone estrogen: Women normally respond with an elevation of the pituitary hormone LH (luteinizing hormone), whereas men show no such elevated responsiveness. In their studies, Dorner and colleagues found a femalelike LH response in homosexual men. This so-called positive-feedback response in LH to estrogen was presumed to be due to differences in brain development during prenatal life. This remarkable finding, and the consequent reasoning that homosexual men have a "female" hypothalamus, although overly simplistic, suggested a new approach toward exploring biological predispositions for homosexuality.

But nearly a decade passed before this extraordinary finding was confirmed. My colleagues and I injected heterosexual and homosexual men, and a comparative group of heterosexual women, with estrogen and tracked their LH levels over the next few days. We found that homosexual men did show an LH response to estrogen well above that of heterosexual men, but still less than that shown by women. We suspected that these neuroendocrine (LH) differences might be mediated by some gonadal process, possibly dynamics of testosterone production in the testes. Testosterone is well known to influence the production and release of LH. In response to an estrogen injection, testosterone levels in all men plummeted rapidly (a typical male response). However, over the next few days, testosterone levels returned to baseline levels more slowly in the homosexual men than in the heterosexuals, indicating that the brain-pituitary-gonadal interactions associated with sexual orientation were much more complex than suggested earlier.

The conventional wisdom, based on the neurohormonal theory of sexual differentiation, suggested that lesbians would show a diminished, or malelike, LH response to an injection of estrogen. Instead, we found that lesbians had an atypical enhanced LH response to estrogen, far greater than that of heterosexual women. Certainly, these data need independent confirmation, but they suggest that brain hormones function differently in people with different sexual orientations, and that brain hormone functioning in lesbians may not be a simple mirror-image variation of such functioning in gay men.

Although the results of these neuroendocrine studies were not perfect evidence for biological determinants for homosexuality in men and women, they did set the stage for a new wave of neuroscience inquiries into the origins of homosexuality. Differences in anatomy of brain regions responsible for such neuroendocrine functioning became the next area of exploration.

NEUROANATOMICAL EVIDENCE

Only a decade ago, the notion that men and women have anatomically different brains seemed preposterous, bordering on some kind of "new phrenology." Within the past decade, however, several neuroanatomical sex differences have been revealed. The most recent and relevant findings are summarized in Table 1. Variations in brain weight, fiber tracts connecting the two cerebral hemispheres, and areas of the corpus callosum have been shown to differ in men and women. Deeper within

Table 1. *Sex differences in neuroanatomy and related sexual orientation findings*

Brain region	Sex difference		Sexual orientation difference	
Sexually dimorphic nucleus of the preoptic area	Volume:	M = 2.5 × F	Volume:	No difference
	Cell number:	M = 2.2 × F	Cell number:	No difference
Interstitial nucleus of the anterior hypothalamus, Area 3	Volume:	M = 2.8 × F (Study 1) M = 2.1 × F (Study 2)	Volume:	HET-M = 2.3 × HOM-M (Study 2)
Suprachiasmatic nucleus	Volume:	No difference	Volume:	HOM-M = 1.7 × HET-M
	Cell number:	No difference	Cell number:	HOM-M = 2.1 × HET-M
	Shape:	Elongated in females, spherical in males	Shape:	More elongated in homosexual than in heterosexual males
Anterior commissure	Area:	F = 1.12 × M	Area:	HOM-M = 1.18 × HET-F HOM-M = 1.34 × HET-M

Note. M = value for males; F = value for females; HOM-M = value for homosexual males; HET-M = value for heterosexual males; HET-F = value for heterosexual females.

the brain, the anterior commissure (AC), a fiber tract connecting the temporal lobes from the two hemispheres, is about 12% larger in females than in males. Still deeper within the brain are sex differences in regions of the hypothalamus. Direct relationships between sex differences in neuroanatomy and sex differences in behavior have yet to be demonstrated. However, because certain hypothalamic areas influence pituitary responsiveness, maternal behavior, and sexual behavior in many mammalian species, behavioral implications in humans seem likely.

Eventually, these findings set the stage for a search for within-sex differences in brain areas of heterosexuals and homosexuals. The first report of neuroanatomical differences between homosexual and heterosexual men showed that the suprachiasmatic nucleus (SCN), a deep brain area associated with generating and coordinating hormonal, physiological, and behavioral rhythms, was larger and more elongated in homosexuals than in heterosexuals, and that this elongated SCN shape was characteristically found in women. Shortly thereafter, a specific region of the hypothalamus, the interstitial nucleus of the anterior hypothalamus (INAH-3), an area typically smaller in women than in men, was also found to be smaller in homosexual men than in heterosexual men. Finally, another research team reported that the AC (as mentioned, a structure typically larger in women than in men) was also larger in homosexual men than in either heterosexual men or heterosexual women. However, the sexually dimorphic nucleus of the preoptic area (SDN), an area of the hypothalamus known to be larger in men than women, does not differ in heterosexual and homosexual men. Thus far, the emerging neuroanatomical picture is that, in some brain areas, homosexual men are more likely to have female-typical neuroanatomy than are heterosexual men.

But are such brain differences a cause or a consequence of behavior? Although it is likely that these structures are established early in life and have later influences on behavior, certain postnatal social and environmental stimuli can alter responses to hormones, which in turn can influence early postnatal neural development. Further, differential development of these structures may not be causal but simply correlational. The particular development of the SCN, INAH-3, and AC in men may not cause a specific sexual orientation but rather reflect other developmental processes associated with sexual orientation.

Several critics of biological explanations for homosexuality have argued that demonstrations of neuroanatomical differences between people of different sexual orientation are not conclusive. This is true, yet several independent findings of female-typical neuroanatomical patterns in an assortment of brain areas in homosexual men cannot be dismissed easily. And as the nervous system differentiates (some regions as late as 4 years of age) under the influence of hormones, genetics, and environmental (i.e., nongenetic) factors, the psychosexuality of heterosexuals and homosexuals is probably influenced by many forces and processes. Essentially, these recent neuroanatomical discoveries add weight to the idea that the bases for sexual orientation are primarily biological.

NEUROPSYCHOLOGICAL EVIDENCE

In addition to neuroanatomical and neuroendocrine sex differences, there are sex differences in certain cognitive skills, primarily in spatial abilities, widely regarded to be influenced by neural and hormonal factors. Perhaps the biological bases for these sex differences might also influence neuropsychological differences in people with different psychosexual orientation. Recent studies from several research groups suggest differences in spatial ability related to differences in sexual orientation. A series of spatial performance tasks, in which males tend to outperform females, was administered to heterosexual and homosexual men and women. Of particular interest was the mental rotations task, in which subjects identify a target figure out of a group of similarly shaped figures rotated in three dimensions. Subjects were also tested for spatial visualization of horizontality using the so-called water level task, in which they are asked to indicate the level (but not volume) of water in a vessel tilted at different angles from the horizontal. My colleagues and I found that homosexual men underperformed heterosexual men on both tasks measuring spatial ability, and were comparable to heterosexual women on these measures. Lesbians were generally similar to heterosexual women, although the lesbians performed more poorly than the heterosexual women on the water level task (thus showing more femalelike scores). Other laboratories have reported similar findings of homosexual men underperforming relative to heterosexual men on most spatial tasks. Overall, these spatial ability data suggest possible biological and neuropsychological factors co-related to the development of sexual orientation.

Recall that the AC, a structure associated with the processing of information between the two hemispheres of the brain, is, on average, larger in women than in men, and even larger in homosexual men. A relationship between the AC and cognitive abilities may reflect early neural developmental pathways that are related to similar neural events associated with psychosexual development. With real-time brainscanning technologies, potential connections between anatomy and function in men and women who differ in their psychosexual developmental paths can be explored. Data on the neuroanatomy and neuropsychology of women who differ in sexual orientation are badly needed; our understanding of human psychosexual development will be incomplete without such studies.

ON BIOLOGICAL THEORIES OF SEXUAL ORIENTATION

Discussions about the origins of diversity in sexual orientation center around the mode of causation: Is it nature or nurture? Because most scholars agree that biology must play some role in human behavioral diversity, a biopsychosocial approach seems most useful as an overall theme. Such a model would incorporate genetic, endocrine, and neural developmental factors along with life-span social learning components of behavioral development. Still, what model or theory can both meaningfully account for the present body of biological evidence and prepare us for the new findings sure to emerge? One approach has been to embrace a continuum model in which sex and sexual orientation are cast on a bipolar male-female line. In this scheme, heavily influenced by the neurohormonal theory of sexual differentiation, homosexual men fit somewhere between heterosexual men and women, and lesbians theoretically fall somewhere between heterosexual women and men. The neuroanatomical data seem to fit this model. For the hypothalamic region INAH-3, the neuroanatomy of homosexual men is intermediate to that of heterosexual men and women. For other structures, such as the SCN, homosexual men have a femalelike sex-dimorphic shape. The AC, typically larger in women than in men, is also large in homosexual men compared with heterosexual men. Some of the neuroendocrine data fit this model as well: An LH response pattern intermediate to that of heterosexual men and women was found for some (but not all) homosexual men. And many of the neuropsychological data fit: Spatial abilities of homosexual men appear similar to those of heterosexual women. Most recently, key elements of human mating psychology, involving characteristics of evolutionary psychology and psychobiology, in homosexual men and women were shown to be intermediate between those of heterosexual men and women.

But not every sexually dimorphic neural structure, hormone response pattern, behavioral characteristic, or cognitive ability fits neatly into this model. In short, the evidence does not support a total, simplistic sex reversal. The SDN is similar in homosexual and heterosexual men. Homosexuals, men or women, do not appear to differ from their samesex heterosexual counterparts on measures of trait aggression, despite large sex differences on this measure. And although this male-female continuum model works fairly well for male homosexuals, it does not accommodate many of the data for lesbians. On measures of spatial ability, a sex-dimorphic characteristic, lesbians appear to be generally no different from heterosexual women. Lesbians also show a markedly enhanced LH response to estrogen, not at all a malelike response pattern. It may be that a different set of processes is associated with the development of sexual orientation in women than in men, and that lesbians may represent the more female region of such male-female continua.

In any event, for most of the data, the continuum model may be a useful working system. To be sure, the number of studies exploring the psychobiology of lesbians is appallingly small. Until we expand our inquiries to explore neuroanatomical, neuroendocrine, and neuropsychological processes in homosexual women, the continuum will be missing some key points. No doubt, substantial modifications in the model will be required as findings emerge.

CONCLUSION

The presence of biological factors in the development of homosexuality (and heterosexuality) is becoming increasingly obvious. Already we have a set of reliable findings, from many laboratories, demonstrating that human sexual orientation has a genetic basis, that certain brain areas and neuroendocrine processes known to be sexually dimorphic appear to differ in homosexual and heterosexual men, and that there are corresponding neuropsychological disparities as well. With a larger data base of multiple measurements in heterosexual and homosexual men and women (most studies so far have examined only one or a few variables of interest in a sample of subjects), we may be able to construct a biosocial model in which different events—genetic, hormonal, and environmental—occurring at critical times are weighted for their impact on the development of sexual orientation. Associated with this model would be the idea that not all men and women arrive at their sexual orientation following the same path. A continual and humbling reminder of the complexity (even enormity) of the task of developing a model is that heterosexuals, like homosexuals, vary in their psychosexual milestones of genital, neuropsychological, erotic, and reproductive development. But there is an ever-slowly emerging pattern of findings associated with psychosexual development, and although sexual orientation may not be a strict case in which anatomy is destiny, biological contributions are clearly in play.

Acknowledgments—I thank James Council, J. Michael Bailey, and the anonymous reviewer for their helpful advice and comments regarding this manuscript. Research conducted by my laboratory and reported in this review was supported by funds from the National Institute of Mental Health; the National Science Foundation (Neuroscience Program); the National Science Foundation's EPSCoR Program (Experimental Program to Stimulate Competitive Research) in North Dakota, also known as the ASEND Project (Achieving Science Excellence in North Dakota); and assistance from the Office of Graduate Studies and Research at North Dakota State University.

Notes

1. Address correspondence to B. Gladue, Senior Scientist, Science Directorate, American Psychological Association, 750 1st St., N.E., Washington, DC 20002–4242; e-mail: bzg.apa@email.apa.org (INTERNET).

2. B.A. Gladue. Hormones in relationship to homosexual/bisexual/heterosexual gender orientation, in *Handbook of Sexology: Vol. 6. The Pharmacology and Endocrinology of Sexual Function*, J.M.A. Sitesen, Ed. (Elsevier, Amsterdam, 1988).

3. For reviews of the family studies literature, see R.C. Pillard and J.D. Weinrich, Evidence of familial nature of male homosexuality, *Archives of General Psychiatry, 43*, 808–812 (1986).

4. For detailed reviews of the genetics literature on male homosexuality, see J.M. Bailey and R.C. Pillard. A genetic study of male sexual orientation, *Archives of General Psychiatry, 48*, 1089–1096 (1991); for twin studies on lesbians, see J.M. Bailey, R.C. Pillard, M.C. Neale, and Y. Agyei, Heritable factors influence sexual orientation in women, *Archives of General Psychiatry, 50*, 217 223 (1993).

5. F.L. Whitam, M. Diamond, and J. Martin, Homosexual orientation in twins: A report on 61 pairs and three triplet sets, *Archives of Sexual Behavior, 22*, 187–206 (1993).

6. D.H. Hamer, S. Hu, V.L. Magnuson, N. Hu, and A.M.L. Pattatucci, A linkage between DNA markers on the X chromosome and male sexual orientation, *Science, 261*, 321–327 (1993).

7. G. Dorner, W. Rhode, F. Stahl, L. Krell, and W.G. Masius, A neuroendocrine predisposition for homosexuality in men, *Archives of Sexual Behavior, 4*, 1–8 (1975); G. Dorner, *Hormones and Brain Sexual Differentiation* (Elsevier, Amsterdam, 1976).

8. B.A. Gladue, R. Green, and R.E. Hellman, Neuroendocrine response to estrogen and sexual orientation, *Science, 225*, 1496–1499 (1984): B.A. Gladue, *Neuroendocrine response to estrogen in lesbians compared to heterosexual women,* paper presented at the XIV Annual Meeting of the International Academy of Sex Research, Minneapolis (August 1988).

9. For brevity's sake, not all information presented in Table 1 is described in this review. For a general review of this area, see S.M. Breedlove, Sexual dimorphism in the vertebrate nervous system, *Journal of Neuroscience, 12,* 4133–4142 (1992); also see L.S. Allen and R.A. Gorski, Sexual dimorphism of the anterior commissure and massa intermedia of the human brain, *Journal of Comparative Neurology, 312,* 97–104 (1991).

10. D.F. Swaab and M.A. Hofman, An enlarged suprachiasmatic nucleus in homosexual men, *Brain Research, 537,* 141–148 (1990); S. LeVay, A difference in hypothalamic structure between heterosexual and homosexual men. *Science, 253,* 1034–1037 (1991).

11. L.S. Allen and R.A. Gorski, Sexual orientation and the size of the anterior commissure in the human brain, *Proceedings of the National Academy of Sciences, 89,* 7199–7202 (1992).

12. D.F. Swaab, L.G. Gooren, and M.A. Hofman, The human hypothalamus in relation to gender and sexual orientation, in *Progress in Brain Research,* Vol. 93, D.F. Swaab, M.A. Hofman, M. Mirmiran, R. Ravid, and F.W. van Leeuwen, Eds. (Elsevier, Amsterdam, 1992).

13. W. Byne and B. Parsons, Human sexual orientation: The biologic theories reappraised, *Archives of General Psychiatry, 50,* 228–239 (1993).

14. D.F. Halpern, *Sex Differences in Cognitive Abilities,* 2nd ed. (Erlbaum, Hillsdale, NJ, 1992).

15. B.A. Gladue, W.W. Beatty, J. Larson, and R.D. Slaton, Sexual orientation and spatial ability in men and women, *Psychobiology, 18,* 101–108 (1990).

16. C.M. McCormick and S.F. Witelson, A cognitive profile of homosexual men compared to heterosexual men and women, *Psychoneuroendocrinology, 16,* 459–473 (1991); J. Tkachuk and K.J. Zucker, *The relation among sexual orientation, spatial ability, handedness, and recalled childhood gender identity in women and men,* paper presented at the XVII Annual Meeting of the International Academy of Sex Research, Barrie, Ontario (July 1991); G. Sanders and M. Wright, *Sexual orientation differences in targeted throwing and manual dexterity tasks,* paper presented at the XIX Annual Meeting of the International Academy of Sex Research, Pacific Grove, CA (June 1993); J. Hall and D. Kimura, *Performance by homosexual males and females on sexually-dimorphic motor tasks,* Research Bulletin No. 718 (University of Western Ontario, London. Ontario, 1993).

17. J.M. Bailey, S. Gaulin, Y. Agyei, and B.A. Gladue, Effects of gender and sexual orientation on evolutionarily relevant aspects of human mating psychology, *Journal of Personality and Social Psychology, 66,* 1081–1093 (1994).

18. B.A. Gladue, Aggressive behavioral characteristics, hormones, and sexual orientation in men and women, *Aggressive Behavior, 17,* 313–326 (1991).

Critical Thinking Questions

1. If sexual orientation were found to have a completely biological etiology, what would be the social, legal, religious, and political implications?

2. Although this article was originally published in 1994, there has not been a significant amount of progress identifying the biological determinants of sexual orientation. What do you think are some of the impediments for research in this area?

3. If you had unlimited funding and resources, what sort of study would you conduct in an attempt to enhance our understanding of the determinants of sexual orientation?

This article has been reprinted as it originally appeared in *Current Directions in Psychological Science.* Citation information for this article as originally published appears above.

What Do We Know About Gay and Lesbian Couples?

Lawrence A. Kurdek[1]
Wright State University

Abstract

Research on gay and lesbian couples is highlighted with regard to household labor, conflict, satisfaction, perceived social support, stability, and the variables that predict relationship quality. Relative to partners from married heterosexual couples, partners from gay and lesbian couples tend to assign household labor more fairly, resolve conflict more constructively, experience similar levels of satisfaction, and perceive less support from family members but more support from friends. The limited data available indicate that gay and lesbian couples may be less stable than married heterosexual couples. The factors that predict relationship quality tend to be the same for gay, lesbian, and heterosexual married couples. Overall, research paints a positive picture of gay and lesbian couples and indicates that they tend to be more similar to than different from heterosexual couples.

Keywords

gay couples; lesbian couples; relationship quality; relationship stability

In November 2004, Americans in 11 states voted on whether marriage should be legal for only heterosexual couples. The resounding message from the voters in each of these states was that marriage as a legal institution should, indeed, be reserved only for couples consisting of a man and a woman. One interpretation of voters' response to the gay-marriage issue is that most Americans regard gay and lesbian couples as being different from heterosexual couples. But what does research on gay and lesbian couples say on this matter? Does evidence support the view that gay and lesbian couples work in ways that are different from the way that heterosexual couples work? Before I examine aspects of these questions, I will address the question of the number of gay and lesbian couples in America.

HOW MANY AMERICAN GAY AND LESBIAN COUPLES ARE THERE?

Because of the stigma associated with homosexuality, many gay and lesbian persons are reluctant to disclose their sexual orientation. Consequently, there are no definitive data on the number of gay and lesbian Americans. Perhaps the best available estimates were derived by Laumann, Gagnon, Michael, and Michaels (1994), who interviewed a national sample of 1,511 men and 1,921 women. Of this sample, 4.9% of the men and 4.1% of the women reported having engaged in sexual behavior with a person of their own sex since the age of 18, 6.2% of the men and 4.4% of the women reported having been attracted to a person of their own sex, and 2.8% of the men and 1.4% of the women identified themselves with a label denoting same-sex sexuality (e.g., homosexual).

Given the difficulty in estimating the number of gay and lesbian Americans, it is not surprising that there are also no definitive data on the number of gay and lesbian American couples. However, changes in the way information about households is collected in the United States Census have allowed estimates of the number of households headed by a person with a same-sex partner to be obtained. Data from the Census of 2000 (Simons & O'Connell, 2003) indicate that of the 5.5 million couples who were living together but not married, about 1 in 9 were same-sex couples. Of these couples, 301,026 involved male partners and 293,365 involved female partners. Children under the age of 18 resided with 22% of the male couples and with 33% of the female couples.

Because presenting oneself publicly as gay or lesbian opens the door to discrimination and even violence, estimates of the number of gay and lesbian individuals and couples are most assuredly underestimates. Nonetheless, it is clear that, despite a generally inhospitable social climate, being part of a couple is integral to the lives of many gay men and lesbians. Next, topics of particular relevance to gay and lesbian couples are reviewed.

TOPICS RELEVANT TO GAY AND LESBIAN COUPLES

Household Labor

One perception of partners from happy couples is that each partner does something to contribute to the overall well-being of the couple. When members of a couple live together, the extent to which they depend on each other increases, making it likely that the general issue of "Who does what?" has to be confronted. For many heterosexual couples, biological sex is one major factor that determines which roles partners assume. For example, despite major changes in the number of American women who work outside the home, wives still do the majority of household tasks (Artis & Pavalko, 2003). Given the persistence with which biological sex is used to assign roles relevant to household labor in heterosexual couples, the division of household labor for gay and lesbian couples provides one way to examine how roles in relationships get assigned independently of biological sex.

Three conclusions emerge from studies of how members of gay and lesbian couples divide household labor (e.g., Carrington, 1999). First, members of gay and lesbian couples do not assign roles for household labor such that one partner is the "husband" and the other partner is the "wife." Second, although members of gay and lesbian couples do not divide household labor in a perfectly equal manner, they are more likely than members of heterosexual couples to negotiate a balance between achieving a fair distribution of household labor and accommodating the different interests, skills, and work schedules of particular partners. This pattern of negotiation holds true even when couples have children living with them (Patterson, 2000). Third, as couples become more established, partners are likely to specialize in the household tasks they do, perhaps as one way of getting household tasks done efficiently.

Conflict

Conflict is inevitable in any relationship. In heterosexual couples, conflict is often thought to occur because of systematic differences in how men and women perceive their worlds. If this view of relationship conflict is valid, then one might expect that partners from same-sex couples would resolve conflict better than partners from heterosexual couples do because they perceive their worlds through similar lenses. Research supports this expectation.

Gottman et al. (2003) videotaped partners from gay, lesbian, and married heterosexual couples discussing problems in their relationships and then coded the emotions expressed by the partners in the course of the discussions. The researchers found that, relative to heterosexual partners, gay and lesbian partners began their discussions more positively and were more likely to maintain a positive tone throughout the course of the discussion. Findings from survey data also indicate that partners from gay and lesbian couples resolve conflict more positively than spouses from married couples do: They argue more effectively, are less likely to use a style of conflict resolution in which one partner demands and the other partner withdraws, and are more likely to suggest possible solutions and compromises (Kurdek, 2004a). Gottman et al. speculated that partners from gay and lesbian couples handle conflict more positively than spouses from heterosexual couples do because they value equality more and have fewer differences in power and status between them.

It is of note that, although partners from gay and lesbian couples tend to resolve conflict more positively than spouses from married couples do, partners from gay, lesbian, and heterosexual couples are likely to disagree over the same issues. In a study in which partners rated how frequently they fought over 20 specific issues (Kurdek, 2004b), differences between gay, lesbian, and heterosexual couples were largely nonexistent. Equally striking was the finding that partners from gay, lesbian, and heterosexual couples identified the same areas as sources of the most conflict: finances, affection, sex, being overly critical, driving style, and household tasks. Thus, differences in conflict resolution appear to be due to how conflict is handled rather than to what the conflict is about.

Perceived Support for the Relationship

Based on evidence that the level of support from members of one's social network affects the health of one's relationship, current theories about relationships (e.g., Huston, 2000) recognize that relationships develop within social contexts. Several studies have examined the extent to which members of gay and lesbian couples perceive support for their relationships (e.g., Kurdek, 2004a). Relative to spouses from heterosexual couples, partners from gay and lesbian couples are less likely to name family members as support providers and are more likely to name friends as support providers. These differences are notable because they are among the largest differences found in comparisons between heterosexual and gay or lesbian couples. The lack of family support for one's primary close relationship is often viewed as a unique stressor for gay men and lesbians and perhaps represents the overall lack of legal, social, political, economic, and religious support that gay and lesbian partners experience for their relationships. On the other hand, the high level of support that gay and lesbian partners enjoy from friends has been viewed as one way in which they compensate for the absence of institutionalized support.

Satisfaction

Nearly all available evidence indicates not only that gay men and lesbians are, on average, satisfied with their relationships, but that their level of satisfaction is at least equal to that reported by spouses from married heterosexual couples (Blumstein & Schwartz, 1983; Kurdek, 2001). Further, longitudinal data from partners from gay, lesbian, and heterosexual couples indicate that, for each type of couple, self-reported relationship quality is relatively high at the start of the relationship but decreases over time (Kurdek, 1998).

Stability

Perhaps the most important "bottom-line" question asked about gay and lesbian couples is whether their relationships last. Because survey data (see Kurdek, 2004b) indicate that between 8% and 21% of lesbian couples and between 18% and 28% of gay couples have lived together 10 or more years, it is clear that gay men and lesbians can and do build durable relationships. More detailed information on the stability of gay and lesbian relationships is limited because few studies have followed the same samples of gay and lesbian couples over time. Nonetheless, findings from three studies are relevant.

Kurdek (2004a) reported that for 126 gay couples and 101 lesbian couples assessed annually up to 12 times, 24 of the gay couples (19%) and 24 of the lesbian couples (24%) dissolved their relationships. With controls for demographic variables (e.g., length of cohabitation), the difference in the rate of dissolution for gay and lesbian couples was not significant. Over a comparable period of 11 annual assessments, 70 of 483 heterosexual married couples (15%) ended their relationships. With controls for demographic variables, the dissolution rate for heterosexual couples was significantly lower than that for either gay or lesbian couples.

In their 18-month follow-up survey of partners from 1,021 married heterosexual couples, 233 cohabiting heterosexual couples, 493 cohabiting gay couples, and 335 cohabiting lesbian couples, Blumstein and Schwartz (1983) found that 4% of the married couples, 14% of the cohabiting heterosexual couples, 13% of the cohabiting gay couples, and 18% of the co-habiting lesbian couples had dissolved their relationships. Although these authors reported no statistical comparisons, my analyses of their data indicated that, although rates of dissolution did not differ for either gay couples versus lesbian couples or for gay and lesbian couples versus cohabiting heterosexual couples, both gay and lesbian couples were more likely to dissolve their relationships than married heterosexual couples were.

Andersson, Noack, Seierstad, and Weedon-Fekjaer (2004) examined differences in the dissolution rates of gay and lesbian registered partnerships in Norway and in Sweden. Because registered partnerships were first made available in Norway in 1993 and in Sweden in 1995, dissolution rates are necessarily based on couples with legal unions of relatively short duration. For both countries, dissolution rates were significantly higher for lesbian couples than they were for gay couples. In Norway, 56 out of 497 lesbian partnerships were dissolved (11.26%) as compared to 62 out of 796 gay partnerships (7.78%). In Sweden, 117 out of 584 lesbian partnerships were dissolved (20.03%) as compared to 135 out of 942 gay partnerships (14.33%). In comparison, the percentage of dissolved heterosexual marriages in Sweden was 8%. For both countries, the higher rate of dissolution for lesbian couples than for gay couples persisted even when statistical analyses controlled for length of the partnership (which, if different between the two groups, can produce illusory differences in gay and lesbian couples' stability).

In sum, the data are too scant to warrant any conclusions about the relative stability of gay and lesbian couples. However, it is of note that Blumstein and Schwartz's (1983) data indicated that the dissolution rate for cohabiting heterosexual couples was similar to that for both cohabiting gay couples and cohabiting lesbian couples. Unlike spouses from married heterosexual couples who experience social, religious, and legal barriers to leaving their relationships, cohabiting couples—whether gay, lesbian, or heterosexual—have no such institutionalized barriers. Further, although some gay and lesbian couples raise children, the majority do not (Simons & O'Connell, 2003), thereby removing another significant barrier to dissolution. Thus, perhaps what is most impressive about gay and lesbian couples is not that they may be less stable than heterosexual married couples, but rather that they manage to endure without the benefits of institutionalized supports.

Factors Predicting Relationship Quality

One way of determining whether the relationships of gay men and lesbians work the same way the relationships of heterosexual persons do is to see if the links between variables known to be relevant to relationship functioning and relationship quality are as strong for gay and lesbian partners as they are for heterosexual married partners. The predictors of relationship quality that have been examined usually come from four classes of variables commonly used in research on relationships (e.g., Huston, 2000). These include characteristics each partner brings to the relationship (such as personality traits), how each partner views the relationship (such as level of trust), how partners behave toward each other (such as communication and conflict-resolution styles), and perceived level of support for the relationship (such as that from family members and friends).

The relevant findings are easily summarized. Nearly all studies (e.g., Kurdek, 2004a) find that the links between variables from the four classes just listed and relationship quality for gay and lesbian couples do not differ from the parallel links for heterosexual married couples. That is, the extent to which relationship quality is predicted by these four kinds of variables tends to be as strong for gay and lesbian couples as it is for heterosexual couples. Thus, despite external differences in how gay, lesbian, and heterosexual couples are constituted, the relationships of gay and lesbian partners appear to work in much the same way as the relationships of heterosexual partners do.

Based on evidence that gay and lesbian relationships are influenced by the same set of factors that influence heterosexual marriages, institutionalized support for gay and lesbian relationships might be expected to enhance the stability of these relationships just as it does for heterosexual marriages. In fact, this reasoning formed one of the bases for the American Psychological Association's passing a resolution declaring it unfair and discriminatory to deny same-sex couples legal access to civil marriage and all its attendant benefits, rights, and privileges (American Psychological Association, 2004).

ISSUES FOR FUTURE RESEARCH

Future research on gay and lesbian couples needs to address several key issues. One is sampling: Because most studies have used convenience samples of mostly white and well-educated partners, the extent to which findings generalize to the larger population of gay and lesbian couples is unknown. Problems with regard to sampling may be eased as specialized populations—such as couples with civil unions from states with open records—become identified. Another issue is research methods: Most studies on gay and lesbian couples have used self-report surveys. Future work could address some of the biases associated with self-report data by employing behavioral observations as well as peer or partner ratings.

The life course of gay and lesbian relationships is another area requiring further research. Because gay and lesbian courtship is a fairly hidden process, little is known about how gay and lesbian relationships develop from courtship to cohabitation to marriage-like unions with high commitment. Recruiting dating couples for longitudinal research, however, remains a challenge. It is also necessary to establish what variables are unique to gay and lesbian persons. Most research has used theories and methods derived from work with heterosexual couples, so little is known about how variables unique to gay and lesbian persons— such as negotiating a private and public identity as a gay or lesbian person—affect the quality of their relationships. Finally, it is necessary to learn more about the forces that help stabilize relationships. Because it is unlikely that all American gay and lesbian couples will soon have the option to marry, they will need to continue to rely on less institutionalized forces to maintain the stability of their relationships. These include psychological processes such as commitment and social processes such as level of integration into the support systems of family, friends, and coworkers.

Recommended Reading

Kurdek, L.A. (2001). (See References)
Kurdek, L.A. (2003). Differences between gay and lesbian cohabiting couples. *Journal of Social Personal Relationships, 20,* 411–436.
Kurdek, L.A. (2004a). (See References)
Patterson, C.J. (2000). (See References)
Peplau, L.A., & Beals, K.P. (2004). The family lives of lesbians and gay men. In A.L. Vangelisti (Ed.), *Handbook of family communication* (pp. 233–248). Mahwah, NJ: Erlbaum.

Note

1. Address correspondence to Larry Kurdek, Department of Psychology, Wright State University, Dayton, OH 45435-0001; e-mail: larry. kurdek@wright.edu.

References

American Psychological Association (2004). *Resolution on sexual orientation and marriage*. Retrieved November 14, 2004 from http://www.apa.org/pi/lgbc/policy/marriage.pdf

Andersson, G., Noack, T., Seierstad, A., & Weedon-Fekjaer, H. (2004). *The demographics of same-sex "marriages" in Norway and Sweden*. Rostock, Germany: Max-Planck Institute for Demographic Research. Retrieved November 14, 2004 from http://www.demogr.mpg.de/papers/working/wp-2004-018.pdf.

Artis, J.E., & Pavalko, E.K. (2003). Explaining the decline in women's household labor: Individual change and cohort differences. *Journal of Marriage and Family, 65*, 746–761.

Blumstein, P., & Schwartz, P. (1983). *American couples: Money, work, sex*. New York: William Morrow.

Carrington, C. (1999). *No place like home: Relationships and family life among lesbians and gay men*. Chicago: University of Chicago Press.

Gottman, J.M., Levenson, R.W., Swanson, C., Swanson, K., Tyson, R., & Yoshimoto, D. (2003). Observing gay, lesbian, and heterosexual couples' relationships: Mathematical modeling of conflict interaction. *Journal of Homosexuality, 45*, 65–91.

Huston, T.L. (2000). The social ecology of marriage and other intimate unions. *Journal of Marriage and the Family, 62*, 298–320.

Kurdek, L.A. (1998). Relationship outcomes and their predictors: Longitudinal evidence from heterosexual married, gay cohabiting, and lesbian cohabiting couples. *Journal of Marriage and Family, 60*, 553–568.

Kurdek, L.A. (2001). Differences between heterosexual-nonparent couples and gay, lesbian, and heterosexual-parent couples. *Journal of Family Issues, 22*, 727–754.

Kurdek, L.A. (2004a). Are gay and lesbian cohabiting couples *really* different from heterosexual married couples? *Journal of Marriage and Family, 66*, 880–900.

Kurdek, L.A. (2004b). Gay men and lesbians: The family context. In M. Coleman & L.H. Ganong (Eds.), *Handbook of contemporary families: Considering the past, contemplating the future* (pp. 96–115). Thousand Oaks, CA: Sage.

Laumann, E.O., Gagnon, J.H., Michael, R.T., & Michaels, S. (1994). *The social organization of sexuality: Sexual practices in the United States*. Chicago: University of Chicago Press.

Patterson, C.J. (2000). Family relationships of lesbians and gay men. *Journal of Marriage and Family, 62*, 1052–1069.

Simons, T., & O'Connell, M. (2003). *Married-couple and unmarried-partner households: 2000*. Washington, DC: U.S. Census Bureau. Retrieved November 14, 2004, from http://www.census.gov/prod/2003pubs/censr-5.pdf

Critical Thinking Questions

1. If and when marriage between same-sex couples becomes legal in most countries, what do you think would change about same-sex relationships? What would not change?

2. Kurdek did not address the sexual relationships and satisfaction of gay and lesbian couples. Based on what you now know about sex differences in sexuality, what differences might you expect in the sexual relationships of lesbians and gay men?

This article has been reprinted as it originally appeared in *Current Directions in Psychological Science*. Citation information for this article as originally published appears above.

Lesbian and Gay Families

Charlotte J. Patterson[1]
University of Virginia

A pervasive stereotype about lesbians and gay men is that they do not take part in family life. From this perspective, they are thought to live their lives outside the reach of family pleasures and obligations, and the concept of gay and lesbian families is viewed as an oxymoron. Despite widespread prejudice and discrimination, however, lesbians and gay men do belong to, participate in, and create families. As research in the social sciences begins to address issues posed by sexual orientation, a more inclusive understanding of families is beginning to take shape.

In the United States alone, many millions of people belong to families that include gay or lesbian members. One well-known estimate holds that about 10% of the approximately 260 million people who live in the United States may be considered predominantly gay or lesbian. Starting from this estimate, we can consider the likelihood that each of these 26 million gay men and lesbians has two parents plus siblings and other relatives, such as aunts, uncles, cousins, and grandparents. These figures suggest that well over 100 million Americans either identify themselves as gay or lesbian or have a relative who does. Inasmuch as recent research suggests that the 10% figure may be high and that allowance should be made for the possibility of aggregation due to genetic factors, these numbers may be too large. Even if the estimates are reduced by half, though, it is clear that substantial numbers of Americans belong to families that include gay men or lesbians. For simplicity, I call these gay and lesbian families.

What is known of these families? Psychological research has begun to address issues relevant to lesbian and gay individuals' families of origin, to couple relationships formed by gay men and lesbians, and to gay and lesbian parenthood. In this article, I outline some principal issues and findings in each of these areas.

FAMILIES OF ORIGIN

In issues concerning families of origin, the extent of disclosure of gay and lesbian identities—commonly called "coming out"–is a pivotal concern. Coming out to self, friends, family members, and other people is a central process in the evolution of gay or lesbian identity, and its course may be influenced strongly by a variety of factors. Many studies have found that gay men and lesbians who identify themselves as such early in adolescence may nevertheless wait years to disclose their gay or lesbian identities to anyone. The resulting cognitive, emotional, and social isolation experienced by many gay and lesbian teenagers has been linked to psychological distress, substance abuse, and an elevated probability of suicide, especially among gay youths.

When they do come out, most adolescents disclose first to friends, and only later—if at all—to parents. Other things being equal, young lesbians and gay men are more likely to report having come out to their mothers than to their fathers, and young lesbians are more likely than young gay men to report having disclosed their sexual identity to a wide variety of people. Research findings about the consequences of coming out are mixed, with the impact depending on the balance between prejudice and stigmatization on the one hand and caring support on the other. All observers agree that coming out to family members usually challenges the existing family equilibrium and is generally seen by the lesbian or gay individual as carrying the risk of rejection by heterosexual family members.

The disequilibrium often created can be expected to have effects on heterosexual as well as gay or lesbian family members. Many parents feel shock and surprise that their son or daughter is assuming a stigmatized identity, and they may respond with anger, denial, or shame. Parents, in particular, may also mourn the loss of a hoped-for heterosexual future for their child. In many cases, concerns about AIDS and HIV (the virus that causes AIDS) are also important issues. Heterosexual family members also face questions about disclosing their own identities as relatives of lesbians or gay men. The ways in which existing personal, familial, ethnic, and cultural patterns may affect these processes are as yet little understood.

Lesbian and gay families also face questions about integration of gay or lesbian and heterosexual aspects of a lesbian or gay family member's life. For adolescents who are living with their parents, these questions may focus on the extent to which a gay or lesbian teenager is allowed or encouraged to make contact with nonheterosexual parts of his or her community. Among young adults, these issues may concern the extent to which comfortable interactions among heterosexual and non-heterosexual friends and family members are possible. Among middle-aged and older adults, issues may focus on the degree to which members of the family of origin know the individual's lovers, partners, children, and friends. At every age, recognition by heterosexual family members of the legitimacy and significance of gay and lesbian relationships is likely to be a central issue.

GAY AND LESBIAN COUPLES

Prominent among the significant family relationships of gay men and lesbians are, of course, those with lovers or life partners. According to data from large-scale surveys, the formation and maintenance of close relationships are high priorities for most gay and lesbian adults. In view of obstacles to lasting relationships (e.g., stigmatization of gay relationships, denial of marriage rights to same-sex couples), it is perhaps remarkable that most gay and lesbian adults say that they are involved in a relationship at any given moment, and that at least some of these relationships are sustained over a period of many years.

Research to date has documented many ways in which lesbian and gay close relationships are similar to those of heterosexual couples. Studies by Peplau and her associates and by Kurdek and his associates have shown that many of the same variables that are important in heterosexual couple relationships are also significant for lesbian and gay couples. For example, in one series of studies, Kurdek found that among a sample of lesbian, gay, heterosexual married, and heterosexual unmarried but cohabiting couples, length of relationship was better than couple type as a predictor of relationship variables such as satisfaction. Thus, some types of relationship dynamics do not seem to vary as a function of partners' sexual orientation.

Despite many similarities among lesbian, gay, and heterosexual couple relationships, however, a number of differences have also been noted. For instance, although heterosexual couples are likely to assign the majority of household labor to the wife or female partner, lesbian and gay couples—who cannot divide labor as a function of gender—are more likely to share household labor evenly. Another difference is that gay couples report greater frequency of sexual relations than do heterosexual couples, who in turn report higher frequency than do lesbian couples. Findings such as these point to the ways in which the study of lesbian and gay couples may help to address diverse questions about the role of gender in heterosexual as well as gay and lesbian family life.

In the past several years, the AIDS epidemic has affected lesbian and gay couple relationships in very different ways. Although many lesbians have been active in medical, social service, and community efforts in response to the AIDS epidemic, and although many lesbians have lost friends and family members, the impact of AIDS has been greater in gay communities. Especially in urban areas hardest hit by the AIDS epidemic, the illness itself and the losses sustained as a result of it have affected gay relationships at every level.

In sickness and in health, lesbian and gay individuals and couples are believed to be more likely than heterosexuals to count close friends and ex-lovers as family members. Especially in the face of prejudice and discrimination from members of the family of origin, lesbians and gay men may be more likely than heterosexuals to turn to networks of friends for support. Though evidence on this point is lacking, some observers have suggested that ex-lovers are particularly likely to be represented in such networks, especially among lesbians. Though viewed as family relationships by many participants in them, little is known as yet about the functioning of such networks.

PARENTHOOD AND CHILDREN

Although prevalent stereotypes suggest that lesbians and gay men do not become parents, there are almost certainly millions of lesbian mothers and gay fathers in the United States today. Most became parents in the context of heterosexual marriages before coming out as gay or lesbian, but increasing numbers of lesbians and gay men are also believed to be becoming parents after having come out. The largest increase in numbers of lesbians who are becoming parents is occurring by means of donor insemination, though other routes to parenthood, such as adoption, are also involved. This trend is seen by many observers as significant enough to be termed a "lesbian baby boom." Through surrogacy, adoption, and foster care, some gay men are also seeking to become parents. In contrast to the stereotype, then, it seems that the numbers of lesbian and gay parents, already substantial, are on the rise.

Although judicial and legislative bodies in this country have often denied child custody and visitation rights on the basis of parental sexual orientation, empirical studies have revealed no association between sexual orientation and psychological characteristics relevant to parenting. Courts in particular have sometimes assumed that gay men and lesbians are mentally ill and hence not fit to be parents, that lesbians are less maternal than heterosexual women and hence do not make good mothers, and that lesbians' and gay men's relationships with sexual partners leave little time for parenting behavior. Findings from systematic research have failed to confirm any of these fears. The idea that homosexuality constitutes a mental illness or disorder has long been repudiated by every major psychological and psychiatric professional association. Lesbians and heterosexual women have been found not to differ markedly either in their overall mental health or in their approaches to child rearing, nor have lesbians' romantic relationships been found to detract from their ability to care for children. Research on gay fathers has similarly failed to unearth any reasons to believe them unfit as parents. On the basis of research to date, then, negative assumptions about gay and lesbian adults' fitness as parents appear to be without empirical foundation.

Judicial decision making and public policies in many jurisdictions have also reflected various concerns about the well-being of children raised by gay or lesbian parents. Judges have voiced fears about the development of children's sexual identity, about other aspects of children's personal or psychological development, and about the social relationships of children reared by gay or lesbian parents. Reflecting common prejudices, judges have sometimes expressed concerns that children living with lesbian or gay parents would be at heightened risk of sexual abuse or be more likely to grow up to be gay or lesbian themselves (an outcome they apparently view as negative). There is, however, no evidence that the development of children with lesbian or gay parents is compromised in any significant way relative to that of children with heterosexual parents in otherwise comparable circumstances. Indeed, the available evidence suggests that home environments provided by gay and lesbian parents are as likely as those provided by heterosexual parents to support and enable children's psychological growth.

Just as other families exhibit tremendous diversity, so too do lesbian and gay families with children. Sources of diversity include individual differences in parents' psychological well-being, whether parents are involved in stable romantic relationships, degree of conflict among important adults in a child's life, and related variables. Other important forms of diversity include the economic circumstances and the racial, ethnic, religious, and cultural identities of lesbian and gay families. The scant research to date suggests that children of lesbian mothers are better off if their mothers are in good psychological health, living with a lesbian partner in a supportive milieu, than if their mothers are depressed, not in a relationship, and lacking good social support. Much remains to be learned, however, about the many forms of diversity among lesbian and gay families.

CONCLUSION

With increasing openness about lesbian and gay identities, the issues of lesbian and gay families are beginning to be recognized. Lesbians and gay men are born into families of origin, participate in those families, and in turn create their own families. In some ways, lesbian and gay issues in families are the same ones that heterosexual individuals face; in other ways, the issues are quite different. There is also great diversity among lesbian and gay families. Psychological research is just beginning to examine the role of sexual orientation in family lives. Despite some notable advances, much important work remains to be done.

Recommended Reading

D'Augelli, A.R., and Patterson, C.J., Eds. (in press). *Lesbian, Gay and Bisexual Identities Across the Lifespan* (Oxford University Press, New York).
Gonsiorek, J.C., and Weinrich, J.D., Eds. (1991). *Homosexuality: Research Implications for Public Policy* (Sage, Beverly Hills, CA).

Notes

1. Address correspondence to Charlotte J. Patterson at the Department of Psychology, Gilmer Hall, University of Virginia, Charlottesville, VA 22903; e-mail: cjp@virginia.edu.

2. J.C. Gonsiorek and J.D. Weinrich, Eds., *Homosexuality: Research Implications for Public Policy* (Sage, Beverly Hills, CA, 1991); J. Laird, Lesbian and gay families, in *Normal Family Processes*, 2nd ed., F. Walsh, Ed. (Guilford Press, New York, 1993); K. Weston, *Families We Choose: Lesbians, Gays, Kinship* (Columbia University Press, New York, 1991).

3. J.M. Bailey, Biological perspectives on sexual orientation, in *Lesbian, Gay and Bisexual Identities Across the Lifespan*, A.R. D'Augelli and C.J. Patterson, Eds. (Oxford University Press, New York, in press); Gonsiorek and Weinrich, note 2.

4. A.M. Boxer, J.A. Cook, and G. Herdt, Double jeopardy: Identity transitions and parent-child relations among gay and lesbian youth, in *Parent-Child Relations Throughout Life*, K. Pillemer and K. McCartney, Eds. (Erlbaum, Hillsdale, NJ, 1991); G. Herdt, Ed., *Gay and Lesbian Youth* (Harrington Park Press, New York, 1989); G. Remafedi, Risk factors for attempted suicide in gay and bisexual youth, *Pediatrics*, 87, 869–875 (1991); R.C. Savin-Williams, Lesbian, gay and bisexual adolescents, in *Lesbian, Gay and Bisexual Identities Across the Lifespan*, A.R. D'Augelli and C.J. Patterson, Eds. (Oxford University Press, New York, in press).

5. L. Kurdek, Lesbian and gay couples, in *Lesbian, Gay and Bisexual Identities Across the Lifespan*, A.R. D'Augelli and C.J. Patterson, Eds. (Oxford University Press, New York, in press); L.A. Peplau, Lesbian and gay relationships, in Gonsiorek and Weinrich, note 2.

6. S. Morin, AIDS: The challenge to psychology, *American Psychologist*, 43, 838–842 (1988); J.P. Paul, R.B. Hays, and T.J. Coates, The impact of the HIV epidemic on U.S. gay male communities, in *Lesbian, Gay and Bisexual Identities Across the Lifespan*, A.R. D'Augelli and C.J. Patterson, Eds. (Oxford University Press, New York, in press).

7. A.R. D'Augelli and L. Garnets, Lesbian and gay communities, and D. Kimmel and B. Sang, The adult years, both in *Lesbian, Gay and Bisexual Identities Across the Lifespan*, A.R. D'Augelli and C.J. Patterson, Eds. (Oxford University Press, New York, in press); Weston, note 2.

8. C.J. Patterson, Children of lesbian and gay parents, *Child Development*, 63, 1025–1042 (1992).

9. P.J. Falk, Lesbian mothers: Psychosocial assumptions in family law, *American Psychologist*, 44, 941–947 (1989); C.J. Patterson, Lesbian mothers, gay fathers, and their children, in *Lesbian, Gay and Bisexual Identities Across the Lifespan*, A.R. D'Augelli and C.J. Patterson, Eds. (Oxford University Press, New York, in press).

Critical Thinking Questions

1. If, in fact, there is little difference in the family relationships of gays and lesbians as opposed to heterosexuals, why does the general public persist in believing that there are differences?

2. Patterson discusses the process of "coming out" in a family context. How is the success of that process likely to influence subsequent family relationships?

This article has been reprinted as it originally appeared in *Current Directions in Psychological Science*. Citation information for this article as originally published appears above.

The Psychology of Sexual Prejudice

Gregory M. Herek[1]

Department of Psychology, University of California, Davis, California

Abstract

Sexual prejudice refers to negative attitudes toward an individual because of her or his sexual orientation. In this article, the term is used to characterize heterosexuals' negative attitudes toward (a) homosexual behavior, (b) people with a homosexual or bisexual orientation, and (c) communities of gay, lesbian, and bisexual people. Sexual prejudice is a preferable term to *homophobia* because it conveys no assumptions about the motivations underlying negative attitudes, locates the study of attitudes concerning sexual orientation within the broader context of social psychological research on prejudice, and avoids value judgments about such attitudes. Sexual prejudice remains widespread in the United States, although moral condemnation has decreased in the 1990s and opposition to antigay discrimination has increased. The article reviews current knowledge about the prevalence of sexual prejudice, its psychological correlates, its underlying motivations, and its relationship to hate crimes and other antigay behaviors.

Keywords

attitudes; homosexuality; prejudice; homophobia; heterosexism

In a 6-month period beginning late in 1998, Americans were shocked by the brutal murders of Matthew Shepard and Billy Jack Gaither. Shepard, a 21-year-old Wyoming college student, and Gaither, a 39-year-old factory worker in Alabama, had little in common except that each was targeted for attack because he was gay. Unfortunately, their slayings were not isolated events. Lesbians, gay men, and bisexual people—as well as heterosexuals perceived to be gay—routinely experience violence, discrimination, and personal rejection. In all, 1,102 hate crimes based on sexual orientation were tallied by law-enforcement authorities in 1997. Because a substantial proportion of such crimes are never reported to police, that figure represents only the tip of an iceberg (Herek, Gillis, & Cogan, 1999).

People with homosexual or bisexual orientations have long been stigmatized. With the rise of the gay political movement in the late 1960s, however, homosexuality's condemnation as immoral, criminal, and sick came under increasing scrutiny. When the American Psychiatric Association dropped homosexuality as a psychiatric diagnosis in 1973, the question of why some heterosexuals harbor strongly negative attitudes toward homosexuals began to receive serious scientific consideration.

Society's rethinking of sexual orientation was crystallized in the term *homophobia*, which heterosexual psychologist George Weinberg coined in the late 1960s. The word first appeared in print in 1969 and was subsequently discussed at length in a popular book (Weinberg, 1972).[2] Around the same time, *heterosexism* began to be used as a term analogous to sexism and racism, describing an ideological system that casts homosexuality as inferior to heterosexuality.[3] Although usage of the two words has not been uniform, homophobia has typically been employed to describe individual antigay attitudes and behaviors, whereas heterosexism has referred to societal-level ideologies and patterns of institutionalized oppression of nonheterosexual people.

By drawing popular and scientific attention to antigay hostility, the creation of these terms marked a watershed. Of the two, homophobia is probably more widely used and more often criticized. Its critics note that homophobia implicitly suggests that antigay attitudes are best understood as an irrational fear and that they represent a form of individual psychopathology rather than a socially reinforced prejudice. As antigay attitudes have become increasingly central to conservative political and religious ideologies since the 1980s, these limitations have become more problematic. Yet, heterosexism, with its historical macro-level focus on cultural ideologies rather than individual attitudes, is not a satisfactory replacement for homophobia.

Thus, scientific analysis of the psychology of antigay attitudes will be facilitated by a new term. I offer *sexual prejudice* for this purpose. Broadly conceived, sexual prejudice refers to all negative attitudes based on sexual orientation, whether the target is homosexual, bisexual, or heterosexual. Given the current social organization of sexuality, however, such prejudice is almost always directed at people who engage in homosexual behavior or label themselves gay, lesbian, or bisexual. Thus, as used here, the term sexual prejudice encompasses heterosexuals' negative attitudes toward (a) homosexual behavior, (b) people with a homosexual or bisexual orientation, and (c) communities of gay, lesbian, and bisexual people. Like other types of prejudice, sexual prejudice has three principal features: It is an attitude (i.e., an evaluation or judgment); it is directed at a social group and its members; and it is negative, involving hostility or dislike.

Conceptualizing heterosexuals' negative attitudes toward homosexuality and bisexuality as sexual prejudice—rather than homophobia—has several advantages. First, sexual prejudice is a descriptive term. Unlike homophobia, it conveys no a priori assumptions about the origins, dynamics, and underlying motivations of antigay attitudes. Second, the term explicitly links the study of antigay hostility with the rich tradition of social psychological research on prejudice. Third, using the construct of sexual prejudice does not require value judgments that antigay attitudes are inherently irrational or evil.

PREVALENCE

Most adults in the United States hold negative attitudes toward homosexual behavior, regarding it as wrong and unnatural (Herek & Capitanio, 1996; Yang, 1997). Nevertheless, poll data show that attitudes have become more favorable over the past three decades. For example, whereas at least two thirds of respondents to the General Social Survey (GSS) considered homosexual behavior "always wrong" in the 1970s and 1980s, that figure declined noticeably in the 1990s. By 1996, only 56% of GSS respondents regarded it as always wrong (Yang, 1997).

Much of the public also holds negative attitudes toward individuals who are homosexual. In a 1992 national survey, more than half of the heterosexual respondents expressed disgust for lesbians and gay men (Herek, 1994). Respondents to the ongoing American National Election Studies have typically rated lesbians and gay men among the lowest of all groups on a 101-point feeling thermometer, although mean scores increased by approximately 10 points between 1984 and 1996 (Yang, 1997).

Despite these examples of negative attitudes, most Americans believe that a gay person should not be denied employment or basic civil liberties. The public is reluctant to treat homosexuality on a par with heterosexuality, however. Most Americans favor giving same-sex domestic partners limited recognition (e.g., employee health benefits, hospital visitation rights), but most oppose legalizing same-sex marriages. And whereas the public generally supports the employment rights of gay teachers, they do not believe that lesbians and gay men should be able to adopt children (Yang, 1997).

Unfortunately, most studies have not distinguished between lesbians and gay men as targets of prejudice. The available data suggest that attitudes toward gay men are more negative than attitudes toward lesbians, with the difference more pronounced among heterosexual men than women (Herek & Capitanio, 1996; Kite & Whitley, 1998). This pattern may reflect sex differences in the underlying cognitive organization of sexual prejudice (Herek & Capitanio, 1999).

CORRELATES

Laboratory and questionnaire studies have utilized a variety of measures to assess heterosexuals' attitudes toward gay men and lesbians (e.g., Davis, Yarber, Bauser-man, Schreer, & Davis, 1998). Consistent with findings from public opinion surveys, they have revealed higher levels of sexual prejudice among individuals who are older, less educated, living in the U.S. South or Midwest, and living in rural areas (Herek, 1994). In survey and laboratory studies alike, heterosexual men generally display higher levels of sexual prejudice than heterosexual women (Herek & Capitanio, 1999; Kite & Whitley, 1998; Yang, 1998).

Sexual prejudice is also reliably correlated with several psychological and social variables. Heterosexuals with high levels of sexual prejudice tend to score higher than others on authoritarianism (Altemeyer, 1996; Haddock & Zanna, 1998). In addition, heterosexuals who identify with a fundamentalist religious denomination and frequently attend religious services typically manifest higher levels of sexual prejudice than do the non-religious and members of liberal denominations (Herek & Capitanio, 1996). Since the 1980s, political ideology and party affiliation have also come to be strongly associated with sexual prejudice, with conservatives and Republicans expressing the highest levels (Yang, 1998).

Sexual prejudice is strongly related to whether or not a heterosexual knows gay people personally. The lowest levels of prejudice are manifested by heterosexuals who have gay friends or family members, describe their relationships with those individuals as close, and report having directly discussed the gay or lesbian person's sexual orientation with him or her. Interpersonal contact and prejudice are reciprocally related. Not only are heterosexuals with gay friends or relatives less prejudiced, but heterosexuals from demographic groups with low levels of sexual prejudice (e.g., women, highly educated people) are more likely to experience personal contact with an openly gay person (Herek & Capitanio, 1996).

Relatively little empirical research has examined racial and ethnic differences. Sexual prejudice may be somewhat greater among heterosexual African Americans than among heterosexual whites, mainly because of white women's relatively favorable attitudes toward lesbians and gay men. The correlates of sexual prejudice may vary by race and ethnicity. Interpersonal contact may be more important in shaping the attitudes of whites than of blacks, for example, whereas the belief that homosexuality is a choice may be a more influential predictor of heterosexual blacks' sexual prejudice (Herek & Capitanio, 1995).

UNDERLYING MOTIVATIONS

Like other forms of prejudice, sexual prejudice has multiple motivations. For some heterosexuals, it results from unpleasant interactions with gay individuals, which are then generalized to attitudes toward the entire group. This explanation probably applies mainly to cases in which interpersonal contact has been superficial and minimal. For other heterosexuals, sexual prejudice is rooted in fears associated with homosexuality, perhaps reflecting discomfort with their own sexual impulses or gender conformity. For still others, sexual prejudice reflects influences of in-group norms that are hostile to homosexual and bisexual people. Yet another source of prejudice is the perception that gay people and the gay community represent values that are directly in conflict with one's personal value system.

These different motivations can be understood as deriving from the psychological functions that sexual prejudice serves, which vary from one individual to another. One heterosexual's sexual prejudice, for example, may reduce the anxiety associated with his fears about sexuality and gender, whereas another heterosexual's prejudice might reinforce a positive sense of herself as a member of the social group "good Christians." Such attitudes are functional only when they are consistent with cultural and situational cues, for example, when homosexuality is defined as inconsistent with a masculine identity or when a religious congregation defines hostility to homosexuality as a criterion for being a good Christian (Herek, 1987).

PREJUDICE AND BEHAVIOR

Hate crimes and discrimination are inevitably influenced by complex situational factors (Franklin, 1998). Nevertheless, sexual prejudice contributes to antigay behaviors. In experimental studies, sexual prejudice correlates with antigay behaviors, although other factors often moderate this relationship (Haddock & Zanna, 1998; Kite & Whitley, 1998). Voting patterns on gay-related ballot measures have been generally consistent with the demographic correlates of sexual prejudice described earlier (Strand, 1998). Recognizing the complex relationship between sexual prejudice and antigay behavior further underscores the value of anchoring this phenomenon in the scientific literature on prejudice, which offers multiple models for understanding the links between attitudes and behavior.

CONCLUSION AND DIRECTIONS FOR RESEARCH

Although more than a quarter century has passed since Weinberg first presented a scholarly discussion of the psychology of homophobia, empirical research on sexual prejudice is still in its early stages. To date, the prevalence and correlates of sexual prejudice have received the most attention. Relatively little research has been devoted to understanding the dynamic cognitive processes associated with antigay attitudes and stereotypes, that is, how heterosexuals think about lesbians and gay men. Nor has extensive systematic inquiry been devoted to the underlying motivations for sexual prejudice or the effectiveness of different interventions for reducing sexual prejudice. These represent promising areas for future research.

In addition, there is a need for descriptive studies of sexual prejudice within different subsets of the population, including ethnic and age groups. Given the tendency for antigay behaviors to be perpetrated by adolescents and young adults, studies of the development of sexual prejudice early in the life span are especially needed. Finally, commonalities and convergences in the psychology of sexual prejudice toward different targets (e.g., men or women, homosexuals or bisexuals) should be studied. Much of the empirical research in this area to date has been limited because it has focused (implicitly or explicitly) on heterosexuals' attitudes toward gay men.

Stigma based on sexual orientation has been commonplace throughout the 20th century. Conceptualizing such hostility as sexual prejudice represents a step toward achieving a scientific understanding of its origins, dynamics, and functions. Perhaps most important, such an understanding may help to prevent the behavioral expression of sexual prejudice through violence, discrimination, and harassment.

Recommended Reading

Herek, G.M. (Ed.). (1998). *Stigma and sexual orientation: Understanding prejudice against lesbians, gay men, and bisexuals*. Newbury Park, CA: Sage.

Herek, G.M., & Berrill, K. (Eds.). (1992). *Hate crimes: Confronting violence against lesbians and gay men*. Thousand Oaks, CA: Sage.

Herek, G.M., Kimmel, D.C., Amaro, H., & Melton, G.B. (1991). Avoiding heterosexist bias in psychological research. *American Psychologist, 46,* 957–963.

Herman, D. (1997). *The antigay agenda: Orthodox vision and the Christian Right*. Chicago: University of Chicago Press.

Rothblum, E., & Bond, L. (Eds.). (1996). *Preventing heterosexism and homophobia*. Thousand Oaks, CA: Sage.

Acknowledgments—Preparation of this article was supported in part by an Independent Scientist Award from the National Institute of Mental Health (K02 MH01455).

Notes

1. Address correspondence to Gregory Herek, Department of Psychology, University of California, Davis, CA 95616-8775.

2. Although Weinberg coined the term homophobia, it was first used in print in 1969 by Jack Nichols and Lige Clarke in their May 23rd column in *Screw* magazine (J. Nichols, personal communication, November 5, 1998; G. Weinberg, personal communication, October 30, 1998).

3. Heterosexism was used as early as July 10, 1972, in two separate letters printed in the *Great Speckled Bird,* an alternative newspaper published in Atlanta, Georgia. I thank Joanne Despres of the Merriam Webster Company for her kind assistance with researching the origins of this word.

References

Altemeyer, B. (1996). *The authoritarian specter.* Cambridge, MA: Harvard University Press.

Davis, C.M., Yarber, W.L., Bauserman, R., Schreer, G., & Davis, S.L. (Eds.). (1998). *Handbook of sexuality-related measures.* Thousand Oaks, CA: Sage.

Franklin, K. (1998). Unassuming motivations: Contextualizing the narratives of antigay assailants. In G.M. Herek (Ed.), *Stigma and sexual orientation: Understanding prejudice against lesbians, gay men, and bisexuals* (pp. 1–23). Newbury Park, CA: Sage.

Haddock, G., & Zanna, M. (1998). Authoritarianism, values, and the favorability and structure of antigay attitudes. In G.M. Herek (Ed.), *Stigma and sexual orientation: Understanding prejudice against lesbians, gay men, and bisexuals* (pp. 82–107). Newbury Park, CA: Sage.

Herek, G.M. (1987). Can functions be measured? A new perspective on the functional approach to attitudes. *Social Psychology Quarterly, 50,* 285–303.

Herek, G.M. (1994). Assessing attitudes toward lesbians and gay men: A review of empirical research with the ATLG scale. In B. Greene & G.M. Herek (Eds.), *Lesbian and gay psychology* (pp. 206–228). Thousand Oaks, CA: Sage.

Herek, G.M., & Capitanio, J. (1995). Black heterosexuals' attitudes toward lesbians and gay men in the United States. *Journal of Sex Research, 32,* 95–105.

Herek, G.M., & Capitanio, J. (1996). "Some of my best friends": Intergroup contact, concealable stigma, and heterosexuals' attitudes toward gay men and lesbians. *Personality and Social Psychology Bulletin, 22,* 412–424.

Herek, G.M., & Capitanio, J.P. (1999). Sex differences in how heterosexuals think about lesbians and gay men: Evidence from survey context effects. *Journal of Sex Research, 36,* 348–360.

Herek, G.M., Gillis, J., & Cogan, J. (1999). Psychological sequelae of hate crime victimization among lesbian, gay, and bisexual adults. *Journal of Consulting and Clinical Psychology, 67,* 945–951.

Kite, M.E., & Whitley, E., Jr. (1998). Do heterosexual women and men differ in their attitudes toward homosexuality? A conceptual and methodological analysis. In G.M. Herek (Ed.), *Stigma and sexual orientation: Understanding prejudice against lesbians, gay men, and bisexuals* (pp. 39–61). Newbury Park, CA: Sage.

Strand, D. (1998). Civil liberties, civil rights, and stigma: Voter attitudes and behavior in the politics of homosexuality. In G.M. Herek (Ed.), *Stigma and sexual orientation: Understanding prejudice against lesbians, gay men, and bisexuals* (pp. 108–137). Newbury Park, CA: Sage.

Weinberg, G. (1972). *Society and the healthy homosexual.* New York: St. Martin's.

Yang, A. (1997). Trends: Attitudes toward homosexuality. *Public Opinion Quarterly, 61,* 477–507.

Yang, A. (1998). *From wrongs to rights: Public opinion on gay and lesbian Americans moves toward equality.* Washington, DC: National Gay and Lesbian Task Force Policy Institute.

Critical Thinking Questions

1. Why do you think there are so many people who have a high level of sexual prejudice?

2. What do you think are the similarities and differences between sexual prejudice and racial prejudice?

This article has been reprinted as it originally appeared in *Current Directions in Psychological Science.* Citation information for this article as originally published appears above.

Section 5: Relationship Formation and Maintenance

The fifth section of this reader contains articles that seek to answer questions about how relationships function: When and how do we begin to form romantic/sexual relationships? What are the obstacles to forming relationships? What factors allow us to develop intimacy and trust in our relationships? How do we know whether our relationships are working or not?

One way to understand how romantic and sexual relationships develop is to understand how they begin. What is the impact of our first relationship on our subsequent relationships? This section begins with an article in which Wyndol Furman describes research on adolescent romantic relationships, noting that such relationships become important to the development and functioning of four important behavioral systems: affiliation, sex-reproduction, attachment, and caregiving. Furman highlights how adolescents' relationships are shaped by the developmental and social contexts in which they occur, and notes how adolescents' experiences with relationships may ultimately shape their adult relationships.

In the next article, Sandra Murray argues that relationships involve a conflict between our need to be intimate with others and our desire to protect ourselves from the pain of rejection. She notes that this conflict creates numerous choices surrounding whether to risk rejection and promote the relationship or protect the self and potentially damage the relationship. Individual and situational differences that influence the degree of confidence that one will not be rejected play a powerful role in determining whether one will take the necessary risks to promote the relationship or protect oneself to the detriment of the relationship.

One factor that plays a role in determining this sort of confidence is trust. Indeed, in the next article, Jeffry Simpson notes that trust is integral to virtually all theories of relationships. Nevertheless, as Simpson indicates, very little empirical work has addressed how trust is created, kept, and diminished, possibly because of its complexity. In an attempt to facilitate such work, Simpson lays out a dyadic model of trust that describes how the dynamics of self, partner, and relationship contribute to patterns of behavior that may build trust or cause it to deteriorate.

With regard to the evaluation of our sexual and romantic relationships, whether the outcomes we receive from our relationships are good enough for us often depends on how well they agree with the standards we have for those relationships. Garth Fletcher and Jeffry Simpson review evidence consistent with the idea that such standards play a crucial role not only in determining how happy we are with our relationships, but how we are likely to behave in our relationships. Specifically, Fletcher and

Simpson review evidence consistent with the idea that standards for our romantic partners fall into one of three categories—(1) warmth, (2) attractiveness, and (3) status—and function to help us (1) evaluate, (2) explain, and (3) regulate our relationships. The authors explain that a key factor in the judgments we make about our romantic partners is whether we are more concerned with seeing things positively or seeing things accurately.

The Emerging Field of Adolescent Romantic Relationships

Wyndol Furman[1]

Department of Psychology, University of Denver, Denver, Colorado

Abstract

Romantic relationships are central in adolescents' lives. They have the potential to affect development positively, but also place adolescents at risk for problems. Romantic experiences change substantially over the course of adolescence; the peer context plays a critical role as heterosexual adolescents initially interact with the other sex in a group context, then begin group dating, and finally have dyadic romantic relationships. Adolescents' expectations and experiences in romantic relationships are related to their relationships with their peers as well as their parents. Although research on adolescents' romantic relationships has blossomed in the past decade, further work is needed to identify the causes and consequences of romantic experiences, examine the diversity of romantic experiences, and integrate the field with work on sexuality and adult romantic relationships.

Keywords

romantic relationships; attachment; love; friendships; adolescent adjustment

A review of the literature on adolescent romantic relationships a decade ago would have uncovered very little empirical research. The work that had been conducted consisted primarily of descriptive studies on the frequency of dating or other romantic behaviors. A substantial amount of work on sexual behavior had been conducted, but much of that was descriptive as well, and did not say much about the relational context in which the sexual behavior occurred. In other words, the literature contained a lot of information about the proportions of adolescents of different ages or backgrounds who were sexually active, but much less about who their partners were and what their relationships with them were like.

Happily, the field has changed substantially in the past decade. A cadre of social scientists have been studying adolescents' romantic relationships, and the number of articles and conference presentations seems to increase each year. The fields of adolescent romantic relationships and sexual behavior are still not well integrated, but the connections between them are increasing. Most of the work has been done on heterosexual relationships, but research on lesbian, gay, and bisexual relationships is beginning as well.

The increasing interest in adolescents' romantic relationships may partially stem from a recognition that these relationships are not simply trivial flings. As young people move from preadolescence through late adolescence, their romantic relationships become increasingly central in their social world. Preadolescents spend an hour or less a week interacting with the other sex. By the 12th grade, boys spend an average of 5 hr a week with the other sex, and girls spend an average of 10 hr a week. Furthermore, 12th-grade boys and girls spend an additional 5 to 8 hr a week thinking about members of the other sex when not with them (Richards, Crowe, Larson, & Swarr, 1998). Romantic partners are also a major source of support for many adolescents. Among 10th graders, only close friends provide more support. During the college years, romantic relationships are the most supportive relationships for males, and among the most supportive relationships for females (Furman & Buhrmester, 1992).

Romantic relationships may also affect other aspects of adolescents' development. For example, they have been hypothesized to contribute to the development of an identity, the transformation of family relationships, the development of close relationships with peers, the development of sexuality, and scholastic achievement and career planning (Furman & Shaffer, in press). One particularly interesting question is whether adolescent romantic experiences influence subsequent romantic relationships, including marriages. Unfortunately, there is limited empirical data on these possible impacts.

Adolescent romantic relationships are not, however, simple "beds of roses." One fifth of adolescent women are victims of physical or sexual abuse by a dating partner (Silverman, Raj, Mucci, & Hathaway, 2001). Breakups are one of the strongest predictors of depression (Monroe, Rhode, Seeley, & Lewinsohn, 1999). Sexually transmitted diseases and teenage pregnancy are also major risks.

Of course, the benefits and risks of particular romantic experiences vary. Having romantic experience at an early age and having a high number of partners are associated with problems in adjustment (see Zimmer-Gembeck, Siebenbruner, & Collins, 2001), although researchers do not know yet the direction of the influence. That is, the romantic experiences may lead to the difficulties, but it is also possible that adolescents who are not well adjusted are more likely than their better adjusted peers to become prematurely or overly involved in romantic relationships. Moreover, little is known about how the length or qualities of romantic relationships may be linked to adjustment.

DEVELOPMENTAL COURSE

Adolescents vary widely in when they become interested in romantic relationships, and the experiences they have once they begin dating. Accordingly, there is not one normative pattern of development. Some commonalities in the nature and sequence of heterosexual experiences can be seen, however. Prior to adolescence, boys and girls primarily interact with same-sex peers. In early adolescence, they begin to think more about members of the other sex, and then eventually to interact more with them (Richards et al., 1998). Initial interactions typically occur in mixed boy-girl groups; then group dating begins, with several pairs engaging in some activity together; finally, dyadic romantic relationships begin to form (Connolly, Goldberg, & Pepler, 2002). Having a large network of other-sex friends increases the likelihood of developing a romantic relationship with someone (Connolly, Furman, & Konarski, 2000).

The developmental course of romantic experiences for gay, lesbian, and bisexual youths is less charted, but is likely to be somewhat different. Most have some same-sex sexual experience, but relatively few have same-sex romantic relationships because of both the limited opportunities to do so and the social disapproval such relationships may generate from families or heterosexual peers (Diamond, Savin-Williams, & Dubé, 1999). Many sexual-minority youths date other-sex peers; such experiences can help them clarify their sexual orientation or disguise it from others.

The nature of heterosexual or homosexual romantic relationships changes developmentally. Early relationships do not fulfill many of the functions that adult romantic relationships often do. Early adolescents do not commonly turn to a partner for support or provide such caregiving for a partner. In fact, what may be important is simply having such a relationship, especially if the partner is a popular or desired one.

Eventually, adolescents develop some comfort in these interactions and begin to turn to their partners for specific social and emotional needs. Wehner and I proposed that romantic relationships become important in the functioning of four behavioral systems—affiliation, sex-reproduction, attachment, and caregiving (Furman & Wehner, 1994). The affiliative and sexual-reproductive systems are the first to become salient, as young adolescents spend time with their partners and explore their sexual feelings. The attachment and caretaking systems become more important during late adolescence and early adulthood, as relationships become more long term. Several findings are consistent with our proposal. When asked to describe their romantic relationships, adolescents mention affiliative features more often than attachment or caregiving features (Feiring, 1996). Similarly, in another study, young adults retrospectively described their romances in adolescence in terms of companionship and affiliation, and described their relationships in young adulthood in terms of trust and support (Shulman & Kipnis, 2001).

The work on the developmental course of romantic experiences illustrates several important points. First, these relationships do not occur in isolation. Relationships with peers typically serve as a social context for the emergence of heterosexual relationships, and often are a deterrent for gay and lesbian relationships. Second, adolescents' romantic relationships are more than simple sexual encounters; at the same time, one could not characterize most of them as the fullblown attachment relationships that committed adult relationships become (Shaver & Hazan, 1988). Affiliation, companionship, and friendship seem to be particularly important aspects of most of these relationships. Finally, the developmental changes in these relationships are striking. Although at first they are based on simple interest, in the course of a decade, adolescents go from simply being interested in boys or girls to having significant relationships that are beginning to be characterized by attachment and caregiving. Because the changes are qualitative as well as quantitative, they present challenges for investigators trying to describe them or to compare the experiences of different adolescents. Wehner and I (Furman & Wehner, 1994) have tried to provide a common framework for research by examining adolescents' expectations for and beliefs about these relationships, a point I discuss more extensively in the next section.

LINKS WITH OTHER RELATIONSHIPS

Much of the current research on adult romantic relationships has been guided by attachment theory. More than a decade ago, Shaver and Hazan (1988) proposed that committed romantic relationships could be characterized as attachments, just as relationships between parent and child were. Moreover, they suggested that experiences with parents affect individuals' expectations of romantic relationships. Individuals who had secure relationships with parents would be likely to have secure expectations of romantic relationships and, in fact, would be likely to develop secure romantic attachments, whereas those who had adverse experiences with parents would be expected to develop insecure expectations of romantic relationships.

Although researchers generally emphasized the links between relationships with parents and romantic relationships, Wehner and I suggested that friendships would be related to romantic relationships as well (Furman & Wehner, 1994). Friendships and romantic relationships are both egalitarian relationships characterized by features of affiliation, such as companionship and mutual intimacy. Accordingly, we proposed that adolescents' experiences with friends and expectations concerning these relationships influence their expectations of romantic relationships. Subsequently, several studies using multiple methods of assessment demonstrated links between adolescents' expectations of friendships and romantic relationships (see Furman, Simon, Shaffer, & Bouchey, 2002). In fact, these links were more consistent than those between parent-child relationships and romantic relationships. Interestingly, the latter links were found to strengthen over the course of adolescence. Such a developmental shift may occur as the attachment and caregiving features of romantic relationships become increasingly salient.

These studies were cross-sectional, and thus cannot support inferences about causality. However, the findings again underscore the importance of recognizing that romantic relationships are peer relationships and thus, links with friendships are likely as well.

At the same time, various types of relationships have only moderate effects on one another. Experiences in other relationships may influence romantic relationships, but romantic relationships also present new challenges, and thus past experiences are not likely to be simply replicated. What influence do past romantic relationships have on future romantic relationships? Individuals' perceptions of support and negative interaction in their romantic relationships have been found to be stable over the span of a year, even across different relationships (Connolly et al., 2000), but otherwise researchers know little about what does and does not carry over from one romantic relationship to the next.

CURRENT AND FUTURE DIRECTIONS

The existing literature on romantic relationships has many of the characteristics of initial research on a topic. One such characteristic is the methodologies used to date: Investigators have principally relied on questionnaires, administered at one point in time. Interview and observational studies are now beginning to appear, though, and investigators conducting longitudinal studies have begun to report their results concerning adolescent romantic relationships. For example, Capaldi and Clark (1998) found that having a parent whose behavior is antisocial and who is unskilled in parenting is predictive of antisocial behavior in midadolescence, which in turn is predictive of aggression toward dating partners in late adolescence. Reports from other ongoing longitudinal studies of the childhood precursors of adolescent romantic relationships and the consequences of these relationships for subsequent development should appear shortly.

In this article, I have described some of the common developmental changes characteristic of adolescent romantic relationships and how these relationships may be influenced by relationships with friends and parents. At the same time, the diversity of romantic experiences should be underscored. The links between romantic experiences and adjustment vary as a function of the timing and degree of romantic involvement (Zimmer-Gembeck et al., 2001). Investigators are beginning to examine how romantic experiences may be associated with characteristics of the adolescent, such as antisocial or bullying behavior, health status, or sensitivity to being rejected. To date, most of the work has focused on heterosexual youths from middle-class Euro-American backgrounds, and further work with other groups is certainly needed. Additionally, almost all of the research has been conducted in Western societies, yet romantic development is likely to be quite different in other societies where contacts with the other sex are more constrained, and marriages are arranged.

Efforts to integrate the field with related ones are needed. Just as research on sexual behavior could profit from examining the nature of the relationships between sexual partners, investigators studying romantic relationships need to examine the role of sexual behavior in romantic relationships. Ironically, few investigators have done so, and instead these relationships have been treated as if they were platonic. Similarly, research on adolescent relationships could benefit from the insights of the work on adult romantic relationships, which has a rich empirical and theoretical history. At the same time, investigators studying adult relationships may want to give greater consideration to the developmental changes that occur in these relationships and to their peer context—themes that have been highlighted by adolescence researchers. In sum, research on adolescent romantic relationships has blossomed in the past decade, but a broad, integrative perspective will be needed to fully illuminate their nature.

Recommended Reading

Bouchey, H.A., & Furman, W. (in press). Dating and romantic experiences in adolescence. In G.R. Adams & M. Berzonsky (Eds.), *The Blackwell handbook of adolescence*. Oxford, England: Blackwell.

Florsheim, P. (Ed.). (in press). *Adolescent romantic relations and sexual behavior: Theory, research, and practical implications*. Mahwah, NJ: Erlbaum.

Furman, W., Brown, B.B., & Feiring, C. (Eds.). (1999). *The development of romantic relationships in adolescence*. New York: Cambridge University Press.

Shulman, S., & Collins, W. (Eds.). (1997). *Romantic relationships in adolescence: Developmental perspectives*. San Francisco: Jossey-Bass.

Shulman, S., & Seiffge-Krenke, I. (Eds.). (2001). Adolescent romance: From experiences to relationships [Special issue]. *Journal of Adolescence, 24*(3).

Acknowledgments—Preparation of this manuscript was supported by Grant 50106 from the National Institute of Mental Health.

149

Note

1. Address correspondence to Wyndol Furman, Department of Psychology, University of Denver, Denver, CO 80208; e-mail: wfurman@nova.psy.du.edu.

References

Capaldi, D.M., & Clark, S. (1998). Prospective family predictors of aggression toward female partners for at-risk young men. *Developmental Psychology, 34,* 1175–1188.

Connolly, J., Furman, W., & Konarski, R. (2000). The role of peers in the emergence of romantic relationships in adolescence. *Child Development, 71,* 1395–1408.

Connolly, J., Goldberg, A., & Pepler, D. (2002). *Romantic development in the peer group in early adolescence.* Manuscript submitted for publication.

Diamond, L.M., Savin-Williams, R.C., & Dubé, E.M. (1999). Sex, dating, passionate friendships, and romance: Intimate peer relations among lesbian, gay, and bisexual adolescents. In W. Furman, B.B. Brown, & C. Feiring (Eds.), *The development of romantic relationships in adolescence* (pp. 175–210). New York: Cambridge University Press.

Feiring, C. (1996). Concepts of romance in 15-year-old adolescents. *Journal of Research on Adolescence, 6,* 181–200.

Furman, W., & Buhrmester, D. (1992). Age and sex differences in perceptions of networks of personal relationships. *Child Development, 63,* 103–115.

Furman, W., & Shaffer, L. (in press). The role of romantic relationships in adolescent development. In P. Florsheim (Ed.), *Adolescent romantic relations and sexual behavior: Theory, research, and practical implications.* Mahwah, NJ: Erlbaum.

Furman, W., Simon, V.A., Shaffer, L., & Bouchey, H.A. (2002). Adolescents' working models and styles for relationships with parents, friends, and romantic partners. *Child Development, 73,* 241–255.

Furman, W., & Wehner, E.A. (1994). Romantic views: Toward a theory of adolescent romantic relationships. In R. Montemayor, G.R. Adams, & G.P. Gullota (Eds.), *Advances in adolescent development: Vol. 6. Relationships during adolescence* (pp. 168–175). Thousand Oaks, CA: Sage.

Monroe, S.M., Rhode, P., Seeley, J.R., & Lewinsohn, P.M. (1999). Life events and depression in adolescence: Relationship loss as a prospective risk factor for first onset of major depressive disorder. *Journal of Abnormal Psychology, 108,* 606–614.

Richards, M.H., Crowe, P.A., Larson, R., & Swarr, A. (1998). Developmental patterns and gender differences in the experience of peer companionship during adolescence. *Child Development, 69,* 154–163.

Shaver, P., & Hazan, C. (1988). A biased overview of the study of love. *Journal of Social and Personal Relationships, 5,* 473–501.

Shulman, S., & Kipnis, O. (2001). Adolescent romantic relationships: A look from the future. *Journal of Adolescence, 24,* 337–351.

Silverman, J.G., Raj, A., Mucci, L.A., & Hathaway, J.E. (2001). Dating violence against adolescent girls and associated substance use, unhealthy weight control, sexual risk behavior, pregnancy, and suicidality. *Journal of the American Medical Association, 286,* 572–579.

Zimmer-Gembeck, M.J., Siebenbruner, J., & Collins, W.A. (2001). Diverse aspects of dating: Associations with psychosocial functioning from early to middle adolescence. *Journal of Adolescence, 24,* 313–336.

Critical Thinking Questions

1. How did your first romantic relationship influence your subsequent relationships?

2. How have your needs and your abilities to fulfill the needs of others changed since early adolescence?

3. What can we learn about adult relationships by studying adolescent relationships?

4. How are adolescent relationships different from and similar to adult relationships?

This article has been reprinted as it originally appeared in *Current Directions in Psychological Science*. Citation information for this article as originally published appears above.

Regulating the Risks of Closeness:
A Relationship-Specific Sense of Felt Security

Sandra L. Murray[1]
University at Buffalo, State University of New York

Abstract

To feel secure in romantic relationships, people need to believe that their partners see qualities in them that merit attention, nurturance, and care. This article examines how finding (or failing to find) this sense of security affects three facets of romantic life: (a) the inferences people draw about their partners' regard for them in threatening situations, (b) the inferences people draw about their own value in situations in which they feel rejected, and (c) the kinds of behavioral strategies (whether protective of the self or promotive of the relationship) that people adopt to minimize the likelihood of feeling hurt or rejected again.

Keywords

rejection; security; dependence regulation; relationships

"Marriage is like life in this—that it is a field of battle, and not a bed of roses."
—Robert Louis Stevenson, *Virginibus Puerisque*

Just as romantic life is filled with situations that can bolster self-esteem, it is also filled with situations that highlight the risks of rejection and the potential practical and self-esteem costs of depending on another person's fallible good will (Holmes, 2002). When Harry is feeling uncertain of his professional aptitudes, he needs to decide whether to keep his doubts to himself or risk disclosing his doubts to Sally in the hope of eliciting her reassurance. When Harry has broken a promise, Sally must decide whether to risk future disappointment by relying on Harry again for the fulfillment of her needs.

In romantic life, it is situations like these—situations of dependence, in which a partner's responsiveness to one's needs is in question—that most often activate the threat of rejection. In such situations, the choice that best protects against the likelihood and pain of rejection is the choice that minimizes closeness to the partner. When Harry has let Sally down, for example, Sally may decide not to trust Harry's promises anymore, and may reduce her reliance on him for the satisfaction of her goals, to protect herself from feeling rejected or let down by him again. However, such a self-protective choice also compromises Sally's trust in Harry and limits his future opportunities to demonstrate his trustworthiness, thereby putting the well-being of the relationship at greater risk than if she risked trusting him again.

Here, in a nutshell, is the nature of the dilemma that romantic partners face: Thinking and behaving in ways that best protect against the pain of rejection interfere with thinking and behaving in ways that promote closeness. Romantic relationships thus present a central context where two fundamental motives—

the need to protect against the pain of rejection and the need to establish satisfying connections to other people—can frequently conflict. This article provides a thumbnail sketch of the theoretical framework on felt security my colleagues and I have developed to explain how people balance these competing motivations (Murray, Holmes, & Collins, 2004).

WHY IS FELT SECURITY A FUNDAMENTAL MOTIVATION?

People's sense of their own self-worth is bound up in the quality of their relationships with others (Leary & Baumeister, 2000). Even signs of a stranger's rejection can hurt and threaten self-esteem, so some degree of wariness or caution should be expected in romantic relationships. Consequently, the threat of rejection implicit in such relationships will generally activate self-protection concerns, leaving people primed to perceive rejection and hesitant to think or behave in ways that might make the prospect of rejection more likely or more painful (Murray, Holmes, & Griffin, 2000).

To commit to a specific romantic partner, however, people need a strong sense of certainty or clarity of purpose (Murray, 1999). Most relationships, being imperfect, are unlikely to afford this sense of certainty, so people need to overstate the case for commitment to feel connected to their partners. They discount and reframe the very signs of negativity that self-protection motivations seek to highlight. Such leaps of faith are evident in the relationship-promoting ways people think and behave in satisfying and stable romantic relationships.

At a behavioral level, people in satisfying relationships routinely put themselves in situations in which they could be hurt or exploited by their partners. For instance, people in such relationships inhibit their self-protective inclinations to respond in kind to partners' misdeeds, instead responding constructively (Rusbult, Verette, Whitney, Slovik, & Lipkus, 1991). Rather than responding to Sally's criticism with a reciprocal snipe, for instance, a satisfied Harry might instead ask what is troubling her. At the level of interpreting a partner's behavior or traits, people in satisfying relationships attribute their partners' misdeeds to transient features of the situation (Bradbury & Fincham, 1990), and they even see strengths in imperfect partners that are not apparent to the partners themselves (Murray, Holmes, & Griffin, 1996).

The Dependence-Regulation Process

The catch, again, is that thinking and behaving in ways that promote the relationship (i.e. responding constructively, seeing strengths in the partner) and satisfy the need for connectedness also increase the short-term risk and long-term pain of rejection, activating self-protection concerns. For people to put such concerns aside, they need to be able to give themselves some sort of assurance that the risks of rejection are minimal. My colleagues and I believe that a sense of security in a partner's positive regard and caring provides this psychological insurance policy (Murray et al., 2000). To feel safe, people actively regulate or balance dependence with felt security, allowing themselves to risk thinking and behaving in ways that enhance closeness only when they can believe that their partners are motivated to be available and responsive to them.

To feel secure in a specific relationship, people need to believe that their partners see positive qualities in them worth valuing (Murray et al., 2000). Establishing this sense of confidence is likely to be more difficult for some people than others, however. People generally assume that others see them as they see themselves. Accordingly, if Sally sees herself as not particularly smart, or warm, or patient, she is likely to have difficulty believing that Harry sees her any differently. In fact, people with low self-esteem incorrectly assume that their partners see them in the same relatively negative light as they see themselves. In contrast, people with high self-esteem better appreciate their partners' positive regard (Murray et al., 2000).

For people who chronically feel less positively regarded by their partners, the goal of satisfying needs for felt security is likely to be chronically accessible—that is, constantly in mind. The accessibility of this goal sensitizes them to rejection, structuring perception and behavior in specific situations in ways that put a premium on self-protection. In contrast, for people who chronically feel positively regarded by their partners, felt-security goals are likely to be largely satiated, structuring perception and behavior in ways that put a greater premium on relationship promotion. The essence of felt security thus lies in the "if-then" procedural rules or specific cognitive models that are activated automatically and that govern people's attempts to restore a sense of safety in threatening situations (Baldwin, 1992). A similar logic holds in child development: Developmental scholars argue that the quality of a child's attachment to a caregiver is revealed in the behavioral strategies the child adopts to maintain some sense of security in interactions with that caregiver (Sroufe & Waters, 1977).

THE RELATIONAL SIGNATURE OF FELT SECURITY

Figure 1 (see p. 157) illustrates dynamics that are likely to unfold in the course of a given marital interaction for people who chronically feel less positively regarded by their partners. This model emerged from experiments with people in dating relationships, in which my colleagues and I manipulated specific threats to acceptance such as discovering new faults in oneself or becoming aware of a partner's annoyance (Murray, Holmes, Mac-Donald, & Ellsworth, 1998; Murray, Rose, Bellavia, Holmes, & Kusche, 2002); and from a naturalistic study of daily life in married couples (Murray, Bellavia, Rose, & Griffin, 2003; Murray, Griffin, Rose, & Bellavia, 2003). In the latter study, each partner in 154 married couples completed a standardized daily diary for 21 days. Participants indicated which threatening events had occurred that day (e.g., "had a minor disagreement," "partner criticized me") and answered daily questions about self-esteem, about how rejected or accepted they felt by their partners, and about how they felt and behaved toward their partners. In the experiments, we used global self-esteem as a substitute or proxy measure to tap how positively regarded participants felt by their partners. In the diary study, participants described how positively their partners saw them on a series of interpersonal traits, such as warmth or criticalness, as a direct measure of the partner's perceived regard.

Imagine that Sally comes home after being criticized at work and finds Harry in an irritable mood, grumbling about the lack of food in the refrigerator. As Sally needs and wants to feel better about Harry's regard, we would expect her to be in a hypothesis-testing mode, scrutinizing the available evidence (e.g., her work-related self-doubts, Harry's moody behavior) for what it might reveal about his evaluation of her. Rather than brushing off Harry's grumbling as a sign of fatigue, Sally might worry that his mood signifies broader displeasure with her, and she might also fear that disclosing her recent problems at work will only heighten Harry's ire.

Path A in Figure 1 illustrates this hypothesized sensitivity to interpreting threatening events as signs of rejection. Consistent with the hypothesis that people who feel less positively regarded by their partners treat isolated experiences as meaningful data, one study found that people in dating relationships who were low in global self-esteem (and likely to doubt their partners' regard for them) reacted to experimentally induced doubts about their own intelligence or considerateness by expressing greater concerns about their partners' rejection as compared to control participants (Murray et al., 1998). Low-self-esteem participants in another study also reacted to experimentally induced signs of a partner's annoyance or irritation by anticipating rejection (Murray et al., 2002). Similarly, married people who believed (incorrectly) that their partners regarded them relatively negatively on specific interpersonal traits (such as how warm or tolerant they were) felt more rejected on days after they thought their partners had behaved particularly badly or had been in a worse-than-average mood than they did after days low in such perceived threats (Murray, Bellavia, et al., 2003).

As self-esteem is tied to anticipated evaluations by other people (Leary & Baumeister, 2000), perceiving Harry's displeasure should be particularly hurtful or painful for Sally if she feels less positively regarded by Harry. Path B in Figure 1 illustrates this hypothesized sensitivity of self-esteem to rejection. Feeling less than fully valued by Harry, Sally enters any interaction with him with a less-than-fully-stocked reserve of self-esteem in place. Any specific threat of Harry's rejection is a heavy blow because it poses a disproportionately large loss to an already-impoverished self-esteem resource. Analyses of the diary data in the marriage study revealed that people who felt less positively regarded by their partners internalized their partners' perceived rejections, feeling worse about themselves on days after they experienced greater-than-normal levels of anxiety about their partner's rejection than after low-anxiety days (Murray, Griffin, et al., 2003).

How does taking such a hit to self-esteem then affect Sally's capacity to put the needed positive cognitive and behavioral spin on things when she is already feeling acutely rejected? In such situations, Sally's primary motivation is to protect herself from feeling hurt again. Accordingly, she could try to restore a sense of safety by reducing her sense of connection to Harry, thereby inoculating herself against future rejections. Such self-protective efforts might involve privately devaluing Harry's qualities, or lashing out at him in ways that communicate such diminished sentiments. Path C in Figure 1 reflects this defensive-devaluation hypothesis.

In a study supporting this logic, people with low self-esteem reacted to experimentally induced doubts about their partners' acceptance by derogating their partners' traits (Murray et al., 2002). Similarly, when people in the diary study who chronically felt less positively regarded felt acutely rejected by their partners on a particular day, they tended to devalue their partners the next day by treating them more coldly and critically than usual. Unfortunately, these defensive reactions emerged even when the partners had not actually been upset with them. However, once those who felt less positively regarded started behaving badly, their partners did become annoyed with them the next day—suggesting that Sally's self-protective behavior may have the self-fulfilling consequence of annoying Harry (Murray, Griffin, et al., 2003).

Figure 2 illustrates what dynamics are likely to unfold in the course of a specific marital interaction for people who chronically feel highly regarded by their partners. Imagine now that Harry comes home after getting criticized at work and finds Sally in a generally bad mood, grumbling about the lack of food in the refrigerator. Confident of Sally's regard, Harry is not likely to wonder what he did to elicit Sally's apparent upset. Instead, he is likely to see such events in ways that confirm and reinforce his generally positive expectations about Sally's positive regard. Consequently, Harry will readily turn to Sally for comfort and explain away her grumpy behaviors, and he might even tell himself that such foibles are actually a sign of Sally's acceptance and love. Path A in Figure 2 shows this potential benefit of such relationship-promoting perceptions. Indeed, a study showed that people with high self-esteem compensated for failure on a purported intelligence test by exaggerating their partners' love (Murray et al., 1998). Similarly, people in the diary study who chronically felt more positively regarded felt more loved and accepted by their partners on days after they reported higher-than-normal levels of conflict and negative behavior by their partners (and thus, more reason to feel rejected) as compared to low-threat days (Murray, Bellavia, et al., 2003).

In situations in which Sally's behavior is more egregious, and Harry does end up feeling rejected or hurt, the resource of generally feeling valued should lessen the sting of rejection for Harry in a way that allows him to put defending his connection to Sally ahead of self-protection. Paths B through C in Figure 2 represent this relationship-promoting avenue to restoring a sense of safety. Rather than responding to feeling hurt by distancing, people who chronically felt more valued by their partners in the diary study actually reported feeling even closer to their partners on days after they felt more rejected by their partners than they normally did (Murray, Bellavia, et al., 2003).

PRACTICAL AND THEORETICAL IMPLICATIONS

As the findings discussed here illustrate, the dynamics outlined in Figures 1 and 2 can easily be used to explain why people who are troubled by dispositional insecurities, such as low self-esteem, are involved in less satisfying romantic relationships than people who feel more secure (Murray et al., 2000). Because they are chronically thinking about their need for security, people with low self-esteem seem to put self-protection first, thinking and behaving in ways that dull the pain of rejection in the short term but effectively undermine their relationships over the longer term (as illustrated in Fig. 1). Over time, they become less satisfied (and more distressed) because they cannot escape needless doubts about their partners' regard (Murray et al., 2000). In contrast, being more confident of their partners' regard, people with high self-esteem put relationship

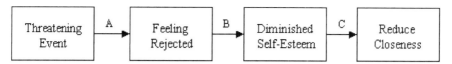

Fig. 1. The dependence-regulation process for people who feel negatively regarded.

promotion first, increasing closeness in response to signs of rejection (as illustrated in Fig. 2).

Apart from explaining why relationship difficulties are more likely for some people than for others, focusing on how feeling positively regarded by one's specific partner resolves the tension between self-protection and connectedness motives has the added benefit of expanding existing perspectives on self-esteem. Interpersonal perspectives on the origins of self-esteem sometimes assume that self-esteem and connectedness motivations are interchangeable (Leary & Baumeister, 2000). Accordingly, when the threat of rejection is salient, people will seek closeness to restore self-esteem. Attachment theory instead assumes that people can respond to rejection anxiety that stems from low self-esteem by either seeking or avoiding closeness (Fraley & Shaver, 2000). The dependence-regulation model integrates these positions by specifying the types of specific expectations that determine whether or not people will be likely to seek greater closeness to the source of perceived rejections or slights.

CONCLUSION

Stevenson's cynicism aside, dating and marital relationships have the potential to be a bed of roses. Whether this potential is realized may depend on the strategies intimates adopt to balance the tension between their need for self-protection and their need for connectedness. When people are able to quell their concerns

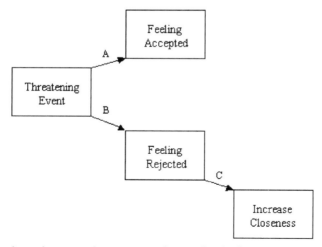

Fig. 2. The dependence-regulation process for people who feel positively regarded.

about self-protection, they are free to think and behave in ways that create the kinds of bonds that will satisfy their need for connectedness (and bolster their self-esteem). When people cannot escape the need for self-protective caution, however, they set the stage for cycles of negative interactions that are likely to erode their relationships (and, in turn, their self-esteem). Until now, the ways in which these motivational conflicts play out have received little conceptual or empirical attention. This area is a promising one for future research.

Recommended Reading

Baldwin, M.W. (1992). (See References)
Holmes, J.G. (2002). (See References)
Leary, M.R., & Baumeister, R.F. (2000). (See References)
Murray, S.L., Bellavia, G., Rose, P., & Griffin, D. (2003). (See References)

Acknowledgments—Preparation of this article was supported by the National Science Foundation (SBR 9817282) and National Institutes of Mental Health (MH 60105-02).

Note

1. Address correspondence to Sandra Murray, Psychology Department, Park Hall, State University of New York, Buffalo, NY 14260–4110; e-mail: smurray@buffalo.edu.

References

Baldwin, M.W. (1992). Relational schemas and the processing of social information. *Psychological Bulletin, 112,* 461–484.
Bradbury, T.N., & Fincham, F.D. (1990). Attributions in marriage: Review and critique. *Psychological Bulletin, 107,* 3–23.
Fraley, R.C., & Shaver, P.R. (2000). Adult romantic attachment: Theoretical developments, emerging controversies, and unanswered questions. *Review of General Psychology, 4,* 132–154.
Holmes, J.G. (2002). Interpersonal expectations as the building blocks of social cognition: An interdependence theory perspective. *Personal Relationships, 9,* 1–26.
Leary, M.R., & Baumeister, R.F. (2000). The nature and function of self-esteem: Sociometer theory. In M.P. Zanna (Ed.), *Advances in experimental social psychology* (Vol. 32. pp. 2–51). San Diego, CA: Academic Press.
Murray, S.L. (1999). The quest for conviction: Motivated cognition in romantic relationships. *Psychological Inquiry, 10,* 23–34.
Murray, S.L., Bellavia, G., Rose, P., & Griffin, D. (2003). Once hurt, twice hurtful: How perceived regard regulates daily marital interaction. *Journal of Personality and Social Psychology, 84,* 126–147.
Murray, S.L., Griffin, D.W., Rose, P., & Bellavia, G. (2003). Calibrating the sociometer: The relational contingencies of self-esteem. *Journal of Personality and Social Psychology, 85,* 63–84.
Murray, S.L., Holmes, J.G., & Collins, N.L. (2004). The relational signature of felt security. Unpublished manuscript, University at Buffalo, SUNY.
Murray, S.L., Holmes, J.G., & Griffin, D. (1996). The benefits of positive illusions: Idealization and the construction of satisfaction in close relationships. *Journal of Personality and Social Psychology, 70,* 79–98.
Murray, S.L., Holmes, J.G., & Griffin, D.W. (2000). Self-esteem and the quest for felt security: How perceived regard regulates attachment processes. *Journal of Personality and Social Psychology, 78,* 478–498.
Murray, S.L., Holmes, J.G., MacDonald, G., & Ellsworth, P. (1998). Through the looking glass darkly? When self-doubts turn into relationship insecurities. *Journal of Personality and Social Psychology, 75,* 1459–1480.

Murray, S.L., Rose, P., Bellavia, G., Holmes, J., & Kusche, A. (2002). When rejection stings: How self-esteem constrains relationship-enhancement processes. *Journal of Personality and Social Psychology, 83,* 556–573.

Rusbult, C.E., Verette, J., Whitney, G.A., Slovik, L.F., & Lipkus, I. (1991). Accommodation processes in close relationships: Theory and preliminary research evidence. *Journal of Personality and Social Psychology, 60,* 53–78.

Sroufe, L.A., & Waters, E. (1977). Attachment as an organizational construct. *Child Development, 48,* 1184–1199.

Stevenson, R.L. (1996, January). *Virginibus Puerisque* (pt. 1). Retrieved April 6, 2005, from http://www.gutenberg.org/dirs/etext96/virpr10.txt

Critical Thinking Questions

1. Think of a time when you took a risk to promote your relationship and a time when you protected yourself. Why did you make each decision?

2. In addition to qualities of the self (e.g., self-esteem), what other qualities of a person might lead one to take risks or to protect oneself?

3. Are there times when people should protect themselves rather than promote their relationships?

4. Compared to a non-romantic relationship, does a romantic relationship offer unique risks to the self? Does it offer greater payoffs for the self in return?

This article has been reprinted as it originally appeared in *Current Directions in Psychological Science*. Citation information for this article as originally published appears above.

Psychological Foundations of Trust

Jeffry A. Simpson[1]

University of Minnesota, Twin Cities Campus

Abstract

Trust lies at the foundation of nearly all major theories of interpersonal relationships. Despite its great theoretical importance, a limited amount of research has examined how and why trust develops, is maintained, and occasionally unravels in relationships. Following a brief overview of theoretical and empirical milestones in the interpersonal-trust literature, an integrative process model of trust in dyadic relationships is presented.

Keywords

trust; interdependence; strain tests; felt security

Trust: "confidence that [one] will find what is desired [from another] rather than what is feared." (Deutsch, 1973, p.148)

Trust involves the juxtaposition of people's loftiest hopes and aspirations with their deepest worries and fears. It may be the single most important ingredient for the development and maintenance of happy, well-functioning relationships. Several major theories, including attachment theory (Bowlby, 1969) and Erikson's (1963) theory of psychosocial development, are built on the premise that higher levels of trust in relationships early in life lay the psychological foundation for happier and better-functioning relationships in adulthood. Tooby and Cosmides (1996) claim that trust-relevant emission and detection mechanisms should have evolved in humans, given the importance of gauging accurately the intentions of others.

Considering the centrality of trust in relationships across the lifespan, one might expect the topic would have received widespread theoretical and empirical attention. Surprisingly, it has not. Although there have been significant pockets of theory (e.g., Holmes & Rempel, 1989) and research (e.g., Mikulincer, 1998; Rempel, Holmes, & Zanna, 1985) on the subject, relatively little is known about how and why interpersonal trust develops, is maintained, and unravels when betrayed.

Why has trust received such limited attention? To begin with, trust is a complex, multidimensional construct, making it difficult to operationalize, measure, and interpret. Second, trust can be construed in different ways, and it might have varying importance at different stages of relationship development. Third, trust emerges and changes in situations that are difficult to observe and study, such as in "strain test" situations (Holmes, 1981). In strain-test situations, one individual is highly outcome dependent on his or her partner, but the actions that would promote the individual's own interests differ from those that would benefit the partner. For example, if Chris desperately needs Susan's help to complete an important task and Susan willingly helps despite the fact that doing so impedes what she really wants or needs to accomplish, Susan has "passed" a strain test and, accordingly, Chris should trust her more.

In this article, I first discuss major theoretical and empirical accounts of interpersonal trust from which four basic principles can be distilled. I then describe a new process model of dyadic trust that integrates these principles.

THEORETICAL AND EMPIRICAL CONCEPTUALIZATIONS OF TRUST

Historically, there have been two main approaches to conceptualizing interpersonal trust. The earliest work adopted a dispositional (person-centered) view. According to this perspective, trust entails general beliefs and attitudes about the degree to which other people are likely to be reliable, cooperative, or helpful in experimental game situations (Deutsch, 1973) or in daily-life contexts (Rotter, 1971). Beginning in the early 1980s, conceptualizations and measures of trust started to focus on specific partners and relationships (Holmes & Rempel, 1989; Rempel et al., 1985). According to the dyadic (interpersonal) perspective, trust is a psychological state or orientation of an actor (the truster) toward a specific partner (the trustee) with whom the actor is in some way interdependent (that is, the truster needs the trustee's cooperation to attain valued outcomes or resources). What makes trust particularly difficult to study is that it involves three components (e.g., "I trust *you* to do *X*"; Hardin, 2003). Thus, trust is a function of properties of the self (I), the specific partner (you), and the specific goal in a current situation (to do X).

Kramer and Carnevale (2001) argue that trust involves a set of beliefs and expectations that a partner's actions will be beneficial to one's long-term self-interest, especially in situations in which the partner must be counted on to provide unique benefits or valuable outcomes. Trust-relevant situations typically activate two cognitive processes: (a) feelings of vulnerability; and (b) expectations of how the partner is likely to behave across time, particularly in strain-test situations. When the partner promotes the individual's best interests rather than his or her own, both parties should experience heightened trust. Trust is also likely to be higher in a relationship when (a) each member's self-interested outcomes match those that are best for their partner or the relationship, or (b) both members believe that their partner will act on what is best for the relationship even when the members' personal self-interests diverge.

Kelley et al. (2003) claim that trust can be assessed in certain interpersonal situations. Trust situations involve the configuration of high interdependence (such that the actions of each partner strongly impact the other), a blend of rules for coordination and exchange that sustain interdependence, and moderately corresponding interests (see Kelley et al., 2003, for further details). One prototypical trust situation is depicted in Figure 1. In this situation, trust should be facilitated when partners in a relationship repeatedly make A1/B1 (i.e., mutually beneficial) decisions that yield maximum rewards for both individuals.[2]

Most previous research on interpersonal trust has been guided by dispositional or interpersonal perspectives. Dispositionally oriented work has revealed

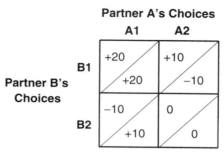

Partner A's Choices

		A1	A2
Partner B's Choices	**B1**	+20 / +20	+10 / −10
	B2	−10 / +10	0 / 0

Fig. 1. The payoffs (outcomes) in Kelley et al.'s (2003) trust situation. Payoffs above the diagonal in each cell are for Partner A; those below the diagonal are for Partner B. If both partners choose option 1 (e.g., they work together on a difficult but important task, reflected in the A1/B1 cell), each partner receives 20 units of benefit because the task gets done and partners enjoy each other's company. If both partners select option 2 (neither works on the task, represented by the A2/B2 cell), neither partner receives benefits because nothing gets accomplished. If partner A chooses option 2 (not to work on the task: A2) whereas partner B chooses option 1 (works solo on the task: B1), partner A benefits by 10 units because progress is made on the task, but partner B experiences a net loss of 10 units because he or she is saddled with all the work. The reverse pattern exists when partner A chooses A1 (to work on the task) and partner B chooses B2 (to not work on the task). Trust situations have three special properties: First, they involve collective rationality in that cooperative behavior by both partners (A1/B1) always yields better outcomes than when partners fail to cooperate (A1/B2 or A2/B1). Second, the best outcome always occurs when both partners make the cooperative choice (A1/B1). Third, cooperative choices are risky, because if one's partner decides to make a noncooperative choice, the cooperative choice generates the worst possible outcomes because one has been exploited.

that individuals who are more insecurely attached, have lower self-esteem, or have more poorly differentiated self-concepts (i.e., self-concepts that are less diversified, more imbalanced, and poorly tied together) trust their relationship partners less (see Simpson, 2007, for a review). Interpersonally oriented work has confirmed that trust is typically higher when individuals believe their partners are more committed to the relationship and have more benevolent intentions and motivations. It is also higher when partners regularly display prorelationship transformations of motivation (that is, turn initial gut-level negative reactions to caustic partner behaviors into constructive responses that benefit the relationship), which then generate self-sacrificial or accommodative behaviors. Research testing Holmes and Rempel's (1989) dyadic model of trust has also indicated that the development of trust involves a process of uncertainty reduction as individuals move from having confidence in their partner's general predictability to having confidence in their prorelationship values, motives, goals, and intentions (Holmes & Rempel, 1989).

Based on a recent review of the interpersonal trust literature (Simpson, 2007), four core principles of interpersonal trust stand out.

First, individuals gauge the degree to which they can trust their partners by observing whether partners display proper transformation of motivation in *trust-diagnostic* situations (that is, in trust or strain-test situations in which partners make decisions that go against their own personal self-interest and support the best interests of the individual or the relationship).

Second, trust-diagnostic situations often occur naturally and unintentionally during the ebb and flow of everyday life. Depending on situational circumstances, however, individuals may enter, transform, or occasionally create trust-diagnostic situations to test whether their current level of trust in a partner is warranted.

Third, individual differences in attachment orientations, self-esteem, or self-differentiation (i.e., working models of self and others as relationship partners) should affect the growth or decline of trust over time in relationships. People who are more securely attached, have higher self-esteem, or have more differentiated self-concepts should be more likely to experience trust as well as increases in trust in relationships across time.

Fourth, neither the level nor the trajectory of trust in relationships can be fully understood without considering the dispositions and actions of *both* relationship partners, especially in trust-diagnostic situations.

A DYADIC MODEL OF TRUST

A model of how these core principles may be linked together in dyadic social interactions is shown in Figure 2. The Dyadic Model of Trust in Relationships (Simpson, 2007) contains both normative (typical) and individual-difference components. The normative components are depicted in the five boxes (constructs) in the middle of the figure. The individual-difference components reflect the relevant dispositions of each relationship partner (e.g., attachment orientations, self-esteem, self-differentiation) and their connections to each normative construct. Feedback loops from the final normative construct in the model (each partner's degree of felt security following an interaction) to the construct that launches future trust-relevant interactions (each partner's decision regarding whether or not to enter the next trust-relevant situation) are not shown, but are presumed to exist. According to the model, each individual's perceptions of his or her own and the partner's standing on each construct are necessary to explain and understand what happens for each partner further along in the model.

The model assumes that information about the relevant dispositions of *both* partners is essential to understanding and explaining the growth of trust—or lack thereof—in a relationship across many interactions. The dispositional tendencies discussed above should motivate or enable individuals to enter, transform, and occasionally create social interactions that enhance trust over time. Two types of situations should give individuals a particularly good opportunity to gauge the level of trust warranted in a partner or relationship: (a) *trust situations* (Kelley et al., 2003), in which partners can repeatedly make or fail to make A1/B1 (i.e., mutually beneficial) decisions (see Fig. 1); and (b) strain-test situations (Holmes, 1981), in which partners can demonstrate or fail to demonstrate their willingness to make personal sacrifices for the good of the partner or relationship. Before trust-diagnostic situations can be entered, transformed, or created, however, one or both partners must have enough confidence to take the interpersonal risks necessary to confirm or reaffirm that the partner *can* be

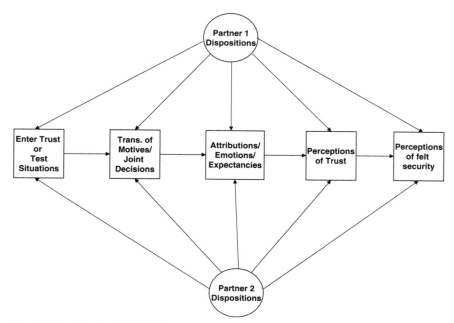

Fig. 2. The Dyadic Model of Trust in Relationships (Simpson, 2007). Individuals who have certain dispositions (positive working models) should be more likely to enter, transform, or occasionally create trust-diagnostic situations in their relationships. When encountered, such situations should provide good opportunities for these individuals to experience relationship-enhancing transformations of motivation, which should increase their willingness to enter mutually beneficial decisions (promoting the goals of the partner and/or the relationship over the self). If both partners make mutually beneficial decisions, this should generate positive patterns of attributions, emotions, and future expectancies, which in turn should enhance perceptions of trust and felt security, at least temporarily. The working models of each partner in the relationship are likely to affect outcomes at each stage of the model. Feedback loops from the final construct in the model (each partner's perceived degree of felt security) to the construct that launches future trust-relevant interactions (each partner's decision whether or not to enter, transform, or create the next trust-relevant situation) are not depicted, but are presumed to exist.

trusted. People who have more positive working models should be more inclined to take these risks and leaps of faith.

Once in trust-diagnostic situations, individuals who display the transformation of motivation necessary to make decisions that benefit the partner or relationship at some cost to the self should experience greater trust and felt security. Partners who have more positive working models ought to display partner- or relationship-based transformations more often and more extensively. Consequently, they should be more motivated and capable of steering trust-relevant social interactions toward mutually beneficial decisions. Once such decisions have been made, working models should influence how individuals interpret the amount of transformation that the self and the partner have undergone. Those who have more positive working models may grant themselves and their partners "fuller credit" for each partner's willingness to prioritize partner or relationship outcomes over egocentric interests, whereas the reverse should be true of those who harbor more negative models (Murray, Holmes, & Collins, 2006).

This process should then trigger benevolent attributions of one's own and the partner's relationship motives. For example, after Susan makes a major personal sacrifice to help Chris complete his important task, Chris should infer that he needs and values Susan and the relationship and that she genuinely cares about him. Such attributions may result in more constructive problem solving, more adaptive emotion regulation, and/or more optimistic expectations about future trust-diagnostic interactions. Patterns of attribution, emotion regulation, and situation-specific expectancies are presented in a single box in Figure 2 because the temporal order of these processes may depend on specific aspects of the inter-action, the working models of each partner, or unique properties of the relation-ship. These positive outcomes, in turn, should increase perceptions of trust, which should elevate felt security at least temporarily. At this point, positive working mod-els might further boost perceptions of trust and felt security. These perceptions should then set up the next trust-relevant interaction, determining whether or when the next trust situation or strain test is entered, transformed, or created.

In many instances, individuals enter, transform, or create trust or strain-test situations without forethought or deliberation. Deliberate attempts to create such situations should occur when important, unexpected, or suspicious events lead people to question whether they can truly trust their partners. Though potentially very diagnostic, premeditated tests probably are conducted rather infrequently.

Over time, individuals who repeatedly experience mutually beneficial out-comes with their partners should begin to perceive greater "added value" (see Fig. 1), especially in trust-diagnostic situations. These repeated outcomes may encourage individuals and their partners to engage in further relationship-sustaining or rela-tionship-building acts (e.g., disparaging attractive alternative partners, perceiving the partner in an overly positive light) that might increase the likelihood of more mutually beneficial decisions and outcomes in the future. These effects should diminish, however, if one or both partners have negative working models, repeat-edly decide not to enter into mutually beneficial agreements, or harbor negative attributions regarding their partner's overarching relationship motives.

This raises an interesting paradox. Early in relationships, greater transforma-tion of motivation by both members should be a good barometer of the level of trust that is warranted in a partner or the relationship, especially when both indi-viduals are equally dependent on each other for unique or important outcomes (Holmes & Rempel, 1989) or have similar levels of vulnerability or commitment (Wieselquist, Rusbult, Foster, & Agnew, 1999). As relationships progress, how-ever, most individuals incorporate (merge) their partners and relationships with their own self-concepts. This means that less transformation of motivation should take place in well-established relationships. Couples in long-term relationships, therefore, may occasionally need to identify new trust-diagnostic situations in which each individual's self-interests start out being discrepant from what might be best for his or her partner or the relationship. If partners jointly reaffirm that they are still willing to undergo large transformations when new trust-diagnostic situations arise, this should sustain or increase trust even in longstanding pairs.

FUTURE DIRECTIONS AND CONCLUSIONS

Our knowledge of how trust is generated, sustained, and compromised in relationships remains surprisingly limited. Future theory and research would profit from addressing the following issues. First, we need to gain a better understanding of how the dispositions and behaviors of both individuals in a relationship affect how they think, feel, and behave in trust-relevant situations. Second, research should explore how and why certain combinations of partner attributes promote or impede the development and maintenance of trust. For example, relationships in which one partner has much more power than the other could hinder the development of trust if the powerful person self-servingly takes advantage of the less powerful partner, yet this combination could generate high levels of trust if the high-power partner continually forgoes his or her best self-interest for the best interest of the low-power partner. Third, we need to determine whether the normative component of the Dyadic Model of Trust in Relationships holds with equal effect at different stages of relationship development. Fourth, we need to know more about how normative processes and individual differences reciprocally influence one another over time, particularly in trust-relevant situations. Fifth, we need to disentangle the constructs and processes depicted in the middle box of the model (attributions/emotions/expectancies). Sixth, we must learn more about the roles played by factors critical to the development of intimacy—such as feeling understood, validated, and cared for by one's partner—in fostering trust and felt security (Reis & Shaver, 1988), especially when they occur in trust-relevant interactions. Finally, we need to know more about when and how perceptions of "added value" arise.

In conclusion, there are few constructs in psychology that are more central to interpersonal functioning and outcomes than trust. Indeed, many of the principles discussed in this article might apply to other social contexts and relationships, including coworker relationships, business negotiations, and perhaps even interactions between political groups. Whether the model and psychological processes discussed above extend beyond the realm of close relationships remains unknown. Nevertheless, for the science of relationships to advance, we must gain a deeper and more complete understanding of how trust emerges, changes, is maintained, and declines in different types of relationships across time.

Recommended Reading

Holmes, J.G., & Rempel, J.K. (1989). (See References)
Kelley, H.H., Holmes, J.G., Kerr, N.L., Reis, H.T., Rusbult, C.E., & Van Lange, P.A.M. (2003). (See References)
Ostrom, E., & Walker, J. (Eds.). (2003). *Trust and reciprocity: Interdisciplinary lessons from experimental research.* New York: Russell Sage Foundation.
Simpson, J.A. (2007). (See References)

Acknowledgments—The writing of the article was supported in part by National Institute of Mental Health Grant MH49599-05.

Notes

1. Address correspondence to Jeffry A. Simpson, Department of Psychology, University of Minnesota, Minneapolis, MN 55455-0344; e-mail: simps108@umn.edu.

2. In contrast to Prisoner's Dilemma games in which decision making is independent of the partner, partners in established relationships often engage in joint decision making in which separate (totally independent) action may not be realistic. See Kelley et al. (2003) for how game outcomes involving established partners can be interpreted.

References

Bowlby, J. (1969). *Attachment and loss: Vol. 1. Attachment*. New York: Basic Books.

Deutsch, M. (1973). *The resolution of conflict*. New Haven, CT: Yale University Press.

Erikson, E. (1963). *Childhood and society*. New York: Norton.

Hardin, R. (2003). Gaming trust. In E. Ostrom & J. Walker (Eds.), *Trust and reciprocity: Interdisciplinary lessons from experimental research* (pp. 80–101). New York: Russell Sage Foundation.

Holmes, J.G. (1981). The exchange process in close relationships: Microbehavior and macromotives. In M.J. Lerner & S.C. Lerner (Eds.), *The justice motive in social behavior* (pp. 261–284). New York: Plenum.

Holmes, J.G., & Rempel, J.K. (1989). Trust in close relationships. In C. Hendrick (Ed.), *Close relationships* (pp. 187–220). Newbury Park, CA: Sage.

Kelley, H.H., Holmes, J.G., Kerr, N.L., Reis, H.T., Rusbult, C.E., & Van Lange, P.A.M. (2003). *An atlas of interpersonal situations*. New York: Cambridge University Press.

Kramer, R.M., & Carnevale, P.J. (2001). Trust and intergroup negotiation. In R. Brown & S. Gaertner (Eds.), *Blackwell handbook of social psychology: Intergroup processes* (pp. 431–450). Malden, MA: Blackwell Publishers.

Mikulincer, M. (1998). Attachment working models and the sense of trust: An exploration of interaction goals and affect regulation. *Journal of Personality and Social Psychology, 74*, 1209–1224.

Murray, S.L., Holmes, J.G., & Collins, N.L. (2006). Optimizing assurance: The risk regulation system in relationships. *Psychological Bulletin, 132*, 641–666.

Reis, H.T., & Shaver, P.R. (1988). Intimacy as an interpersonal process. In S.W. Duck (Ed.), *Handbook of personal relationships* (pp. 367–389). Chichester, England: Wiley.

Rempel, J.K., Holmes, J.G., & Zanna, M.P. (1985). Trust in close relationships. *Journal of Personality and Social Psychology, 49*, 95–112.

Rotter, J.B. (1971). Generalized expectancies of interpersonal trust. *American Psychologist, 26*, 443–452.

Simpson, J.A. (2007). Foundations of interpersonal trust. In A.W. Kruglanski & E.T. Higgins (Eds.), *Social psychology: Handbook of basic principles* (2nd ed., pp. 587–607). New York: Guilford.

Tooby, J., & Cosmides, L. (1996). Friendship and the banker's paradox: Other pathways to the evolution of adaptations for altruism. *Proceedings of the British Academy, 88*, 119–143.

Wieselquist, J., Rusbult, C.E., Foster, C.A., & Agnew, C.R. (1999). Commitment, pro-relationship behavior, and trust in close relationships. *Journal of Personality and Social Psychology, 77*, 942–966.

Critical Thinking Questions

1. What qualities of a person are likely to make him or her more trusting?

2. What qualities of a partner are likely to make him or her more worthy of trust?

3. Even a partner in a relationship initially characterized by high levels of trust sometimes loses that trust. How/why does that happen?

4. Is it more harmful to be more trusting than one should or to be less trusting than one should?

This article has been reprinted as it originally appeared in *Current Directions in Psychological Science*. Citation information for this article as originally published appears above.

Ideal Standards in Close Relationships: Their Structure and Functions

Garth J.O. Fletcher[1] and Jeffry A. Simpson

Department of Psychology, University of Canterbury, Christchurch, New Zealand (G.J.O.F.), and Department of Psychology, Texas A&M University, College Station, Texas (J.A.S.)

Abstract

This article describes the Ideals Standards Model, which deals with the content and functions of partner and relationship ideals in intimate relationships. This model proposes that there are three distinct categories of partner ideals (warmth-loyalty, vitality-attractiveness, and status-resources), and that ideals have three distinct functions (evaluation, explanation, and regulation). The model also explains how perceived discrepancies between ideals and perceptions of one's current partner or relationship can have different consequences, depending on which of two motivating forces is active (the need to see the partner or relationship positively or the need to be accurate). Recent empirical studies that support some of the main features of the model are described.

Keywords

ideals; functions; discrepancies; relationships

How do people know whether they are in a good or a bad intimate relationship? On what basis do people decide whether to become more involved, live together, get married, or look for another mate? One answer to such questions is that judgments about a particular relationship might be based on the consistency between ideal standards, on the one hand, and perceptions of the current partner or relationship, on the other. This idea is in common currency in folk wisdom but has received relatively little attention in the scientific literature. Our research and theoretical program over the past few years has confirmed that ideal standards do serve as pivotal knowledge structures in close relationships. However, it has also suggested that the psychological processes through which ideal standards operate are complex.

THE IDEALS STANDARDS MODEL

Relationship and partner ideals are central components of the social mind that people use to guide and regulate their interpersonal worlds. According to our Ideals Standards Model (Simpson, Fletcher, & Campbell, in press), partner and relationship ideals may predate—and causally influence—important judgments and decisions in relationships. These ideals comprise three interlocking components: perceptions of the self, the partner, and the relationship. For example, a person's partner ideal of "handsome and warm" represents a personally held ideal that specifies what the individual hopes and desires (the self), describes a hypothetical other (the partner), and specifies what the ideal would be like in an intimate relationship with the self (the relationship).

According to our model, partner and relationship ideals should be based around three evaluative dimensions: (a) warmth, commitment, and intimacy; (b) health, passion, and attractiveness; and (c) status and resources. We derived these predictions from recent evolutionary models which suggest that each of these dimensions represents a different "route" to obtaining a mate and promoting one's own reproductive fitness (see Gangestad & Simpson, in press). For example, by being attentive to a partner's capacity for intimacy and commitment, an individual should increase his or her chances of finding a cooperative, committed partner who is likely to be a devoted parent. By focusing on attractiveness and health, an individual is likely to acquire a mate who is younger, healthier, and perhaps more fertile (especially in the case of men choosing women). And by considering a partner's resources and status, an individual should be more likely to obtain a mate who can ascend social hierarchies and form coalitions with other people who have—or can acquire—valued social status or other resources.

Why do people not "want it all" in terms of their ideals, seeking out mates who are incredibly attractive, rich, and warm? First, relatively few people fit such a stellar description. Second, most people could not attract such a person, even if one were available. Third, even if someone succeeded in attracting such a paragon, it might be difficult to keep him or her. In short, people must normally make trade-offs between these attributes when deciding whom to date or marry.

Our Ideals Standards Model proposes that partner and relationship ideals serve three functions: evaluation, explanation, and regulation. More specifically, the size of discrepancies between ideal standards and perceptions of the current partner or relationship should be used by individuals to (a) estimate and evaluate the quality of their partners and relationships (e.g., assess the appropriateness of potential or current partners or relationships), (b) explain or provide an understanding of relationship events (e.g., give causal accounts explaining relationship satisfaction, problems, or conflicts), and (c) regulate and make adjustments in their relationships (e.g., predict and possibly control current partners or relationships).

Many relationship theorists have proposed that people need to idealize and enhance their romantic partners and relationships. Indeed, there is good evidence that individuals often do perceive their partners and relationships in an excessively positive, Pollyanna-ish light, and that the tendency to idealize one's partner is associated with greater relationship satisfaction and lower rates of dissolution (see Murray & Holmes, 1996).

It is not difficult to understand why people are motivated to idealize their partners and relationships. To begin with, the costs of relationship conflict and dissolution should motivate most individuals to perceive their partners and relationships in the best possible light. From a rational standpoint, most people know that approximately 50% of marriages end in divorce, at least in Western countries. Despite this realization, the vast majority of people get married and have children at some point in their lives. Committing to a long-term relationship, therefore, requires a leap of faith and a level of confidence that may well be difficult to justify on purely rational grounds. As a result, psychological pressures to make charitable and benevolent judgments about one's partner and relationship must be strong to counteract these forces. This might explain the potency of the enhancement motive in most relationships.

Thomas Huxley (1884) once lamented that "the great tragedy of Science [is] the slaying of a beautiful hypothesis by an ugly fact" (p. 244). In this case, the beautiful hypothesis is the presumed pervasiveness and dominance of the relationship-enhancement motive. The ugly fact is that the vast majority of romantic relationships eventually break up. This latter fact suggests that the relationship-enhancement motive is often either inoperative or displaced by other basic motives in certain contexts.

Our model proposes that partner and relationship idealization will sometimes conflict with the goal of being accurate, especially when the effective prediction, explanation, and control of partners and relationships become important. Attempting to accurately understand and attribute motives and beliefs to others should be highly adaptive in certain situations (such as when deciding whether or not to start or remain in a relationship, or when deciding how best to predict or control the behavior of others). Indeed, evolutionary pressures should have selected humans to ascertain and face the truth—no matter how bleak and depressing—in situations in which it was dangerous or extremely costly to do otherwise.

How can the coexistence of these two contrasting motives be reconciled? We believe that both enhancement and accuracy motives operate, but under different conditions. Relationship interactions that are highly threatening ought to increase the power of esteem-maintenance goals, subverting accurate attributions about the partner or the relationship. However, when the need to make accurate, unbiased judgments becomes critical in relationships (such as when individuals must decide whether or not to date someone, get married, or have a child), the accuracy motive should take precedence. When couples settle into a comfortable relationship phase of maintenance, the enhancement motive should once again become ascendant.

These contrasting motives have important implications for understanding the consequences of discrepancies between ideals and perceptions of the current partner or relationship. For example, when enhancement motives predominate, people should try to reduce ideal-perception discrepancies (and, thus, improve the evaluations that stem from them) by using cognitive strategies that involve rationalizing inconsistencies, altering attributions, or changing what they value in their partner or relationship. We suspect that such processes often occur automatically and largely outside of conscious awareness. However, in situations that demand greater accuracy (e.g., when important relationship decisions must be made, when attractive alternative partners become available, or when difficult relationship problems arise), moderate to large ideal-perception discrepancies should motivate individuals to engage in more in-depth analysis and information processing. To reduce discrepancies, accuracy-motivated individuals are likely to use behavioral strategies, perhaps attempting to change their own or their partners' behavior. If individuals eventually come to the conclusion that the discrepancies are important but simply cannot be reduced, they may leave the relationship, look for new partners, or seek solace in other activities.

EMPIRICAL EVIDENCE FOR THE MODEL

We currently are testing some of our model's basic postulates. We initially set out to identify the structure and content of partner and relationship ideals (Fletcher,

Simpson, Thomas, & Giles, 1999). Adopting an inductive approach to identifying the ideals dimensions that people spontaneously use, in a first study we asked men and women to list all the traits or characteristics that described their ideal romantic partners and their ideal romantic relationships.

In a second study, another sample of men and women then rated the 78 items gathered in the first study in terms of perceived importance for their own standards concerning ideal partners and ideal relationships (using 7-point scales where 1 = *very unimportant* and 7 = *very important*). In order to determine the underlying structure of the perceived-importance ratings of the ideals, we carried out two exploratory factor analyses. A factor analysis of the ideal-partner items revealed the three factors we expected: (a) partner characteristics relevant to intimacy, warmth, trust, and loyalty; (b) personality and appearance characteristics concerning how attractive, energetic, and healthy the partner is; and (c) characteristics relevant to the partner's social status and resources. The ideal-relationship items produced two factors that resembled two of the partner-based ideals: (a) the importance of intimacy, loyalty, and stability in a relationship and (b) the importance of excitement and passion in a relationship. The results of the factor analyses (the correlation, or loading, of each item on each factor) were used to assess which items belonged to which factors. We then summed the scores for items belonging to each factor, separately for each participant, to produce five separate scores representing the perceived importance of each general ideal category. Additional analyses and studies have confirmed the reliability and validity of these derived measures of the five factors.

The final study we reported (Fletcher, Simpson, Thomas, & Giles, 1999) tested a basic postulate of our model—that individuals evaluate their current partners and relationships by comparing them against their ideal standards. To test this hypothesis, we asked a new sample of men and women to rank the importance of various ideal attributes and also to report their perceptions of their current partner or relationship on items taken from the ideal-partner and ideal-relationship scales. In addition, we asked subjects to rate how satisfied they were with their relationships. As predicted, individuals who reported smaller discrepancies between their ideal standards and their perceptions of the current partner and relationship rated their relationships more favorably.

Although these studies provided initial support for our model, they were cross-sectional in design and, therefore, could not test for possible causal relationships. To address this issue, we conducted a longitudinal study (Fletcher, Simpson, & Thomas, 1999). A large sample of individuals in newly formed dating relationships completed a battery of measures assessing perceptions of their current partner or relationship, the quality of their relationship, and their ideal standards once a month for 3 months, and then at 12 months after the beginning of the relationship. The first measurement typically occurred 3 weeks after individuals had started dating someone.

As predicted, greater consistency between ideals and perceptions of the current partner or relationship (assessed at earlier times in the relationship) predicted increases in relationship satisfaction over time. Indeed, how closely partners matched individuals' ideals during the first month of dating strongly predicted how individuals felt about their relationships a full 12 months after the dating started. However, also as expected, higher initial levels of relationship satisfaction did not predict changes in levels of consistency between ideals and perceptions. These results suggest that cognitive comparisons between ideal standards and perceptions of the current partner or relationship are firmly in the cognitive driving seat in the initial stages of dating relationships.

We are currently investigating how self-perceptions, along with the flexibility of ideal standards, are related to how individuals set their ideal standards (Campbell, Simpson, Kashy, & Fletcher, in press). The higher that individuals set their ideal standards, the more demanding they are in terms of how closely they expect their partners to match their ideal standards. Although this may seem paradoxical, it is understandable in terms of other results showing that individuals with more positive self-views (e.g., on the vitality-attractiveness dimension) also possess both higher ideal standards and less flexible ideal standards. For example, if a man perceives himself as very fit and highly attractive, he can set high expectations for obtaining a partner who is also highly fit and attractive. Moreover, if the chosen partner subsequently turns into a "couch potato" and gains weight, and this change is monitored by the man, then he is in a strong position to look for—and possibly find—an alternative partner who meets his exacting standards.

Many intriguing and important questions remain to be investigated. First, our theorizing concerning the different functions of relationship-enhancement and accuracy motives remains speculative. Second, we still know relatively little about how individuals establish and adjust their ideal standards over time. Third, and perhaps most important, there is a need to understand and research how ideals function and change within their natural home—the dyadic relationship. We know very little, for instance, about how ideal standards are communicated to the partner, or what happens when one partner is motivated to be accurate when the other partner is motivated to enhance the relationship. We also know almost nothing about whether possessing ideal standards that are similar to those held by one's partner facilitates a relationship's functioning and quality, or how partners might influence one another concerning the perceived importance of particular ideals.

CONCLUSION

It is hard to think of another domain in social life in which the needs for prediction, control, and explanation are more pressing than in intimate relationships. The research and theory we have reported here are part of a burgeoning area within social psychology that is examining social cognition in close relationships. For years, it has been assumed that judgments and perceptions of relationships depend mainly on the nature of the individuals and interactions involved. Our research shows that there exist hidden "third parties"—mental images of ideal partners and ideal relationships—that also play a critical role in influencing judgments about relationships.

Recommended Reading

Fletcher, G.J.O., Simpson, J.A., Thomas, G., & Giles, L. (1999). (See References)
Fletcher, G.J.O., & Thomas, G. (1996). Lay theories in close relationships: Their structure and function. In G.J.O. Fletcher & J. Fitness (Eds.), *Knowledge structures in close relationships: A social psychological approach* (pp. 3–24). Mahwah, NJ: Erlbaum.
Murray, S.L., & Holmes, J.G. (1996). (See References)
Simpson, J.A., Fletcher, G.J.O., & Campbell, L.J. (in press). (See References)

Note

1. Address correspondence to either Garth Fletcher, Department of Psychology, University of Canterbury, Christchurch, New Zealand, e-mail: g.fletcher@psyc.canterbury.ac.nz, or to Jeffry A. Simpson, Department of Psychology, Texas A&M University, College Station, TX 77843-4235, e-mail: jas@psyc.tamu.edu.

References

Campbell, L.J., Simpson, J.A., Kashy, D.A., & Fletcher, G.J.O. (in press). Ideal standards, the self, and flexibility of ideals in close relationships. *Personality and Social Psychology Bulletin.*
Fletcher, G.J.O., Simpson, J.A., & Thomas, G. (1999). *The role of ideals in early relationship development.* Unpublished manuscript, University of Canterbury, Christchurch, New Zealand.
Fletcher, G.J.O., Simpson, J.A., Thomas, G., & Giles, L. (1999). Ideals in intimate relationships. *Journal of Personality and Social Psychology, 76,* 72–89.
Gangestad, S.W., & Simpson, J.A. (in press). The evolution of human mating: Trade-offs and strategic pluralism. *Behavioral and Brain Sciences.*
Huxley, T.H. (1884). *Biogenesis and abiogenesis; collected essays, Vol. 8.* London: Macmillan.
Murray, S.L., & Holmes, J.G. (1996). The construction of relationship realities. In G.J.O. Fletcher & J. Fitness (Eds.), *Knowledge structures in close relationships: A social psychological approach* (pp. 91–120). Mahwah, NJ: Erlbaum.
Simpson, J.A., Fletcher, G.J.O., & Campbell, L.J. (in press). The structure and functions of ideal standards in close relationships. In G.J.O. Fletcher & M.S. Clark (Eds.), *Blackwell handbook of social psychology: Interpersonal processes.* London: Blackwell.

Critical Thinking Questions

1. What standards do you have for your relationships? How do they influence how you feel toward and behave in those relationships?

2. Would simply lowering our standards make us happier with our relationships?

3. What determines how high our standards for our relationships should be?

4. Where do our standards come from?

This article has been reprinted as it originally appeared in *Current Directions in Psychological Science*. Citation information for this article as originally published appears above.

Section 6: Conflict, Problems, and Risk

With a divorce rate that stands just under 50%, one of the most puzzling questions to be addressed by relationships research is: Why do relationships that are initially satisfying become unsatisfying? That initially gratifying relationships so frequently become dissatisfactory presents both practical and theoretical challenges. From a practical standpoint, dysfunctional relationships present challenges to emotional and mental health. From a theoretical standpoint, deteriorating relationships present challenges to social-cognitive theories that posit that important beliefs are remarkably stable.

What makes a bad relationship bad? One factor that plays a central role in relationship dissatisfaction is conflict. But what types of behaviors during conflict are most harmful for relationships? In the first reading, Frank Fincham reviews research describing the consequences, topics, content, and patterns of marital conflict. Then, in line with contextual approaches to understanding relationships, Fincham argues for more nuanced investigations of the antecedents and consequences of conflict behavior, noting that such correlates are likely to vary according to various qualities of individuals, their partners, and their relationships.

Are these conflicts and other relationship problems present in relationships from the beginning but only start to matter later? Or do relationships and contexts change as they develop in such a way that leads to conflict over time? Ted Huston, Silvia Niehuis, and Shanna Smith address these questions in the second article of this section. Specifically, they present three possible descriptions of the association between the initial and later phases of relationships: (1) the initial relationship is marked by love and affection but disagreements develop later and come to dominate and change how the partner is viewed, (2) the initial, idealized relationship succumbs to feelings of disillusionment and disappointment, and (3) the relationship during courtship is similar to the relationship in marriage, as the partners' strengths and weaknesses were recognized from the outset. Huston and colleagues describe findings from their own research that support the third explanation, which they call the *enduring dynamics model,* by demonstrating that relationships that become unsatisfactory are qualitatively different from relationships that remain more satisfying.

Exploring one of the more distressing outcomes that sometimes emerge over the course of a relationship, Stephen Drigotas and William Barta report on recent scientific approaches to studying and understanding infidelity. They first note that the study of infidelity is fraught with methodological barriers. For example, the use of self-report could result in the underreporting of such behavior, particularly by women (given the historically harsher consequences that have befallen unfaithful women). Then, the authors review descriptive research findings as well as more theoretically driven research that is based on the *normative model*, the *investment model*, and the *evolutionary model*. Drigotas and Barta indicate that a shortcoming of much of the work in this area is the neglect of individual differences that may contribute to a predilection toward infidelity and they suggest that the incorporation of such considerations could enrich both the investment and evolutionary models.

In the next article, Amy Holtzworth-Munroe addresses another disturbing aspect of relationships: violence. Specifically, Holtzworth-Munroe describes research suggesting that there are three types of men who are violent against their relationship partners, but to varying degrees. There are men who are violent only in their intimate relationships, mostly because they lack necessary skills to solve their problems. There are men who are slightly more violent, mostly within their families and largely because of psychological problems and distress. And there are the most violent men of all who are violent both within and outside the family, mostly due to psychopathology and a disregard for others' well-being.

Finally, M. Lynne Cooper examines the effects of alcohol on risky sexual behavior. The findings in this area are an excellent example of why psychological research on sex and relationships is necessary, as the results she describes are counterintuitive and much more complex than one might expect. Specifically, Cooper describes research indicating that the relationship between alcohol and riskier sex is in large part a function of one's beliefs about alcohol's influence *and* one's attitudes toward sexuality, condom use, and sexual risks, rather than simply the alcohol itself.

Marital Conflict: Correlates, Structure, and Context

Frank D. Fincham[1]

Psychology Department, University at Buffalo, Buffalo, New York

Abstract

Marital conflict has deleterious effects on mental, physical, and family health, and three decades of research have yielded a detailed picture of the behaviors that differentiate distressed from nondistressed couples. Review of this work shows that the singular emphasis on conflict in generating marital outcomes has yielded an incomplete picture of its role in marriage. Recently, researchers have tried to paint a more textured picture of marital conflict by studying spouses' backgrounds and charateristics, investigating conflict in the contexts of support giving and affectional expression, and considering the ecological niche of couples in their broader environment.

Keywords

conflict patterns; marital distress; support

Systematic psychological research on marriage emerged largely among clinical psychologists who wanted to better assist couples experiencing marital distress. In the 30 years since this development, marital conflict has assumed a special status in the literature on marriage, as evidenced by three indices. First, many of the most influential theories of marriage tend to reflect the view that "distress results from couples' aversive and ineffectual response to conflict" (Koerner & Jacobson, 1994, p. 208). Second, research on marriage has focused on what spouses do when they disagree with each other, and reviews of marital interaction are dominated by studies of conflict and problem solving (see Weiss & Heyman, 1997). Third, psychological interventions for distressed couples often target conflict-resolution skills (see Baucom, Shoham, Mueser, Daiuto, & Stickle, 1998).

IS MARITAL CONFLICT IMPORTANT?

The attention given marital conflict is understandable when we consider its implications for mental, physical, and family health. Marital conflict has been linked to the onset of depressive symptoms, eating disorders, male alcoholism, episodic drinking, binge drinking, and out-of-home drinking. Although married individuals are healthier on average than the unmarried, marital conflict is associated with poorer health and with specific illnesses such as cancer, cardiac disease, and chronic pain, perhaps because hostile behaviors during conflict are related to alterations in immunological, endocrine, and cardiovascular functioning. Physical aggression occurs in about 30% of married couples in the United States, leading to significant physical injury in about 10% of couples. Marriage is also the most common interpersonal context for homicide, and more women are murdered by their partners than by anyone else. Finally, marital conflict is associated with important family outcomes, including poor parenting, poor adjustment of children, increased likelihood of parent-child conflict, and conflict between siblings. Marital conflicts that are frequent, intense, physical, unresolved, and child related have a particularly negative influence on children, as do marital conflicts that spouses attribute to their child's behavior (see Grych & Fincham, 2001).

WHAT ARE MARITAL CONFLICTS ABOUT?

Marital conflicts can be about virtually anything. Couples complain about sources of conflict ranging from verbal and physical abusiveness to personal characteristics and behaviors. Perceived inequity in a couple's division of labor is associated with marital conflict and with a tendency for the male to withdraw in response to conflict. Conflict over power is also strongly related to marital dissatisfaction. Spouses' reports of conflict over extramarital sex, problematic drinking, or drug use predict divorce, as do wives' reports of husbands being jealous and spending money foolishly. Greater problem severity increases the likelihood of divorce. Even though it is often not reported to be a problem by couples, violence among newlyweds is a predictor of divorce, as is psychological aggression (verbal aggression and nonverbal aggressive behaviors that are not directed at the partner's body).

HOW DO SPOUSES BEHAVE DURING CONFLICT?

Stimulated, in part, by the view that "studying what people say about themselves is no substitute for studying how they behave" (Raush, Barry, Hertel, & Swain, 1974, p. 5), psychologists have conducted observational studies, with the underlying hope of identifying dysfunctional behaviors that could be modified in couple therapy. This research has focused on problem-solving discussions in the laboratory and provides detailed information about how maritally distressed and nondistressed couples behave during conflict.

During conflict, distressed couples make more negative statements and fewer positive statements than nondistressed couples. They are also more likely to respond with negative behavior when their partner behaves negatively. Indeed, this negative reciprocity, as it is called, is more consistent across different types of situations than is the amount of negative behavior, making it the most reliable overt signature of marital distress. Negative behavior is both more frequent and more frequently reciprocated in couples that engage in physical aggression than in other couples. Nonverbal behavior, often used as an index of emotion, reflects marital satisfaction better than verbal behavior, and unlike verbal behavior does not change when spouses try to fake good and bad marriages.

Are There Typical Patterns of Conflict Behavior?

The sequences of behavior that occur during conflict are more predictable in distressed than in nondistressed marriages and are often dominated by chains of negative behavior that usually escalate and are difficult for the couple to stop. One of the greatest challenges for couples locked into negative exchanges is to find an adaptive way of exiting from such cycles. This is usually attempted through responses that are designed to repair the interaction (e.g., "You're not listening to me") but are delivered with negative affect (e.g., irritation, sadness). The partners tend to respond to the negative affect, thereby continuing the cycle. This makes their interactions structured and predictable. In contrast, nondistressed coupled appear to be more responsive to attempts at repair and are thereby able to exit from negative exchanges early on. For example, a spouse may respond to "Wait, you're not letting me finish" with "Sorry . . . please finish what you were saying." Their interaction therefore appears more random and less predicable.

A second important behavior pattern exhibited by maritally distressed couples is the demand-withdraw pattern, in which one spouse pressures the other with demands, complaints, and criticisms, while the partner withdraws with defensiveness and passive inaction. Specifically, behavior sequences in which the husband withdraws and the wife responds with hostility are more common in distressed than in satisfied couples. This finding is consistent with several studies showing that wives display more negative affect and behavior than husbands, who tend to not respond or to make statements suggestive of withdrawal, such as irrelevant comments. Disengagement or withdrawal is, in turn, related to later decreases in marital satisfaction. However, inferring reliable gender differences in demand-withdraw patterns would be premature, as recent research shows that the partner who withdraws varies according to which partner desires change. So, for example, when a man desires change, the woman is the one who withdraws. Finally, conflict patterns seem to be relatively stable over time (see Karney & Bradbury, 1995).

Is There a Simple Way to Summarize Research Findings on Marital Conflict?

The findings of the extensive literature on marital conflict can be summarized in terms of a simple ratio: The ratio of agreements to disagreements is greater than 1 for happy couples and less than 1 for unhappy couples. Gottman (1993) utilized this ratio to identify couple types. He observed husbands and wives during conversation, recording each spouse's positive and negative behaviors while speaking, and then calculated the cumulative difference between positive and negative behaviors over time for each spouse. Using the patterns in these difference scores, he distinguished regulated couples (increase in positive speaker behaviors relative to negative behaviors for both spouses over the course of conversation) from nonregulated couples (all other patterns). The regulated couples were more satisfied in their marriage than the non-regulated couples, and also less likely to divorce. Regulated couples displayed positive problem-solving behaviors and positive affect approximately 5 times as often as negative problem-solving behaviors and negative affect, whereas the corresponding ratio was approximately 1:1 for nonregulated couples.

Interestingly, Gottman's perspective corresponds with the findings of two early, often overlooked studies on the reported frequency of sexual intercourse and of marital arguments (Howard & Dawes, 1976; Thornton, 1977). Both showed that the ratio of sexual intercourse to arguments, rather than their base rates, predicted marital satisfaction.

Don't Research Findings on Marital Conflict Just Reflect Common Sense?

The findings described in this article may seem like common sense. However, what we have learned about marital interaction contradicts the long-standing belief that satisfied couples are characterized by a *quid pro quo* principle according to which they exchange positive behavior and instead show that it is dissatisfied spouses who reciprocate one another's (negative) behavior. The astute reader may also be wondering whether couples' behavior in the artificial setting of the laboratory is a good reflection of their behavior in the real world outside the lab. It is therefore important to note that couples who participate in such studies themselves report that their interactions in the lab are reminiscent of their typical interactions. Research also shows that conflict behavior in the lab is similar to conflict behavior in the home; however, laboratory conflicts tend to be less severe, suggesting that research findings underestimate differences between distressed and nondistressed couples.

THE SEEDS OF DISCONTENT

By the early 1980s, researchers were attempting to address the limits of a purely behavioral account of marital conflict. Thus, they began to pay attention to subjective factors, such as thoughts and feelings, which might influence behavioral interactions or the relation between behavior and marital satisfaction. For example, it is now well documented that the tendency to explain a partner's negative behavior (e.g., coming home late from work) in a way that promotes conflict (e.g., "he thinks only about himself and his needs"), rather than in less conflictual ways (e.g., "he was probably caught in traffic"), is related to less effective problem solving, more negative communication in problem-solving discussions, more displays of specific negative affects (e.g., anger) during problem solving, and steeper declines in marital satisfaction over time (Fincham, 2001). Explanations that promote conflict are also related to the tendency to reciprocate a partner's negative behavior, regardless of a couple's marital satisfaction. Research on such subjective factors, like observational research on conflict, has continued to the present time. However, it represents an acceptance and expansion of the behavioral approach that accords conflict a central role in understanding marriage.

In contrast, very recently, some investigators have argued that the role of conflict in marriage should be reconsidered. Longitudinal research shows that conflict accounts for a relatively small portion of the variability in later marital outcomes, suggesting that other factors need to be considered in predicting these outcomes (see Karney & Bradbury, 1995). In addition, studies have demonstrated a troubling number of "reversal effects" (showing that greater conflict is a predictor of improved marriage; see Fincham & Beach, 1999). It is difficult to account for such findings in a field that, for much of its existence, has focused on providing descriptive data at the expense of building theory.

Rethinking the role of conflict also reflects recognition of the fact that most of what we know about conflict behavior comes from observation of problem-solving discussions and that couples experience verbal problem-solving situations infrequently; about 80% of couples report having overt disagreements once a month or less. As a result, cross-sectional studies of distressed versus nondistressed marriages and longitudinal studies of conflict are being increasingly complemented by research designs that focus on how happy marriages become unhappy.

Finally, there is evidence that marital conflict varies according to contextual factors. For example, diary studies illustrate that couples have more stressful marital interactions at home on days of high general life stress than on other days, and at times and places where they are experiencing multiple competing demands; arguments at work are related to marital arguments, and the occurrence of stressful life events is associated with more conflictual problem-solving discussions.

NEW BEGINNINGS: CONFLICT IN CONTEXT

Although domains of interaction other than conflict (e.g., support, companionship) have long been discussed in the marital literature, they are only now emerging from the secondary status accorded to them. This is somewhat ironic given the simple summary of research findings on marital conflict offered earlier, which points to the importance of the context in which conflict occurs.

Conflict in the Context of Support Giving and Affectional Expression

Observational laboratory methods have recently been developed to assess supportive behaviors in interactions in which one spouse talks about a personal issue he or she would like to change and the other is asked to respond as she or he normally would. Behaviors exhibited during such support tasks are only weakly related to the conflict behaviors observed during the problem-solving discussions used to study marital conflict. Supportive spouse behavior is associated with greater marital satisfaction and is more important than negative behavior in determining how supportive the partners perceive an interaction to be. In addition, the amount of supportive behavior partners exhibit is a predictor of later marital stress (i.e., more supportive behavior correlates with less future marital stress), independently of conflict behavior, and when support is poor, there is an increased risk that poor skills in dealing with conflict will lead to later marital deterioration. There is also evidence that support obtained by spouses outside the marriage can influence positively how the spouse behaves within the marriage.

In the context of high levels of affectional expression between spouses, the association between spouses' negative behavior and marital satisfaction decreases significantly. High levels of positive behavior in problem-solving discussions also mitigate the effect of withdrawal or disengagement on later marital satisfaction. Finally, when there are high levels of affectional expression between spouses, the demand-withdraw pattern is unrelated to marital satisfaction, but when affectional expression is average or low, the demand-withdraw pattern is associated with marital dissatisfaction.

Conflict in the Context of Spouses' Backgrounds and Characteristics

Focus on interpersonal behavior as the cause of marital outcomes led to the assumption that the characteristics of individual spouses play no role in those outcomes. However, increasing evidence that contradicts this assumption has generated recent interest in studying how spouses' backgrounds and characteristics might enrich our understanding of marital conflict.

The importance of spouses' characteristics is poignantly illustrated in the intergenerational transmission of divorce. Although there is a tendency for individuals whose parents divorced to get divorced themselves, this tendency varies depending on the offspring's behavior. Divorce rates are higher for offspring who behave in hostile, domineering, and critical ways, compared with offspring who do not behave in this manner.

An individual characteristic that is proving to be particularly informative for understanding marriage comes from recent research on attachment, which aims to address questions about how the experience of relationships early in life affects interpersonal functioning in adulthood. For example, spouses who tend to feel secure in relationships tend to compromise and to take into account both their own and their partner's interests during problem-solving interactions; those who tend to feel anxious or ambivalent in relationships show a greater tendency to oblige their partner, and focus on relationship maintenance, than do those who tend to avoid intimacy in relationships. And spouses who are preoccupied with being completely emotionally intimate in relationships show an elevated level of marital conflict after an involuntary, brief separation from the partner.

Of particular interest for understanding negative reciprocity are the findings that greater commitment is associated with more constructive, accommodative responses to a partner's negative behavior and that the dispositional tendency to forgive is a predictor of spouses' responses to their partners' transgressions; spouses having a greater tendency to forgive are less likely to avoid the partner or retaliate in kind following a transgression by the partner. Indeed, spouses themselves acknowledge that the capacity to seek and grant forgiveness is one of the most important factors contributing to marital longevity and satisfaction.

Conflict in the Context of the Broader Environment

The environments in which marriages are situated and the intersection between interior processes and external factors that impinge upon marriage are important to consider in painting a more textured picture of marital conflict. This is because problem-solving skills and conflict may have little impact on a marriage in the absence of external stressors. External stressors also may influence marriages directly. In particular, non-marital stressors may lead to an increased number of negative interactions, as illustrated by the fact that economic stress is associated with marital conflict. There is a growing need to identify the stressors and life events that are and are not influential for different couples and for different stages of marriage, to investigate how these events influence conflict, and to clarify how individuals and marriages may inadvertently generate stressful events. In fact, Bradbury, Rogge, and Lawrence (2001), in considering the ecological niche of the couple (i.e., their life events, family constellation, socioeconomic standing, and stressful circumstances), have recently argued that it may be "at least as important to examine the struggle that exists between the couple . . . and the environment they inhabit as it is to examine the interpersonal struggles that are the focus of our work [observation of conflict]" (p. 76).

CONCLUSION

The assumption that conflict management is the key to successful marriage and that conflict skills can be modified in couple therapy has proved useful in propelling the study of marriage into the mainstream of psychology. However, it may have outlived its usefulness, and some researchers are now calling for greater attention to other mechanisms (e.g., spousal social support) that might be responsible for marital outcomes. Indeed, controversy over whether conflict has beneficial or detrimental effects on marriage over time is responsible, in part, for the recent upsurge in longitudinal research on marriage. Notwithstanding diverse opinions on just how central conflict is for understanding marriage, current efforts to study conflict in a broader marital context, which is itself seen as situated in a broader ecological niche, bode well for advancing understanding and leading to more powerful preventive and therapeutic interventions.

Recommended Reading

Bradbury, T.N., Fincham, F.D., & Beach, S.R.H. (2000). Research on the nature and determinants of marital satisfaction: A decade in review. *Journal of Marriage and the Family, 62,* 964–980.
Fincham, F.D., & Beach, S.R. (1999). (See References)
Grych, J.H., & Fincham, F.D. (Eds.). (2001). (See References)
Karney, B.R., & Bradbury, T.N. (1995). (See References)

Acknowledgments—This article was written while the author was supported by Grants from the Templeton, Margaret L. Wendt, and J.M. McDonald Foundations.

Note

1. Address correspondence to Frank D. Fincham, Department of Psychology, University at Buffalo, Buffalo, NY 14260.

References

Baucom, D.H., Shoham, V., Mueser, K.T., Daiuto, A.D., & Stickle, T.R. (1998). Empirically supported couple and family interventions for marital distress and adult mental health problems. *Journal of Consulting and Clinical Psychology, 66,* 53–88.
Bradbury, T.N., Rogge, R., & Lawrence, E. (2001). Reconsidering the role of conflict in marriage. In A. Booth, A.C. Crouter, & M. Clements (Eds.), *Couples in conflict* (pp. 59–81). Mahwah, NJ: Erlbaum.
Fincham, F.D. (2001). Attributions and close relationships: From balkanization to integration. In G.J. Fletcher & M. Clark (Eds.), *Blackwell handbook of social psychology* (pp. 3–31). Oxford, England: Blackwell.
Fincham, F.D., & Beach, S.R. (1999). Marital conflict: Implications for working with couples. *Annual Review of Psychology, 50,* 47–77.

Gottman, J.M. (1993). The roles of conflict engagement, escalation, and avoidance in marital interaction: A longitudinal view of five types of couples. *Journal of Consulting and Clinical Psychology, 61,* 6–15.

Grych, J.H., & Fincham, F.D. (Eds.). (2001). *Interparental conflict and child development: Theory,
research, and applications.* New York: Cambridge University Press.

Howard, J.W., & Dawes, R.M. (1976). Linear prediction of marital happiness. *Personality and Social
Psychology Bulletin, 2,* 478–480.

Karney, B.R., & Bradbury, T.N. (1995). The longitudinal course of marital quality and stability: A
review of theory, method, and research. *Psychological Bulletin, 118,* 3–34.

Koerner, K., & Jacobson, N.J. (1994). Emotion and behavior in couple therapy. In S.M. Johnson &
L.S. Greenberg (Eds.), *The heart of the matter: Perspectives on emotion in marital therapy* (pp.
207–226). New York: Brunner/Mazel.

Raush, H.L., Barry, W.A., Hertel, R.K., & Swain, M.A. (1974). *Communication, conflict, and marriage.* San Francisco: Jossey-Bass.

Thornton, B. (1977). Toward a linear prediction of marital happiness. *Personality and Social Psychology Bulletin, 3,* 674–676.

Weiss, R.L., & Heyman, R.E. (1997). A clinical-research overview of couple interactions. In W.K.
Halford & H. Markman (Eds.), *The clinical handbook of marriage and couples interventions*
(pp. 13–41). Brisbane, Australia: Wiley.

Critical Thinking Questions

1. What problems do correlational data present for discussions of the role of marital conflict in relationships? How can researchers handle these problems?

2. Much of the research reviewed in this article described findings from observations of couples' interactions. Why do you think researchers don't just ask
   people how they behave in their relationships?

3. Can you think of contexts in which typically "negative" behaviors can have
   positive consequences for a relationship?

**This article has been reprinted as it originally appeared in *Current Directions in
Psychological Science*. Citation information for this article as originally published
appears above.**

The Early Marital Roots of Conjugal Distress and Divorce

Ted L. Huston,[1] Sylvia Niehuis, and Shanna E. Smith

Department of Human Ecology, University of Texas at Austin, Austin, Texas

Abstract

This article summarizes research that challenges conventional wisdom about the early roots of marital distress and divorce. We abstract results from a 13-year study that focused on the extent to which long-term marital satisfaction and stability could be forecast from newlywed and early marital data. We explore the usefulness of three models—emergent distress, enduring dynamics, and disillusionment—designed to explain why some marriages thrive and others fail. The dominant paradigm, the emergent-distress model, sees newlyweds as homogeneously blissful and posits that distress develops as disagreements and negativity escalate, ultimately leading some couples to divorce. The results we summarize run counter to this model and suggest instead that (a) newlyweds differ considerably in the intensity of both their romance and the negativity of their behavior toward one another and, for those who remain married, these early dynamics persist over time; and (b) for couples who divorce, romance seems to deteriorate differently depending on how long the marriage lasts. Soon after their wedding, "early exiters" seem to lose hope of improving an unpromising relationship; "delayed-action divorcers" begin marriage on a particularly high note, yet quickly show signs of disillusionment. These delayed-action divorcers reluctantly give up on the marriage long after the romance has faded.

Keywords

marriage; love; longitudinal research; divorce; disillusionment

Courting partners are generally drawn toward marriage by romantic love, affection, and a sense of their prospective mate as a caring and understanding person. Yet many couples who enter marriage with a sense of optimism will some day find themselves divorced or in an unhappy union. Are there early signs that foreshadow whether a marriage will succeed or fail? Three developmental models look to different features of the first few years of marriage for clues.

The paradigm most frequently used by researchers and clinicians over the past 20 years—the *emergent-distress* model—focuses on the deleterious effects of increases in conflict and negative behavior. This model presumes that love draws premarital partners toward marriage; thus, newlyweds are deeply in love and highly affectionate. Yet, as Clements, Cordova, Markman, and Laurenceau (1997) argued, "the positive factors that draw people together are indicative of marital choice, but not marital success. Instead, how couples handle differences is the critical factor" (p. 352). As disagreements become more intense and pervasive, spouses eventually begin to perceive each other as disagreeable, or "contrary." Ultimately, these changes lead couples to marital distress, or even to divorce. The primary support for this model is rooted in research documenting the deleterious effects of negativity on marriage (Karney & Bradbury, 1995). For example, distressed married partners and those headed for divorce tend to use dysfunctional coping mechanisms, such as defensiveness, withdrawal, stonewalling, and contempt, during conflict (Gottman, 1994). Studies in this tradition, however, are typically carried out with couples who have already passed through the early years of marriage, leaving open the question of whether it is negativity that leads to distress or some other early marital process that gives rise to both distress and negativity.

Our own research has led us to elaborate on and explore the usefulness of two models that contrast with the emergent-distress model. The first of these, the *disillusionment* model, suggests that distress and divorce are rooted in the erosion of spouses' feelings of love and the waning of their affection, as well as in the emergence of ambivalent feelings about their marriage. This model, like the emergent-distress model, assumes that courting couples are blissful, optimistic lovers who, in order to sustain their romance, draw attention to their desirable qualities and try to see the best in each other. After the wedding, however, spouses may be less motivated to impress each other; in addition, the growing intimacy of marriage makes it difficult for them to sustain idealized images. As a result, some spouses may become disappointed, and feel a sense of disillusionment.

The second model, the *enduring-dynamics* model, presumes that relationship patterns take form during courtship and persist into marriage (Huston, 1994). This model, unlike the disillusionment model, presumes that courtship patterns foreshadow marital patterns—that the "good courtship" presages the "good marriage." The model suggests that the path to the altar is not a journey fueled by idealization and romance; rather, couples marry with their eyes open to each other's and the relationship's strengths and weaknesses.

ANALYZING THE SIGNIFICANCE OF CHANGES EARLY IN MARRIAGE FOR MARITAL SUCCESS

The three developmental models differ in the significance they attach to initial differences among newlyweds and to differences in how couples' marriages change over the first couple of years. Our long-term study of 168 married couples has allowed us to capture both initial differences and changes in couples' relationships early in marriage and to connect them to long-term marital outcomes (Huston, Caughlin, Houts, Smith, & George, 2001). When couples were first married, we collected extensive data from each spouse about the couple's courtship experiences; in addition, when the couples were newlyweds and then across the next 2 years of marriage, we asked the spouses about their feelings toward one another, their perceptions of each other's personality, and the behavioral climate of their marriage. (Information on the six measures—*love, ambivalence, behavioral negativity,* overt expressions of *affection,* and perceptions of the *contrariness* and *responsiveness* of the partner's personality—can be found in Huston et al., 2001.) We examined each of these aspects of the early years of the couples' marriages in connection with the long-term fate of the relationships.

During the follow-up, which took place a little more than 13 years after the couples were wed, we ascertained whether they were still married and, if so, their marital satisfaction. We used these data to create a more finely differentiated categorization scheme for classifying marital outcomes than has customarily been used. Researchers interested in predicting marital success typically group couples in one of two ways: They either (a) compare couples who remain married with those who divorce, and thus assume that unhappy couples are more similar to happy couples than they are to those who divorce, or (b) lump couples who are either unhappy or divorced into a single group, which is then compared with happy couples. This tactic ignores the possibility that spouses who stay in unhappy marriages differ from those who divorce. Thus, at a minimum, researchers should separate couples into three groups: happy, unhappy, and divorced. However, because couples who divorce early may do so for different reasons than those who divorce late (Karney & Bradbury, 1995), couples should be differentiated, when possible, in terms of the timing of their divorce. These considerations led us to classify our couples into four groups:

- Happily married (both partners were happy)
- Unhappily married (at least one partner was not happy)
- Early exiters (married 2–6 years before divorcing)
- Delayed-action divorcers (married at least 7 years before divorcing)

A handful of couples who divorced within 2 years of their wedding were not included in these longitudinal analyses (see Huston, 1994; Huston et al., 2001). For the remaining couples who divorced, we used a cutoff point of 7 years to distinguish between early exiters and delayed-action divorcers because data collected by the U.S. Bureau of the Census suggest that the median length of marriage for couples who eventually divorce is 7.2 years.

THE ENDURING DYNAMICS OF STABLE MARRIAGES

The emergent-distress and the disillusionment models both posit that newlywed couples start out their marriage as affectionate lovers who live together in harmony. Proponents of these models picture newlyweds as a homogeneous group, and thus believe that newlywed patterns provide few clues as to couples' future marital fates. Our results, however, provide two pieces of evidence to counter these views: First, couples differed considerably, even as newlyweds, in how enamored they were with each other and how well they got along; furthermore, these newlywed differences were rooted in couples' premarital relationships (Huston, 1994). Second, the characteristics that initially differentiated the couples who remained married for 13 years remained stable over the first 2 years of marriage, and foreshadowed later marital happiness (Huston et al., 2001). Specifically, couples who were later happily married were more in love and viewed each other as more responsive early in marriage than did those who were later unhappily married, whereas conversely, those who were later unhappily married were more ambivalent and behaved more negatively toward each other during the first 2 years of marriage. Contrary to both the emergent-distress and the disillusionment models, the two groups did not become increasingly differentiated over time, with one exception: Over the first 2 years of marriage, spouses who would later be classified as happy began to see their partner as having a less contrary nature than they did when they were first married, whereas spouses in the other categories did not change their views of their partner's contrariness.

These findings, consistent with the enduring-dynamics model, show that happy and unhappy couples are distinguishable as newlyweds, that these initial differences persist, and that these early patterns predict the long-term status of the relationship. The enduring-dynamics model, then, explains the early relationship roots of marital unhappiness among stably married couples. The disillusionment model, as we argue in the next section, fares better when we trace the early marital roots of divorce.

DISILLUSIONMENT AND DIVORCE

The disillusionment and emergent-distress models both focus on the importance of change early in marriage, with the former concentrating on the loss of romance and illusion, and the latter on increases in negative behavior. Our findings suggest that disillusionment—not the emergence of distress—fore-shadows divorce (Huston et al., 2001). Couples who showed sharper than average declines in affection and love over the first 2 years of marriage, and those who came to see each other as much less responsive, were more apt to divorce. Moreover, those headed for divorce began to experience stronger feelings of ambivalence about their marital union than those who stayed married. The pattern of change in the character of the romantic bond differed slightly, however, depending on whether couples divorced early or later.

Delayed-action divorcers were highly affectionate and deeply in love as newlyweds, more so even than the couples who would be happily married 13 years later. These delayed-action divorcers, however, became considerably less affectionate over the first 2 years of marriage compared with other couples. The abatement of their affection was mirrored by similar declines in their propensity to see each other as having a caring and responsive personality. Despite these declines, when delayed-action divorcers reached their second anniversary, they were still as affectionate and as much in love as those who stayed married over the entire course of the study. This configuration of findings suggests that we may well have captured these couples in the very early stages of disenchantment, particularly because their decline in affection was not accompanied by a heightening of ambivalence. Spouses may initially respond to declines in romance by seeking to recapture the initial excitement; if these efforts fail, however, they may eventually reevaluate their marriage and focus more on each other's shortcomings (cf. Kayser, 1993).

The relationships of the early exiters, like those of the delayed-action divorcers, began to unravel over the first 2 years of marriage; the two groups differed in that the early exiters' marriages were less promising at the outset, and the deterioration of their relationships progressed somewhat differently. The early exiters were not particularly enamored or affectionate with each other as newlyweds. Instead, their marriages initially resembled those of couples who would later become unhappily married. Although the changes in how early exiters interacted with their spouses—as reflected in affection and negativity—mirrored the relatively small changes seen in the happily and unhappily married groups, these early exiters nonetheless became more ambivalent about their relationship and fell quickly out of love. It almost seems that early exiters may have entered marriage with the hope that their relationship would improve—that they would become more affectionate and less negative with time—and when these hoped-for improvements were not realized, their fragile bond deteriorated further.

WHAT ABOUT EMERGENT DISTRESS?

The emergent-distress model takes as axiomatic the idea that problems surface early in marriage, erode satisfaction, and lead some couples to divorce. Our data provide little evidence for this view (Huston, 1994; Huston et al., 2001). First, advocates of the emergent-distress model argue that groups with different marital outcomes would show negligible differences as newlyweds; in reality, however, the newlyweds we studied varied considerably in both the intensity of their romance and the degree of negativity they displayed toward each other. Second, according to the tenets of emergent distress, couples who are headed toward marital distress and dissolution should become increasingly negative toward each other and should come to see one another as more contrary; thus, in our study, rises in negativity and perceptions of one's partner's contrariness (a) should have differentiated happy from not happy couples and (b) should have been more pronounced for the early exiters than for any other group. However, neither of these propositions was supported; unhappily married couples and early exiters did not increase in either negative behavior or perceived contrariness.

The results of our study suggest that researchers need to expand their theoretical vision beyond the emergent-distress model, with its focus on conflict and negativity. Our research indicates that the positive elements of marriage, and their loss, are particularly worthy of further investigation. This point of view is supported by retrospective qualitative studies, which have emphasized the maintenance of these positive elements as important to marital well-being (e.g., Kayser, 1993). Partners in long-term happy marriages also attribute the success of their marriage to enduring feelings of attachment, pleasure, comfort, emotional closeness, being cared for, and friendship.

SOME FINAL THOUGHTS

The research we have reviewed is the first systematic and prospective effort to examine the early roots of long-term marital distress and disruption. Our findings challenge a number of commonly accepted ideas about the roots of distress and divorce. First, contrary to the idea that newlywed couples are homogeneously blissful, our data indicate that dissatisfaction with the relationship may already exist at the outset of some marriages. Second, newlywed data predict marital happiness among couples who remain married. Third, couples who divorce evidence more dramatic changes in the affective character of their marriage over its first 2 years than do those who remain married. Finally, our data indicate that the early roots of long-term distress and divorce are quite different.

We have only just begun to uncover the developmental processes occurring during early marriage that ultimately lead to marital delight, distress, and divorce. It is quite possible that the processes we observed early in marriage are linked to the later emergence of distress, so that early losses of love and other positive elements in a marriage may set the stage for later disappointment, distrust, and increase in conflict. To further delineate the developmental course of distress and dissolution, future research needs to (a) identify the courtship experiences that set the stage for enduring dynamics, disillusionment, or emergent distress; (b) recruit newlyweds, follow them regularly over an extended period of time, and relate changes in their relationship to long-term marital outcomes; (c) recognize that the early marital roots of marital unhappiness are apt to be different from the roots of divorce; and (d) pay greater attention to the positive elements of marriage and to the degree to which these elements are maintained over time.

Recommended Reading

Bradbury, T.N. (Ed.). (1998). *The developmental course of marital dysfunction*. New York: Cambridge University Press.
Kayser, K. (1993). (See References)
Vaughan, D. (1986). *Uncoupling: Turning points in intimate relationships*. New York: Oxford University Press.

Acknowledgments—We thank Paul Miller and Christopher Rasmussen for comments on a previous draft. This research was supported by Grants to Ted L. Huston from the National Science Foundation (SBR-9311846) and the National Institute of Mental Health (MH-33938).

Note

1. Address correspondence to Ted L. Huston, Department of Human Ecology, The University of Texas at Austin, Austin, TX 78712; e-mail: huston@mail.utexas.edu.

References

Clements, M.L., Cordova, A.D., Markman, H.J., & Laurenceau, J. (1997). The erosion of marital satisfaction over time and how to prevent it. In R.J. Sternberg & M. Hojjat (Eds.), *Satisfaction in close relationships* (pp. 335–355). New York: Guilford Press.
Gottman, J.M. (1994). *What predicts divorce? The relationship between marital processes and marital outcomes*. Hillsdale, NJ: Erlbaum.
Huston, T.L. (1994). Courtship antecedents of marital satisfaction and love. In R. Erber & R. Gilmour (Eds.), *Theoretical frameworks for personal relationships* (pp. 43–65). Hillsdale, NJ: Erlbaum.
Huston, T.L., Caughlin, J.P., Houts, R.M., Smith, S.E., & George, L.J. (2001). The connubial crucible: Newlywed years as predictors of marital delight, distress, and divorce. *Journal of Personality and Social Psychology, 80*, 237–252.
Karney, B.J., & Bradbury, T.N. (1995). The longitudinal course of marital quality and stability: A review of theory, method, and research. *Psychological Bulletin, 118*, 3–34.
Kayser, K. (1993). *When love dies: The process of marital disaffection*. New York: Guilford Press.

Critical Thinking Questions

1. Why would couples who acknowledge problems in their relationships get married in the first place?

2. How does the authors' *enduring-dynamics* model suggest that interventions should go about targeting/preventing distressed marriages?

3. Should we rule out the *emergent-distress* model? Why or why not?

4. What other factors might we examine to understand why and how relationships change over time?

This article has been reprinted as it originally appeared in *Current Directions in Psychological Science*. Citation information for this article as originally published appears above.

The Cheating Heart: Scientific Explorations of Infidelity

Stephen M. Drigotas[1] and William Barta

Department of Psychology, Southern Methodist University, Dallas, Texas

Abstract

Given the potential negative ramifications of infidelity, it is not surprising that researchers have attempted to delineate its root causes. Historically, descriptive approaches have simply identified the demographics of who is unfaithful and how often. However, recent developments in both evolutionary and investment-model research have greatly furthered understanding of infidelity. The field could gain additional insight by examining the similarities of these prominent approaches.

Keywords

infidelity; extradyadic behavior; relationships

Infidelity, in the context of a dyadic relationship, represents a partner's violation of norms regulating the level of emotional or physical intimacy with people outside the relationship. Marital infidelity is a leading cause of divorce, spousal battery, and homicide (e.g., Daly & Wilson, 1988). Despite the obvious personal and societal impact of infidelity, little empirical research examined its dynamics until the late 1970s. At that time, empirical researchers paid increased attention to this phenomenon, presumably because of their changing attitudes. Glass and Wright (1977) observed that prior to the 1970s, infidelity was subsumed under the category of sexually deviant behavior. The increasing visibility of infidelity and growing acceptance of nontraditional families during the 1970s, and a willingness to acknowledge the sheer prevalence of infidelity, served to usher in the perception that risk factors for infidelity are pervasive across nominally exclusive heterosexual relationships.

In this article, we summarize relevant empirical research, highlighting some of the key findings and theoretical perspectives that have emerged, particularly since the 1970s. Additionally, we identify new research directions.

THE DESCRIPTIVE APPROACH

This approach encompasses largely atheoretical efforts to document the demographics and attitudinal correlates of infidelity. Typically, descriptive research relies on retrospective and self-report data. Kinsey and his associates found, for example, that 36% of husbands and 25% of wives reported having been unfaithful (e.g., Kinsey, Pomeroy, Martin, & Gebhard, 1953). A more recent survey, spanning five age cohorts, found that 37% of men and 12.4% of women born between 1933 and 1942 reported having been unfaithful; among individuals born between 1953 and 1974, the figures were 27.6% for men and 26.2% for women (Laumann, Gagnon, Michael, & Michaels, 1994).

Gender differences in motivations for infidelity indicate that marital dissatisfaction tends to be higher among unfaithful women than unfaithful men, and that unfaithful men are more likely to report a sexual rather than emotional motivation for infidelity (e.g., Glass & Wright, 1985). This distinction between "emotional" versus "sexual" motivation is reflected in the finding that a male's infidelity is more likely than a female's to be a "one night stand," to involve someone of limited acquaintance, and to include coitus (Humphrey, 1987).

Gender is also a factor in the likelihood of seeking divorce as a consequence of a partner's infidelity. Shackelford (1998) asked people to rate the attractiveness of their partners ("mate value") and indicate their own anticipated responses to infidelity. Results indicated that men were more likely than women to see infidelity as a reason for divorce. However, the likelihood of a woman (but not a man) seeking divorce covaried with the discrepancy between partners' reported mate values (i.e., to the extent that a female partner was more attractive than her spouse, she was more likely to end a relationship following her partner's infidelity). Women also appear to have broader criteria for their definition of infidelity, being more likely than men to end a marriage if their spouse "dates" or "flirts with" someone else, even if sexual intercourse does not occur.

The observed increase in the frequency of married women being unfaithful may be due to the increasing percentage of women who work outside the home. Opportunity is a contributor to the likelihood of infidelity, and women who work outside the home have greater opportunity to form opposite-sex relationships than do women who stay at home. In addition, as women achieve greater economic independence, marital instability tends to increase (e.g., Humphrey, 1987).

Some caution is necessary, however, when relying on self-reported infidelity to draw conclusions. Historically, social sanctions against female infidelity have been far more severe than sanctions against male infidelity (e.g., Daly & Wilson, 1988). The apparent increase in female infidelity, therefore, may be an artifact of a decline in the severity of these sanctions rather than reflecting a true change in the rate of infidelity (i.e., women may be more likely to report truthfully now that society is more permissive). Self-reports are also subject to biases relating to the respondent's level of trust in the confidentiality of the survey, whether the spouse is present in the room, and whether the infidelity is known to the partner. Laumann et al. (1994) found that individuals whose marriages were intact were markedly less likely to report a history of infidelity than individuals whose marriages had ended.

THE NORMATIVE APPROACH

Like the descriptive approach, the normative approach has tended to rely on self-report data and retrospective accounts. The key distinction between the two approaches is that normative researchers proceed from the hypothesis that the likelihood of engaging in infidelity can be attributed to societal norms. For example, people are more likely to be unfaithful if they are acquainted with someone who has been unfaithful than if they have no acquaintances who have been unfaithful (Buunk & Bakker, 1995). Norms relating to infidelity can be categorized as *injunctive* or *descriptive* (Buunk & Bakker, 1995). Injunctive norms are the formal laws and mores that a society upholds, whereas descriptive norms refer to perceptions of other people's behavior. Research indicates that individuals are more likely to engage in a prohibited activity if they see someone else violating the same prohibition. Buunk and Bakker (1995) found that injunctive and descriptive norms independently influence the likelihood of extradyadic sex, but descriptive norms typically outweigh injunctive norms.

The normative model extends to sex roles. Sexual conquest is a component of the masculine sex role (e.g., Lusterman, 1997). This may account for the fact that historically rates of infidelity have been higher for married men than for married women, and for the fact that men are more likely than women to be unfaithful even if marital satisfaction is high. Furthermore, injunctive norms against both female infidelity and female sexual autonomy have historically been far more strict, and accompanied by more severe social sanctions, than the corresponding norms for men (e.g., Daly & Wilson, 1988). At the same time, the decline in male participation in extradyadic sex observed over the course of the 20th century may reflect changing attitudes toward male sexual entitlement and conquest.

THE INVESTMENT MODEL APPROACH

The investment model (for a review, see Rusbult, Drigotas, & Verette, 1994) represents a theory regarding the process by which individuals become committed to their relationships, as well as the circumstances under which feelings of commitment erode and relationships end. According to this model, the primary force in relationships is commitment, which is a psychological attachment to, and a motivation to continue, a relationship. Forces that serve to make an individual more or less committed to a relationship include satisfaction (how happy the individual is with the relationship), alternative quality (potential satisfaction provided outside the relationship, e.g., dating another person, being alone), and investments (things the individual would lose if the relationship ends, e.g., shared possessions, friends). Research has demonstrated the model's power in accounting for a variety of important behaviors in relationships, including breaking up, willingness to sacrifice, accommodation (the ability to respond to the partner's bad behavior constructively), and derogation of alternatives (the tendency to make attractive others seem worse than they actually are).

In reference to infidelity, commitment may serve as a macromotive, that is, a central motive that guides both long-term and short-term behavior. Highly committed individuals are less likely to be unfaithful because they are motivated to (a) derogate potential alternatives in order to protect the relationship (thus, effectively keeping alternatives unattractive) and (b) consider, when tempted to be unfaithful, the long-term ramifications of such behavior on the relationship and the partner. Thus, commitment serves to both reduce the frequency with which temptations arise and provide resources enabling the individual to shift his or her focus from any potential short-term pleasure to the long-term consequences.

In a direct test of the model's ability to predict infidelity (Drigotas, Safstrom, & Gentilia, 1999), measures of commitment (and of other constructs in the model) successfully predicted subsequent infidelity in dating couples both over the course of a semester and over spring break. This research was important for a variety of reasons: First, it demonstrated successful prediction of actual behavior, rather than relying on the traditional method of asking individuals post hoc why they were unfaithful. Second, it provided additional support for the breadth of the investment model. Third, disparate methods (survey vs. diary) yielded the same findings.

THE EVOLUTIONARY APPROACH

The evolutionary approach, like the investment model, emphasizes the exchange of benefits within the dyad and predicts that satisfaction is largely dependent on the level of equity in this exchange. Evolutionary psychologists also acknowledge that satisfaction is inversely related to the quality of alternatives. The evolutionary model is distinguished, however, by its assumption that the functional basis of these benefits is not to promote satisfaction but to facilitate the production of offspring. From a Darwinian perspective, both morphological and behavioral characteristics of a species are assumed to confer advantages upon the organism in terms of its *reproductive success* (RS). The measure of RS, in turn, is whether the individual produces offspring who themselves reproduce (e.g., Buss, 1998). Heterosexual behavior, evolutionary psychologists argue, is shaped by oftentimes unconscious predispositions functioning to promote an individual's RS.

One assumption of evolutionary psychologists is that men and women do not possess the same motivation to cheat. A man can increase his RS considerably by impregnating an extradyadic partner, whereas once a woman is pregnant or has exclusive access to a male, there is little benefit to her mating with an extradyadic partner (e.g., Buss, 1998). She can still benefit from infidelity, however, if it is advantageous in terms of "trading up" to a superior mate.

A second assumption of evolutionary psychologists revolves around *paternal certainty*. Males never have absolute certainty of their biological parentage, whereas females do. As a result, men are more likely than women to exhibit violent sexual jealousy (e.g., Daly & Wilson, 1988). Women, freed from anxieties surrounding the biological parentage of their offspring, are instead alert to the possibility of male abandonment, inasmuch as this abandonment results in the decreased survivability of their offspring.

A third assumption of evolutionary psychologists is that *parental investment,* or the time and resources devoted to offspring, is inversely correlated with *mating effort,* or the time and resources devoted to seeking out and attracting sexual partners—including extradyadic partners. Because of the inescapable costs associated with gestation and nursing, parental investment is higher for women than for men. Consequently, men have more time and resources than women to devote to mating effort. As a result, at any given time, competition for access to mates is greater among males than among females, and this allows females to be more discriminating than males in their choice of partners.

One contribution of the evolutionary perspective has been to generate research answering questions that have not received attention previously. For example, it has been found that men are more likely to engage in sexual infidelity than in emotional infidelity and consider sexual infidelity to be more upsetting relative to emotional infidelity than women do (e.g., Buss, 1998). Women who engage in casual sex with no intention of having a lasting relationship or children nonetheless show a preference for partners who possess qualities they associate with being a good parent (e.g., Buss, 1998). Women experience heightened levels of libido during the most fertile phase of menstruation, are most likely to be unfaithful during their most fertile days, and use contraceptives more conscientiously with their marital partners than with their extramarital partners (Baker & Bellis, 1995).

NEW DIRECTIONS

Each of the approaches to the study of infidelity has focused on the structural characteristics of the dyad, including the quality of the partners' interactions, the exchange of resources, and the attractiveness of alternatives, and has overlooked the unique personalities of the individuals involved. However, personality dimensions (e.g., narcissism) can be expected to influence perceived satisfaction within a dyad and hence moderate individuals' degree of commitment to their relationship (e.g., Lusterman, 1997). Consideration of individual differences could improve both investment and evolutionary models. For example, individual differences may account for why many females engage in sexually motivated infidelities even though, as noted earlier, this does not directly affect their RS. Additional dimensions of individual differences may serve to influence both expectations regarding one's primary relationship and the assessment of the risks and rewards associated with an extradyadic relationship.

One common criticism of infidelity research is its overreliance on self-report methods. Notable for its methodology is a study by Seal, Agostinelli, and Hannett (1994). Using a sample of couples in exclusive dating relationships, the researchers provided each member of each dyad with an opportunity to surreptitiously make a date with an extradyadic partner. The researchers also measured participants' tendency to dissociate sex and love and to seek sexual variety (i.e., "sociosexuality"). Both these tendencies were correlated with the likelihood of pursuing an extradyadic contact. Interestingly, although men were more likely than women to report a willingness to seek extradyadic contacts, the behavioral measure of actual extradyadic sexual encounters showed no difference between men and women. Innovations in methods, such as the diary method (e.g., Drigotas et al., 1999) or the introduction, in a controlled setting, of an opportunity to be unfaithful (Seal et al., 1994), may allow researchers to overcome participants' biases in reporting their own previous behavior. Greater reliance on behavioral as opposed to subjective data is needed to corroborate and extend existing findings.

The evolutionary model would benefit tremendously from longitudinal research focusing on the frequency of coitus both within and outside the primary relationship. In this age of contraceptives, coital frequency is the best index of RS. Thus, it would strengthen the general evolutionary perspective if data showed that coital frequency within the primary relationship initially declines when a man is unfaithful but eventually returns to an optimal level as coital frequency in the secondary relationship declines. These data would also shed light on whether sexual motivation is truly more characteristic of unfaithful males than unfaithful females.

Finally, the exploration of the root causes of infidelity would benefit from the theoretical combination of the evolutionary and investment approaches. One possible link between the two approaches revolves around the common manner in which they attempt to explain the motivation for infidelity. The specific motivational explanation provided in the investment model is that extradyadic partners may offer the individual a higher level of material and emotional benefits than his or her primary partner provides. Evolutionary theorists emphasize the importance of the same pragmatic benefits, but argue that the ultimate basis for what constitutes a "benefit" is whether it enhances the individual's RS. These two approaches are largely compatible with one another, and future research is likely to benefit from their cross-fertilization.

Recommended Reading

Baker, R., & Bellis, M. (1995). (See References)
Drigotas, S., Safstrom, C., & Gentilia, T. (1999). (See References)
Humphrey, F. (1987). (See References)
Laumann, E., Gagnon, J., Michael, R., & Michaels, S. (1994). (See References)

Note

1. Address correspondence to Stephen Drigotas, Department of Psychology, Southern Methodist University, Dallas, TX 75275; e-mail: sdrigota@mail.smu.edu.

References

Baker, R., & Bellis, M. (1995). *Human sperm competition*. London: Chapman & Hall.

Buss, D. (1998). *Evolutionary psychology*. Needham Heights, MA: Allyn & Bacon.

Buunk, B., & Bakker, A. (1995). Extradyadic sex: The role of descriptive and injunctive norms. *Journal of Sex Research, 32,* 313–318.

Daly, M., & Wilson, M. (1988). *Homicide*. Hawthorne, NJ: Aldine de Gruyter.

Drigotas, S., Safstrom, C., & Gentilia, T. (1999). An investment model prediction of dating infidelity. *Journal of Personality and Social Psychology, 77,* 509–524.

Glass, S., & Wright, T. (1977). The relationship of extramarital sex, length of marriage, and sex differences on marital satisfaction and romanticism: Athanasiou's data reanalyzed. *Journal of Marriage and the Family, 39,* 691–704.

Glass, S., & Wright, T. (1985). Sex differences in type of extramarital involvement and marital dissatisfaction. *Sex Roles, 12,* 1101–1120.

Humphrey, F. (1987). Treating extramarital sexual relationships in sex and couples therapy. In G. Weeks & L. Hof (Eds.), *Integrating sex and marital therapy: A clinical guide* (pp. 149–170). New York: Brunner/Mazel.

Kinsey, A., Pomeroy, W., Martin, C., & Gebhard, P. (1953). *Sexual behavior in the human female*. Philadelphia: Saunders.

Laumann, E., Gagnon, J., Michael, R., & Michaels, S. (1994). *The social organization of sexuality*. Chicago: University of Chicago.

Lusterman, D. (1997). Repetitive infidelity, womanizing, and Don Juanism. In R. Levant & G. Brooks (Eds.), *Men and sex* (pp. 84–99). New York: Wiley.

Rusbult, C.E., Drigotas, S.M., & Verette, J. (1994). The investment model: An interdependence analysis of commitment processes and relationship maintenance phenomena. In D. Canary & L. Stafford (Eds.), *Communication and relational maintenance* (pp. 115–139). San Diego: Academic Press.

Seal, D., Agostinelli, G., & Hannett, C. (1994). Extradyadic romantic involvement: Moderating effects of sociosexuality and gender. *Sex Roles, 31*, 1–22.

Shackelford, T. (1998). Divorce as a consequence of spousal infidelity. In V. De Munck (Ed.), *Romantic love and sexual behavior* (pp. 135–153). Westport, CT: Praeger.

Critical Thinking Questions

1. How could researchers investigate infidelity without having to rely on self-reports?

2. Try to design a study that would provide a definitive test of two or more of the theories of infidelity discussed in this article.

This article has been reprinted as it originally appeared in *Current Directions in Psychological Science*. Citation information for this article as originally published appears above.

A Typology of Men Who Are Violent Toward Their Female Partners: Making Sense of the Heterogeneity in Husband Violence

Amy Holtzworth-Munroe[1]

Department of Psychology, Indiana University, Bloomington, Indiana

Abstract

Although much research on men who are violent toward their wives has involved comparisons of groups of violent and nonviolent men, there is increasing evidence that maritally violent men are not a homogeneous group. Several recent studies support a batterer typology that distinguishes maritally violent subgroups. In an effort to identify different underlying processes resulting in husband violence, this article discusses how these subgroups differ along descriptive dimensions and in terms of their correlates in a developmental model of husband violence. The results suggest the importance of at least two continua (i.e., antisociality and borderline personality features) for understanding the heterogeneity in husband violence. The results also demonstrate the necessity of further studying low levels of husbands' physical aggression and of considering batterer subtypes when designing treatment interventions.

Keywords

batterer typology; husband violence

Violence of husbands toward their wives is a serious problem in this country. Data from nationally representative surveys suggest that, each year, one out of every eight married men will be physically aggressive toward his wife and up to 2 million women will be severely assaulted by their partners (Straus & Gelles, 1990). Although husbands and wives engage in aggression against their partners at very similar prevalence rates, a series of studies has demonstrated that husband violence has more negative consequences than wife violence; for example, husband violence is more likely to result in physical injury and depressive symptomatology (see the review in Holtzworth-Munroe, Smutzler, & Sandin, 1997). In attempting to understand the correlates and potential causes of husband violence, reviewers have noted that the most fruitful efforts have focused on characteristics of the violent man, as opposed to the female partner or the dyad (Hotaling & Sugarman, 1986). Indeed, much of the available data regarding husband violence has been gathered in studies comparing "violent" with "nonviolent" samples of men; in such studies, batterers are usually treated as a homogeneous group.

Recent research, however, has made it clear that maritally violent men are a heterogeneous group, varying along theoretically important dimensions. These findings suggest that the understanding of husband violence will be advanced by drawing attention to these differences. Comparing subtypes of violent men with each other, and pinpointing how each type differs from nonviolent men, may help researchers to identify different underlying processes resulting in violence.

PREDICTED SUBTYPES

After conducting a comprehensive review of 15 previous batterer typologies, Stuart and I observed that batterer subtypes can be classified along three descriptive dimensions: (a) severity and frequency of marital violence, (b) generality of violence (i.e., within the family only or outside the family as well), and (c) the batterer's psychopathology or personality disorders (Holtzworth-Munroe & Stuart, 1994). Using these dimensions, we proposed that three subtypes of batterers could be identified (i.e., family-only, dysphoric-borderline, and generally violent-antisocial).

Family-only batterers were predicted to be the least violent subgroup. We expected that they would engage in the least marital violence, the lowest levels of psychological and sexual abuse, and the least violence outside the home. We also predicted that men in this group would evidence little or no psychopathology. *Dysphoric-borderline* batterers were predicted to engage in moderate to severe wife abuse. Their violence would be primarily confined to the wife, although some extrafamilial violence might be evident. This group would be the most psychologically distressed (e.g., exhibiting depressed and anxious symptoms) and the most likely to evidence borderline personality characteristics (e.g., extreme emotional lability; intense, unstable interpersonal relationships; fear of rejection). Finally, *generally violent-antisocial* batterers were predicted to be the most violent subtype, engaging in high levels of marital violence and the highest levels of extrafamilial violence. They would be the most likely to evidence characteristics of antisocial personality disorder (e.g., criminal behavior and arrests, failure to conform to social norms, substance abuse).

We then integrated several intrapersonal models of aggression into a model outlining the developmental course of these differing types of husband violence (Holtzworth-Munroe & Stuart, 1994). The model highlighted the importance of correlates of male violence as risk factors for the differing batterer subtypes. Both historical correlates (i.e., genetic and prenatal factors, childhood home environment and violence in the family of origin, association with delinquent peers) and proximal correlates (correlates more current and directly related to battering; i.e., attachment and dependency; impulsivity; social skills, in both marital and nonmarital relationships; and attitudes, both hostile attitudes toward women and attitudes supportive of violence) were considered.

Based on this model, we predicted that, among the subtypes of batterers, family-only batterers would evidence the lowest levels of risk factors. We proposed that the violence of these men would result from a combination of stress (personal, marital, or both) and low-level risk factors (e.g., childhood exposure to marital violence, lack of relationship skills), so that on some occasions during escalating marital conflicts, these men would engage in physical aggression. Following such incidents, however, their low levels of psychopathology and related problems (e.g., impulsivity, attachment dysfunction), combined with their positive attitudes toward women and negative attitudes toward violence, would lead to remorse and help prevent their aggression from escalating.

In contrast, we hypothesized that dysphoric-borderline batterers come from a background involving parental abuse and rejection. As a result, these men would have difficulty forming a stable, trusting attachment with an intimate partner. Instead, they would be highly dependent on their wives, yet fearful of losing them and very jealous. They would be somewhat impulsive, lack marital skills, and have attitudes hostile toward women and supportive of violence. This group resembles batterers studied by Dutton (1995), who suggested that their early traumatic experiences lead to borderline personality characteristics, anger, and insecure attachment, which, in times of frustration, result in violence against the adult attachment figure (i.e., the wife).

Finally, we predicted that generally violent-antisocial batterers resemble other antisocial, aggressive groups. Relative to the other subtypes, they were expected to have experienced high levels of violence in their families of origin and association with deviant peers. They would be impulsive, lack relationship skills (marital and nonmarital), have hostile attitudes toward women, and view violence as acceptable. We conceptualized their marital violence as a part of their general use of aggression and engagement in antisocial behavior. In other words, their marital violence might not represent something unique about the dynamics of their intimate relationships, but rather might occur because wives are readily accessible victims for men who are often aggressive toward others.

TESTING THE MODEL

We recently completed a study testing this model (Holtzworth-Munroe, Meehan, Herron, Rehman, & Stuart, in press). From the community, we recruited 102 men who had been physically aggressive toward their wives in the past year; their wives also participated in the study. We included men who had engaged in a wide range of violence, in contrast to previous batterer typologies that were based on either clinical samples (i.e., men in treatment for domestic violence) or severely violent samples. In addition, we recruited two nonviolent comparison samples—couples who were experiencing marital distress and couples who were not.

Using measures of the descriptive dimensions (i.e., marital violence, general violence, personality disorder), we found that the three predicted subgroups of violent men emerged, along with one additional subgroup. There was general consistency in the subgroup placement of men across differing statistical solutions, although three men were placed into subgroups by the researchers, as they could fit into more than one subgroup.

The predicted subgroups generally differed as hypothesized along the descriptive dimensions and in terms of the developmental model's correlates of violence (i.e., childhood home environment, association with deviant peers, impulsivity, attachment, skills, attitudes). In addition, other recent batterer typologies have generally supported our predicted subgroups. Two studies of severely violent men (Jacobson & Gottman, 1998; Tweed & Dutton, 1998) identified subgroups that resembled our most violent subgroups (i.e., dysphoric-borderline and generally violent-antisocial). A third study, of more than 800 batterers entering domestic violence treatment, found three subgroups that closely resembled our proposed subtypes (Hamberger, Lohr, Bonge, & Tolin, 1996). Thus, our original three subgroup descriptions have generally been supported and describe the three main subtypes emerging in recent research.

The fourth, unpredicted cluster that emerged we labeled the *low-level anti-social* group, given their moderate scores on measures of antisociality, marital violence, and general violence. On many measures, this group fell intermediate to the family-only and generally violent-antisocial groups (i.e., family-only men had lower scores; generally violent-antisocial men had higher scores). This new group probably corresponds to our originally proposed family-only group; the levels of violence and antisociality in this fourth group are similar to those predicted for the family-only group, which was derived from previous typologies of severely violent men. In contrast, in our study, in which the low-level antisocial group emerged, the sample was recruited from the community and included less violent men. Consequently, we believe that what was labeled the family-only group in our study had not been included in previous batterer typologies, but rather resembles the less violent men often found in studies of newlyweds, couples in marital therapy, and couples in the community who are not seeking therapy and have not been arrested for violence (i.e., community samples). We hope that our four-cluster typology will bridge a recognized gap in this research area—between research examining generally low levels of violence among community samples and research examining severe violence among clinical samples, that is, people who are seeking help in therapy or have been referred to therapy by the courts (e.g., "common couple violence" vs. "patriarchal terrorism"; Johnson, 1995).

Low levels of physical aggression (such as found among family-only batterers) are so prevalent as to be almost normative (statistically) in U.S. culture; one third of engaged and newly married men engage in low levels of physical aggression (e.g., O'Leary et al., 1989). Yet, we do not understand how these less violent men differ from men who are experiencing marital distress or conflict but who do not engage in physical aggression; for example, on our study measures (e.g., of psychopathology, attachment, impulsivity, skills, attitudes, family of origin, peer experiences, wives' depression, and marital satisfaction), family-only batterers did not differ from nonviolent, maritally distressed men. It is thus tempting to assume that low levels of aggression do not lead to particularly pernicious outcomes, at least not above and beyond effects attributable to marital distress. This, however, is not the case, as a recent longitudinal study of newlyweds demonstrated that even low levels of physical aggression predicted marital separation or divorce better than did marital distress or negative marital communication (Rogge & Bradbury, 1999). Thus, although previous batterer typologies have focused on severely violent samples, we believe that lower levels of male physical aggression also deserve attention.

It is possible to conceptualize three of our violent subtypes (i.e., family-only, low-level antisocial, and generally violent-antisocial) as falling along a continuum of antisociality (e.g., family-only batterers have the lowest levels of violence, antisocial behavior, and risk factors; generally violent-antisocial men have the highest; the new cluster has intermediate levels). However, the dysphoric-borderline group cannot be easily placed along this continuum, as these men had the highest scores on a different set of theoretically coherent variables (i.e., fear of abandonment, preoccupied or fearful attachment, dependency). This raises the possibility that two dimensions (i.e., antisociality and borderline personality characteristics) are needed to describe all of the subgroups.

No previous researchers have examined the stability of batterer typologies, but it has been suggested that the various subtypes could exemplify different developmental phases of violence rather than stable clusters. This point is particularly important when considering the family-only and low-level antisocial groups. We predict that some men will remain in these groups, whereas others will escalate their levels of abuse. Indeed, longitudinal research has demonstrated that although severe husband violence predicts the occurrence of future violence, violence is less stable among less severely violent men (e.g., Quigley & Leonard, 1996). The problem, at this point, is that researchers and clinicians cannot predict which men in the less severely violent groups will escalate their violence.

FUTURE DIRECTIONS

The batterer subtypes were found to have differing levels of marital violence. At this time, however, we need further theoretical development regarding whether the nature of aggression, and the motivation for it, differs across subtypes of maritally violent men. For example, it is possible to speculate that the violence of generally violent-antisocial men is instrumental (e.g., goal motivated, premeditated), whereas the violence of the other groups is more expressive (i.e., motivated by anger, frustration, and emotional dysregulation). The answers to such questions await future research.

At this time, it also is unclear if one unifying variable or theory will be able to explain the development of all subtypes of violent husbands (e.g., Dutton, 1995, has focused on an attachment model; our data suggest the importance of antisociality). Our own model is a multivariate one (e.g., attachment, impulsivity, skills, attitudes), based on our belief that more than one variable will be necessary to explain differing developmental pathways; however, this question is currently untested.

We also do not yet understand how differing types of husband violence emerge in the context of varying settings and environments. Our typology emphasizes characteristics of the individual; it is an intrapersonal model, focusing on individual differences. Yet, husband violence occurs in the context of interpersonal relationships, communities and subcultures, and society. Thus, future researchers may wish to consider the societal and interpersonal, as well as the intrapersonal, causes of violence and the interaction of factors at these differing levels of analysis.

Prospective studies are needed to identify the developmental pathways resulting in different subtypes of violent husbands. Future longitudinal studies should examine constructs assumed to predict the use of violence among adolescents or children and then observe the relationship between these variables and the emergence of relationships violence as study participants enter intimate relationships.

Future researchers also should examine how various subtypes of violent men respond to different treatment programs. At the present time, the overall effectiveness of batterers' treatment is not impressive (e.g., Rosenfeld, 1992). Along with others, we have suggested that this may be due to the fact that therapists do not match interventions to batterer subtypes. Initial supportive evidence comes from a study comparing two different treatments; batterers who scored high on an antisocial measure did better in a structured cognitive-behavioral-feminist intervention (e.g., focusing on skills and attitudes), and batterers scoring high on a measure of dependency did better in a new process-psychodynamic intervention (e.g., examining past traumas in the men's lives; Saunders, 1996).

In summary, research on batterer typologies makes it increasingly clear that violent husbands are not a homogeneous group, and that it is no longer adequate to conduct studies comparing violent and nonviolent men. Instead, researchers must systematically examine variability among violent men, along relevant theoretical dimensions of interest. Such research will help identify the different pathways to violence.

Recommended Reading

Dutton, D.G. (1995). (See References)
Holtzworth-Munroe, A., & Stuart, G.L. (1994). (See References)
Jacobson, N.S., & Gottman, J.M. (1998). (See References)

Note

1. Address correspondence to Amy Holtzworth-Munroe, Department of Psychology, 1101 East 10th St., Indiana University, Bloomington, IN 47405-7007.

References

Dutton, D.G. (1995). Intimate abusiveness. *Clinical Psychology: Science and Practice, 2,* 207–224.
Hamberger, L.K., Lohr, J.M., Bonge, D., & Tolin, D.F. (1996). A large sample empirical typology of male spouse abusers and its relationship to dimensions of abuse. *Violence and Victims, 11,* 277–292.
Holtzworth-Munroe, A., Meehan, J.C., Herron, K., Rehman, U., & Stuart, G.L. (in press). Testing the Holtzworth-Munroe and Stuart batterer typology. *Journal of Consulting and Clinical Psychology.*
Holtzworth-Munroe, A., Smutzler, N., & Sandin, E. (1997). A brief review of the research on husband violence: Part II. The psychological effects of husband violence on battered women and their children. *Aggression and Violent Behavior, 2,* 179–213.
Holtzworth-Munroe, A., & Stuart, G.L. (1994). Typologies of male batterers: Three subtypes and the differences among them. *Psychological Bulletin, 116,* 476–497.
Hotaling, G.T., & Sugarman, D.B. (1986). An analysis of risk markers in husband to wife violence. *Violence and Victims, 7,* 79–88.
Jacobson, N.S., & Gottman, J.M. (1998). *When men batter women.* New York: Simon & Schuster.
Johnson, M.P. (1995). Patriarchal terrorism and common couple violence: Two forms of violence against women. *Journal of Marriage and the Family, 57,* 283–294.
O'Leary, K.D., Barling, J., Arias, I., Rosenbaum, A., Malone, J., & Tyree, A. (1989). Prevalence and stability of physical aggression between spouses. *Journal of Consulting and Clinical Psychology, 57,* 263–268.
Quigley, B.M., & Leonard, K.E. (1996). Desistance of husband aggression in the early years of marriage. *Violence and Victims, 11,* 355–370.
Rogge, R.D., & Bradbury, T.N. (1999). Till violence does us part: The differing roles of communication and aggression in predicting adverse marital outcomes. *Journal of Consulting and Clinical Psychology, 67,* 340–351.
Rosenfeld, B.D. (1992). Court-ordered treatment of spouse abuse. *Clinical Psychology Review, 12,* 205–226.

Saunders, D.G. (1996). Feminist-cognitive-behavioral and process-psychodynamic treatments for men who batter. *Violence and Victims, 4,* 393–414.

Straus, M.A., & Gelles, R.J. (1990). *Physical violence in American families.* New Brunswick, NJ: Transactions.

Tweed, R., & Dutton, D.G. (1998). A comparison of impulsive and instrumental subgroups of batterers. *Violence and Victims, 13,* 217–230.

Critical Thinking Questions

1. Would you expect the different types of men described by Holtzworth-Munroe to demonstrate different levels of problems in other aspects of their relationships?

2. How might interventions to prevent violence differ across each type of batterer?

3. Is one type of batterer likely to be more or less easy to study?

4. Are there other relationship processes that might benefit from a categorization like Holtzworth-Munroe's?

This article has been reprinted as it originally appeared in *Current Directions in Psychological Science.* Citation information for this article as originally published appears above.

Does Drinking Promote Risky Sexual Behavior?: A Complex Answer to a Simple Question

M. Lynne Cooper[1]

University of Missouri–Columbia

Abstract

The present review argues that, popular lore notwithstanding, the well-documented association between usual patterns of alcohol use and risky sex reflects multiple underlying processes that are both causal and noncausal (spurious) in nature. It is further argued that even alcohol's acute causal effects on sexual behavior are more variable than they are commonly assumed to be. Drinking can promote, inhibit, or have no effect on behavior, depending on the interplay of factors governing behavior in a particular situation and the content of individually held beliefs about alcohol's effects.

Keywords

alcohol; risky sex; condom use

With the advent of AIDS, efforts to understand the causes of sexual risk-taking have assumed great urgency. In this context, alcohol and its potential disinhibiting effects have received much attention. In the past 20 years, more than 600 studies have been conducted on the link between drinking and risky sex, and drinking proximal to intercourse has become a standard target of intervention efforts aimed at reducing risky sexual behaviors. Targeting drinking as part of a strategy to reduce risky sex can only be effective if drinking causally promotes such behaviors, however. Does the evidence support this connection? Conventional wisdom aside, the answer to this question is surprisingly complex.

BACKGROUND

The belief that alcohol causally disinhibits sexual behavior is firmly ingrained in our culture. Most people believe that drinking increases the likelihood of sexual activity, enhances sexual experience, and promotes riskier sexual behavior. Many also attribute risky sexual experiences to the fact that they were drinking and report drinking (or plying their partner with alcohol) to exploit alcohol's alleged disinhibiting effects on sexual behavior.

Consistent with popular belief, the overwhelming majority of studies do find an association between the two behaviors (Cooper, 2002; Leigh & Stall, 1993). The typical study examines the cross-sectional association between usual patterns of drinking and risky sex. For example, in such studies, individuals who drink consistently report more partners than those who abstain do. Owing to design limitations, however, these studies tell us little about the underlying causal relationship. Such data cannot even establish a temporal link between drinking and risky sex, a minimum condition for attributing causality to acute alcohol effects. Thus, although people are quick to infer a causal connection between the two behaviors, multiple interpretations are possible. Three will be considered here.

THIRD-VARIABLE EXPLANATIONS

Third variable explanations that involve stable (possibly genetically based) features of the individual or of his or her life situation offer one important explanation. For example, a person might both drink and have risky sex to satisfy sensation-seeking needs, because of poor impulse control or coping skills, or in an effort to cope with negative emotions. Consistent with this possibility, Cooper, Wood, Orcutt, and Albino (2003) showed that one third of the statistical overlap (modeled by a higher-order factor) among diverse risk behaviors, including alcohol use and risky sex, could be explained by low impulse control and an avoidant style of coping with negative emotions. Thrill seeking accounted for a much smaller proportion of the overlap, and significantly predicted the overlap only among white (not black) adolescents. In addition, avoidance coping predicted the onset of drinking among initially abstinent youth, and in interaction with impulsivity it predicted the onset of sexual behavior among those who were initially virgins. Thus, avoidance coping and impulsivity appear to be important common causes that partially account for the link between drinking and risky sex. Although thrill seeking was not a strong predictor in our randomly constituted, biracial adolescent sample, closely related measures (e.g., sensation seeking) have been shown to fully account for the association between drinking and risky sex in some high-risk samples (e.g., heavy drinkers, gay or bisexual men).

An individual might also drink and have risky sex as part of a lifestyle, such as being single or living in a fraternity house, where both behaviors are tacitly or explicitly encouraged. Consistent with this possibility, perceptions of peer norms related to drinking and sex are among the most robust predictors of involvement in both behaviors among youth. Similarly, characteristics of one's home environment—e.g., living in a single-parent or conflict-ridden household—have also been found to predict both behaviors. Thus, direct evidence showing that covariation between the two behaviors can be explained by third variables, and indirect evidence showing that involvement in both behaviors is linked to the same putative causal factors, support the contention that the association between drinking and risky sex is at least partly due to the influence of underlying common causes.

REVERSE CAUSAL EXPLANATIONS

Reverse causal explanations posit that the intention or desire to engage in risky sex causes one to drink when sexual opportunity is perceived. Consistent with this possibility, surveys of college students reveal that up to one half of undergraduates report drinking more than usual to make it easier to have sex and giving their partners alcohol to increase the likelihood of sex (Cooper, 2002). Alternatively, an individual might plan a romantic evening and drink to enhance that experience or plan to pick someone up at a party and drink to provide an excuse (to oneself or others) for behavior that might later be seen as inappropriate. Although different motives (to disinhibit, enhance, or excuse) presumably underlie drinking in each scenario, all accounts nevertheless assume that people who drink strategically hold relevant beliefs about alcohol's capacity to facilitate the desired sexual outcome. Supporting this notion, Dermen and I (Dermen & Cooper, 1994) found that people who believe that alcohol enhances or disinhibits sex are more likely to drink, and to drink to intoxication, in sexual or potentially sexual situations (e.g., on a date). Thus, for at least some people, the intention or desire to have sex may precede and cause drinking, rather than the reverse.

CAUSAL EXPLANATIONS

Two prominent theories depict alcohol as a cause of disinhibited social behaviors: alcohol myopia and expectancy theories. Alcohol-myopia theory (Steele & Josephs, 1990) posits that disinhibited behavior results from an interaction of diminished cognitive capabilities and the specific cues that influence behavior in a given situation. Because alcohol narrows the range of cues perceived and limits the ability to process and extract meaning from these cues, intoxication renders a person susceptible to momentary pressures. Simple, highly salient cues (e.g., sexual arousal) continue to be processed, whereas more distal, complex ones (e.g., fear of pregnancy) are no longer adequately processed. Consequently, alcohol creates a "myopia" in which incompletely processed aspects of immediate experience exert undue influence on behavior and emotion. Accordingly, alcohol has its strongest effect when a behavior is controlled by instigating and inhibiting cues that are strong and nearly equal in force—a circumstance known as inhibition conflict.

In support of this model, Steele and Josephs conducted a meta-analysis (a method for statistically combining effects) of 34 experimental studies testing alcohol's effects on social behavior. Results revealed a small (.14) average standardized effect for alcohol under low-inhibition-conflict conditions versus a large effect (1.06) under high-conflict conditions. Thus, consistent with alcohol-myopia theory, intoxicated participants behaved more extremely than sober ones did primarily under high-conflict conditions.

Whereas alcohol-myopia theory emphasizes pharmacological mechanisms, expectancy theory emphasizes psychological ones. According to this view, an individual's behavior after drinking is driven by pre-existing beliefs (expectancies) about alcohol's effects on behavior, much like a self-fulfilling prophecy (Hull & Bond, 1986). The role of expectancies has been investigated experimentally in studies that independently manipulate alcohol content and expectancy set (the belief that alcohol has been consumed). In a meta-analysis of 36 such studies, Hull and Bond found that people who believed they had consumed alcohol (but had not) behaved similarly to those who had consumed alcohol (and didn't know it). Indeed, expectancy effects were significant and only slightly smaller than alcohol-content effects (.27 vs. .35). Expectancy theory thus highlights the role of individually held beliefs about alcohol's effects, and suggests by extension that alcohol effects on behavior may vary as a function of these beliefs.

The foregoing indicates that alcohol intoxication can cause more extreme social behavior through both pharmacological and psychological mechanisms. Contrary to popular opinion, these effects are not immutable, but are contingent on the nature of instigating and inhibiting cues governing momentary behavior, on the content of one's beliefs about alcohol effects, or possibly on a combination of both. Theoretically, then, alcohol intoxication should lead to riskier sexual behavior only under certain conditions or among certain people, a contention that existing evidence largely supports.

A SELECTIVE REVIEW OF NATURALISTIC STUDIES OF DRINKING AND RISKY SEX

From a public health perspective, one of the most important issues concerns alcohol's potential to facilitate the occurrence of intercourse, especially with new or casual partners. To investigate this issue, Orcutt and I (Cooper & Orcutt, 1997) examined the link between drinking and intercourse on two first-date occasions in a large, representative sample of adolescents. Although these data are correlational, the within-subjects design allowed us to compare a person's behavior on two occasions that, for many, differed in the presence versus absence of alcohol, thus helping us rule out stable individual differences between drinkers and nondrinkers as an alternative explanation for observed differences in sexual behavior. As Fig. 1 illustrates, our results showed that rates of intercourse were higher when the male partner drank and lower when he abstained. Interestingly, however, parallel analyses revealed no such relationship for drinking by the female partner.

Drawing on alcohol-myopia theory, we reasoned that the psychological conditions necessary for alcohol-related disinhibition existed only among men. Specifically, if males experienced a type of conflict in which dominant cues favored behavioral action while peripheral cues favored behavioral inhibition, we would expect (due to the greater difficulty of accessing and processing peripheral cues) alcohol-related disinhibition. In contrast, if females experienced a type of

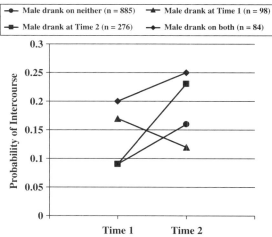

Fig. 1. Male couple-member alcohol use and probability of intercourse on two first-date occasions. From Cooper & Orcutt (1997).

conflict in which dominant cues favored inhibition and peripheral ones activation, then decreased processing of peripheral cues should not disinhibit behavior. Consistent with this logic, we found that men perceived more benefits relative to costs of having sex on their most recent first date, whereas women perceived more costs relative to benefits. Moreover, only the perception of increasing costs predicted conflict among men (for whom benefits were more salient), whereas the reverse was true among women. Thus, men and women appeared to experience qualitatively different forms of conflict about having sex on their most recent first date. Moreover, consistent with the idea that the type of conflict conducive to alcohol-related disinhibition occurred only among men, rates of intercourse on the date were significantly elevated only among highly conflicted men who drank alcohol (Fig. 2).

Together these data indicate that how alcohol affects sexual behavior is determined by the content and relative strength of competing cues that inhibit or activate behavior, and they raise the possibility that alcohol might even promote safer behavior under the right circumstances! Recent experimental evidence lends strong support to this idea, showing that when the potential costs of having sex with an attractive new partner were made salient, intoxicated individuals reported more cautious intentions than did sober ones (MacDonald, Fong, Zanna, & Martineau, 2000).

A second key question from a public health perspective is whether drinking reduces condom use. Somewhat surprisingly, most naturalistic studies directly testing the link between drinking on a specific intercourse occasion and condom use on that occasion find no relationship. Indeed in a quantitative analysis of 29

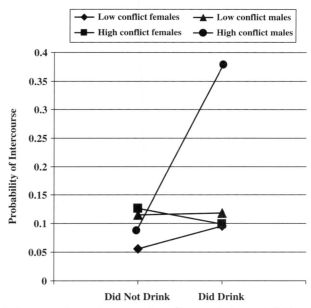

Fig. 2. Alcohol use, gender, and perceived conflict predicting probability of intercourse on the most recent first date. From Cooper & Orcutt (1997).

such tests (Cooper, 2002), alcohol was associated with lower rates of condom (and birth-control) use only under circumscribed conditions: at first intercourse but not on subsequent intercourse occasions, in younger but not older samples, and in studies conducted earlier rather than more recently (Leigh, 2002, reports similar results).

One plausible interpretation of these findings is that few people experience the type of conflict conducive to alcohol-related disinhibition of condom use, though such conflict may have been common in the past and may still be common among sexually inexperienced, younger adolescents. Although no study has directly tested these ideas, a study conducted by Dermen and me (Dermen & Cooper, 2000) provides indirect support. We examined feelings of conflict about using a condom on four occasions of intercourse across two different samples (one of college students; one of community-residing young adults, aged 19–25), and found that fewer than 15% of participants were highly conflicted about using a condom on each occasion. Moreover, although drinking did not predict lower overall rates of condom use on any of these occasions, it predicted significantly lower rates (in three of four tests) among those who felt conflicted about using a condom on that occasion.

In short, these data suggest that drinking can undermine safe sex behaviors, but that it does not invariably do so. Rather, alcohol can promote, inhibit, or have no effect on risky sexual behaviors depending on the specific constellation of salient cues in the moment.

THE ROLE OF ALCOHOL EXPECTANCIES

Although the preponderance of evidence suggests that inhibition conflict plays the larger role in accounting for alcohol's acute causal effects on risky sexual behavior, expectancies also appear important. As previously discussed, those who believe that alcohol disinhibits or enhances sexual experience are more likely to drink in (potentially) sexual situations, suggesting that expectancies are instrumental in setting up situations that may lead to alcohol-related disinhibition of sex. Expectancies (in the absence of alcohol) have also been shown to influence other aspects of sexual experience that could indirectly promote risky behaviors. For example, a recently conducted experiment in which participants were paired with previously unknown, opposite-sex partners found that participants who thought they had consumed alcohol (though none had been consumed) reported greater sexual arousal, perceived their partners as more sexually disinhibited, and showed erotic slides (presumed to be a behavioral analog of sexual interest) to their partners significantly longer, but only if they also held strong beliefs about alcohol's capacity to disinhibit or enhance sexual experience (George, Stoner, Norris, Lopez, & Lehman, 2000). These data suggest that expectancies, once activated by alcohol consumption, may strengthen instigating cues for sex, thereby bringing an individual for whom costs might otherwise greatly outweigh benefits into a state of high inhibition conflict. Finally, expectancies have also been shown to interact with feelings of conflict to jointly predict alcohol-related disinhibition of risky sexual behavior (Dermen & Cooper, 2000). Thus, expectancies and actual alcohol content might work in tandem to disinhibit risky sexual behavior in real-world situations where the two processes always co-occur.

CONCLUSIONS AND FUTURE DIRECTIONS

The relationship between alcohol use and risky sex is complex. It cannot be explained by a single mechanism, but instead reflects multiple underlying causal and noncausal processes. Moreover, even the causal portion of this relationship is not manifest as a main effect but as an interaction.

These complexities have important implications for both research and intervention efforts. The multiplicity of plausible causal mechanisms highlights the need for diverse methodological approaches for exploring alternative models, and for greater sophistication in framing research questions. Rather than focusing on which model better accounts for the link between drinking and risky sex, future research should focus on delineating the conditions under which, and the individuals for whom, different causal (and noncausal) processes are most likely to operate.

At the same time, researchers trying to unravel alcohol's acute effects must adopt more sophisticated methods for studying the complex interplay between drinking, individually held expectancies, and situational cues. Diary methods in which people report on both behaviors across multiple days provide an important and ecologically valid approach for examining this relationship. Such methods not only enable more accurate assessment of the behaviors themselves but also provide a window onto the motivations, emotions, and cognitions that subtly shape these behaviors and set the stage for alcohol's variable effects across individuals and situations.

The existence of multiple causal models also points to the need for diverse intervention strategies, and raises the possibility that different strategies will be optimally effective among individuals for whom different causal processes dominate. For example, among people who chronically drink and engage in risky behaviors, the relationship between drinking and risky sex may primarily reflect the influence of underlying common causes. For such individuals, universal change strategies targeting these common causes should be maximally efficacious. Alternatively, carefully designed interventions aimed at reducing drinking (or manipulating risk cues) in settings where drinking and encountering potential partners co-occur (e.g., college bars) could lower sexual risks associated with alcohol use among those who are most vulnerable to acute intoxication effects, situational influences, or both. To be maximally effective, interventions must be carefully tailored for different populations and circumstances in which different underlying causal processes predominate.

Recommended Reading

Cooper, M.L. (2002). (See References)
George, W.H., & Stoner, S.A. (2000). Understanding acute alcohol effects on sexual behavior. *Annual Review of Sex Research, 11,* 92–122.
Leigh, B.C., & Stall, R. (1993). (See References)
Weinhardt, L.S., & Carey, M.P. (2000). Does alcohol lead to sexual risk behavior? Findings from event-level research. *Annual Review of Sex Research, 11,* 125–157.

Note

1. Address correspondence to M. Lynne Cooper, 105 McAlester Hall, University of Missouri, Columbia, MO, 65211; e-mail: cooperm@missouri.edu.

References

Cooper, M.L. (2002). Alcohol use and risky sexual behavior among college students and youth. *Journal of Studies on Alcohol, 14*(Suppl.), 101–117.

Cooper, M.L., & Orcutt, H.K. (1997). Drinking and sexual experiences on first dates among adolescents. *Journal of Abnormal Psychology, 106,* 191–202.

Cooper, M.L., Wood, P.K., Orcutt, H.K., & Albino, A.W. (2003). Personality and predisposition to engage in risky or problem behaviors during adolescence. *Journal of Personality and Social Psychology, 84,* 390–410.

Dermen, K.H., & Cooper, M.L. (1994). Sex-related alcohol expectancies among adolescents. *Psychology of Addictive Behaviors, 8,* 161–168.

Dermen, K.H., & Cooper, M.L. (2000). Inhibition conflict and alcohol expectancy as moderators of alcohol's relationship to condom use. *Experimental and Clinical Psychopharmacology, 8,* 198–206.

George, W.H., Stoner, S.A., Norris, J., Lopez, P.A., & Lehman, G.L. (2000). Alcohol expectancies and sexuality: A self-fulfilling prophecy analysis of dyadic perceptions and behavior. *Journal of Studies on Alcohol, 61,* 168–176.

Hull, J.G., & Bond, C.F. (1986). Social and behavioral consequences of alcohol consumption and expectancy: A meta-analysis. *Psychological Bulletin, 99,* 347–360.

Leigh, B.C. (2002). Alcohol and condom use: A meta-analysis of event-level studies. *Sexually Transmitted Disease, 29,* 476–482.

Leigh, B.C., & Stall, R. (1993). Substance use and risky sexual behavior for exposure to HIV: Issues in methodology. *American Psychologist, 48,* 1035–1045.

MacDonald, T.K., Fong, G.T., Zanna, M.P., & Martineau, A.M. (2000). Alcohol myopia and condom use: Can alcohol intoxication be associated with more prudent behavior? *Journal of Personality and Social Psychology, 78,* 605–619.

Steele, C.M., & Josephs, R.A. (1990). Alcohol myopia: Its prized and dangerous effects. *American Psychologist, 45,* 921–932.

Critical Thinking Questions

1. Taking Cooper's research findings into account, design a program intended to maximize safer sex (fewer partners, greater condom use) among college students who have been drinking alcohol.

2. What are some of the ethical concerns with experimentally studying sexual behavior after alcohol consumption in an experiment? Try to come up with a design (other than the ones mentioned by Cooper) that would minimize those concerns.

This article has been reprinted as it originally appeared in *Current Directions in Psychological Science*. Citation information for this article as originally published appears above.